THE **BATTLE** FOR THE MEDITERRANEAN

THE BATTLE FOR THE MEDITERRANEAN

ALLIED AND AXIS CAMPAIGNS FROM NORTH AFRICA TO THE ITALIAN PENINSULA, 1940-45

ANTHONY TUCKER-JONES

This edition published in 2021 by Arcturus Publishing Limited
26/27 Bickels Yard, 151–153 Bermondsey Street,
London SE1 3HA

AD007754UK

Printed in the UK

Contents

Foreword by Professor Geoffrey Roberts   9

Introduction: The Cradle of Civilization   13

PART 1: THE MEDITERRANEAN AND NORTH AFRICAN THEATRE OF WAR   21

CHAPTER 1: RUMBLINGS IN THE MED   23
Power sharing in Morocco   24
The Italian bid for power   24
Morocco fights back   27
Italian rule in Libya   28
The Allies take defensive action   29
The invasion of Ethiopia   30

CHAPTER 2: HEMMED IN   35
Mussolini works on his image   38
Mussolini and Hitler cement their relationship   40
Mussolini invades Albania   43
Time to pick a side   45

PART 2: THE WESTERN DESERT   47

CHAPTER 3: DESERT FRONTLINE   49
Things start to go wrong for the Italians   49
A lack of military might   51
The British and Italians come to blows   52
Opening forays in Libya   56
Battle begins   57

CHAPTER 4: FALLEN ALLIES   61
The French under fire   63
Anglo-French relations break down   68
Enemies in multiple theatres   69
Hitler seeks new alliances   70
Hitler offers limited help to the Italians   72
Italy goes it alone in Greece   73

CHAPTER 5: SECOND BLOOD   77
The action hots up in the Adriatic   79
Taranto under attack   80
The Battle of Cape Spartivento   85
Division and distrust   85
Halycon days for the British   86

CHAPTER 6: FOX IS KILLED   89
Operation *Compass*   90
Attention turns to Tobruk and Derna   94
Brute force at Beda Fomm   95
Next steps   97
Hitler assesses his options   99

CHAPTER 7: BACK AT SEA   103
Operation *Lustre*   104
The Battle of Matapan   105
The underwater war   110

CHAPTER 8: UNWANTED DISTRACTIONS   115

Rommel takes the battle to the enemy   116
Battle for the Balkans   118
The German advance in Greece   120
The price of victory   122
The British response   123
Attention shifts to the Eastern Front   125

CHAPTER 9: FALLING FROM THE SKIES   127

Inadequate garrison   127
Battle commences over Crete   129
The Allies withdraw from Crete   132

CHAPTER 10: ADVENTURES IN THE LEVANT   137

Safeguarding Syria   139
Operation *Battleaxe*   141
The fall-out from Operation *Battleaxe*   145
Operation *Crusader*   147

PART 3: THE SICILIAN NARROWS   149

CHAPTER 11: MALTESE SICKNESS   151

The focus of sustained attack   155
Reinforcements arrive in Malta   157
The Germans change tack   160
Operation *Pedestal*   161
Counting the cost   164

CHAPTER 12: BACK TO TRIPOLI   167

Hitler's grand plan fails   169
The Second Battle of El Alamein   171
Operation *Torch*   172
The aftermath of Operation *Torch*   176
Rommel attempts to reason with Hitler   178
The assassination of Admiral Darlan   178
The Axis retreat   180

CHAPTER 13: WHERE NEXT?   185

Strife in the Strait of Sicily   187
Operation *Husky*   189
Il Duce's downfall   192
The Axis withdrawal   194

CHAPTER 14: IL DUCE RESURRECTED   197

The Germans move in   199
The battle for the Aegean   203
An attempt at a Fascist revival   205

CHAPTER 15: AIR, SEA AND LAND   209

Allied 'victory' in Italy   211
Operation *Dragoon*   212
The Germans lose their grip   217

CHAPTER 16: DEADLY SIDESHOW   219

Death of the Mediterranean strongman   220
A series of strategic blunders   222
The road to victory   227
A tumultuous aftermath   228

References   229
Bibliography   241
Index   249

FOREWORD
BY PROFESSOR GEOFFREY ROBERTS

IF THE Second World War was Hitler's war, the vast military conflict that engulfed the Mediterranean between 1940 and 1945 was Mussolini's. It was the Fascist dictator's declaration of war on Britain and France in June 1940 that spread the fighting started by Germany's invasion of Poland in September 1939 to southern Europe, the Balkans, the Middle East and North Africa.

Mussolini's expansion of the conflict cost millions of lives as fierce battles raged in the Mediterranean area – at sea, in the air and on the land. Some of the most memorable actions of the Second World War took place in the Mediterranean theatre: massive tank battles in the deserts of North Africa; the invasion of Crete by German airborne forces; the British torpedo plane attack on Italian battleships at Taranto; the Italo-German bombardment of Malta – the George Cross island; and Allied amphibious landings in North Africa, Sicily, Italy and southern France.

These wartime dramas loomed large – and still do – for Western publics because until the Normandy invasion in June 1944, the Mediterranean provided the main battleground for the American, British and other Allied armies, at least in Europe. It was there that some of the Second World War's most famous generals made their reputations: Erwin Rommel – 'the desert fox' of Afrika Korps fame; Bernard Montgomery and his 8th Army 'desert rats'; Dwight D. Eisenhower, supreme commander Mediterranean and then the D-Day overlord; his British successor in the Mediterranean, Harold Alexander, who led the campaign in Italy; and the flamboyant George S. Patton, whose troops stormed through Sicily in 1943. Less lauded but equally important was Admiral Cunningham, the commander-in-chief of Britain's Mediterranean Fleet whose forces kept open vital supply routes, transported Allied troops and fought a deadly war with German and Italian submarines, bombers and battleships.

Mussolini had allied Italy with Hitler in the 1930s, calling the Italian-German alliance the new 'axis' of European great power politics, but he remained neutral – his preferred term was 'non-belligerent' – until it became clear the Wehrmacht had beaten France and isolated Britain. Mussolini considered the Mediterranean an Italian sea; his aim was a new Roman Empire, which in the first instance entailed occupying Greece and driving the British out of Egypt.

Italy invaded Greece in October 1940 but Mussolini's campaign faltered in the face of strong Greek resistance and British military intervention. Hitler was forced to step in to stop Britain from establishing a foothold in the Balkans and that meant invading Yugoslavia as well as Greece in April 1941. In return for Hitler's support, Mussolini sent an Italian expeditionary corps to fight alongside the Germans on the Soviet–German front in summer 1941.

In North Africa, Mussolini's campaign started well when his forces in Libya (an Italian colony since the 1910s) attacked the British in Egypt, but their offensive was soon turned back. Only the arrival in spring 1941 of Rommel and the Afrika Korps saved the Italians from complete disaster. Rommel then masterminded a campaign that thrust German-Italian forces deep into Egypt only for that invasion to be halted by the allies at El Alamein.

Mid-1942 was the peak of Axis success in North Africa, when Hitler dreamed of capturing the Suez Canal, then marauding through the Middle East and linking up with German armies fighting Stalin's Red Army in the Caucasus. That dream was shattered by the Allied counter-offensive at El Alamein in October 1942 and by the Wehrmacht's disastrous defeat at Stalingrad.

As Rommel retreated back to Libya, Anglo-American forces invaded French North Africa – Morocco, Algeria and Tunisia. Caught in a pincer movement, the Germans and Italians had been forced out of North Africa by spring 1943, but not before they had suffered hundreds of thousands of losses.

The Allies' next target was Italy and their successful invasion of Sicily in summer 1943 proved to be Mussolini's final downfall. He was deposed as leader in July and Italy switched sides in the war. However, the Germans saw this turnabout coming and flooded the country with troops while Mussolini was rescued by Hitler and made head of an Italian puppet state.

When Winston Churchill visited Joseph Stalin in Moscow in August 1942, he drew a picture of a crocodile for the Soviet dictator and argued that the Mediterranean was the soft underbelly of the Axis. Allied troops who fought in the long Italian campaign of 1943–5 had another name: 'tough old gut'.

Mussolini's fate was gruesome. In the very last days of the war he was caught trying to escape to neutral Switzerland by Italian communist partisans. He and his mistress Clara Petacci were summarily executed and their bodies put on public display in Milan.

Anthony Tucker-Jones has written an exciting and illuminating account of the epic struggle for the Mediterranean during the Second World War. His book provides a strategic overview of the war that is interweaved with fascinating personal accounts, its campaigns and battles.

I have long been an admirer of Anthony's writings on military history. His books are always well-informed and judicious. This book guides the reader through some complex threads of action. For a short book, it is amazingly comprehensive and balanced in its treatment of many different theatres and types of operation. Unlike some military historians, Anthony does not get lost in too many technical details, even though he has a firm grasp of them all. To borrow Lewis Namier's phrase, Anthony's latest book is that winning combination of broad outline and significant detail that will engage readers from beginning to end.

Geoffrey Roberts
Emeritus Professor of History
University College Cork

INTRODUCTION:
The Cradle of Civilization

GERMAN RACING driver Hermann Lang stood smiling on the winner's podium at the Tripoli Grand Prix in 1939. It was his third consecutive win in Libya, where there was a fierce sporting rivalry between Italy and Germany. He basked in the glory. Italian driver Giuseppe Farina would triumph in Tripoli in 1940, with Italians coming second and third, but it was to be a hollow victory. That year, the two countries became allies against Britain and France, heralding the rapid escalation of the Second World War.

The Mediterranean is the cradle of Western civilization and the birthplace of littoral warfare. Wars for supremacy over its coastline and adjacent seas are nothing new. Alexander the Great, Caesar, Hannibal and Napoleon all sailed across it. Mighty empires rose and fell along its sun-kissed shores. The Persians were defeated at Salamis, the Phoenicians at Tyre, the Carthaginians at Cannae, the Byzantines at Constantinople, the Moors in Granada, the Ottomans at Lepanto, the French on the Nile, the British at Gallipoli and the Turks at Megiddo. Yet sitting in the pleasant bars, cafes and restaurants along the North African shore in the summer of 1939, it must have been hard to imagine that war was looming once again. Europe's troubled politics seemed so far away. The great Mediterranean ports thrived on trade not war. Commerce brought wealth and prosperity.

Many European colonists had moved there to start a new life, away from the economic uncertainty, political squabbling and persecution. In reality, though, North Africa had been blighted by European conflicts since the late 1800s. In recent years, the French, Italians and Spanish had all carved out empires there, at great cost to the local population. Like a pack of jackals, they had torn apart the still-warm carcass of the moribund Ottoman Empire. Italy in particular had only recently finished conquering Libya. Southern Europe and the Balkans had not been at peace, either. During the early 1920s, war between Greece and Turkey resulted in the formal demise of the Ottoman Empire and the creation of the Turkish republic. This gave the Turks a new-found sense of national pride. In the mid-1930s, Spain was riven by a bloody civil war that spilled over into the Mediterranean. There seemed to be no end to the conflicts along its shores.

On the waters of the Mediterranean throughout the 1920s and 1930s there was an uneasy armed detente between the major powers. This was thanks to the presence of British, French and Italian battleships. Many of them were enormous dreadnoughts dating from the First World War. These monsters were armed with batteries of massive 15-in guns capable of firing shells to a range of almost 20 miles (32 km). These castles of steel were the ultimate armed deterrent and symbols of unassailable naval prowess. The Mediterranean powers had also been busy constructing newer generations of more agile warships and submarines. Britain, for one, realized the value of aircraft carriers and was quietly building a new generation of modern vessels. Again, those living in the Mediterranean chose to ignore the fact that there was a naval arms race going on.

Italian dictator Benito Mussolini's invasion of Ethiopia in the mid-1930s almost sparked war between Britain and Italy – something neither side wanted. The Royal Navy, at the time, was unprepared and Mussolini did not want to be distracted from his campaign of colonial conquest. The British faced him down, but at the 11th hour lost their nerve. Mussolini got his way and added Ethiopia to his African empire. Afterwards, Mussolini and Hitler, feeling they had a free hand, sprang to the support of General Franco during the Spanish Civil War. Mussolini, flouting international law, sent his submarines to sink Spanish Republican shipping. Britain and France had to work hard again to avoid this becoming a much wider conflict.

Britain was severely rattled by Mussolini's behaviour in Ethiopia and Spain. As a result, the British government became obsessed with maintaining the military balance in the Mediterranean at any cost. To this end, on the eve of the Second World War, they cut a shameless deal with Mussolini.

Foreign Secretary Lord Halifax wrote: 'Signor Mussolini assured us that he was well satisfied with the Anglo-Italian Agreement, by which both parties undertook to respect the existing *status quo* in the Mediterranean.'[1] In return, Mussolini told Prime Minister Chamberlain and Halifax that all Italy wanted was peace. Later, Chamberlain was to be duped in a similar manner by Hitler's hollow promises over Europe.

Mussolini, amid the faded glories of Rome, eyed the Mediterranean greedily. He longed for a return to the days when the entire Mediterranean coast had been under the sway of the Roman Empire. The colonization of Libya had given him a sense of what could be achieved. In his speeches to packed crowds, Mussolini told his countrymen that the Mediterranean was the 'Italian Sea'. This was not a hollow boast; there was a network of air and naval bases stretching in a vast arch formed by Sardinia, Sicily, Libya, mainland Italy and Rhodes. Publicly at least, this looked to be an impressive array of military muscle.

Britain and France, though, stood in the way of Mussolini's imperial aspirations. The French, with their powerful navy and naval bases in the Riviera and North Africa, dominated the western Mediterranean. Britain's reach was even greater. From Alexandria and Suez, the Royal Navy was master of the eastern Mediterranean. The British naval base at Malta dominated the central Mediterranean in defiance of Sicily, while from the Rock of Gibraltar the British controlled the very entrance to the Sea. In Mussolini's mind, Britain and France had deliberately made the Mediterranean into an Italian prison. Italy could not grow and flourish because of this deliberate stranglehold.

Then, in 1940, Adolf Hitler defeated France and Admiral Darlan's French fleet was swiftly neutralized. Darlan and his commanders found themselves confined to port with orders to disarm. Gibraltar and Malta suddenly became dangerously isolated and exposed. This placed Mussolini in a tempting position to challenge Britain's command of the Mediterranean and its hold on Egypt.

The last thing Winston Churchill needed was the war in Europe spreading across the Mediterranean. 'Given the crisis which we now faced with the disastrous Battle of France,' he wrote, 'it was clearly my duty, as Prime Minister, to do everything possible to keep Italy out of the conflict...'[2] It was wishful thinking. Some politicians vainly hoped that Mussolini could broker a peace deal with Hitler. They were woefully misguided. It misguided. It was a delusion to believe that Mussolini had any sway over the actions of Hitler. Instead, Mussolini, encouraged by the speed of Hitler's victory over France, wanted to share in the spoils. In North Africa, many colonial administrators – particularly in Algiers, Cairo, Tripoli and Tunis – vainly hoped that the region would be left in peace.

Libya's flamboyant Italian governor, Air Marshal Italo Balbo, had made Tripoli into a playground for the rich and wealthy. The Grand Hotel Tripoli and the Uaddan Hotel and Casino were the places to be seen. It was as if he had transplanted an Italian city to North Africa where every hedonistic pleasure was catered for. The annual Tripoli Grand Prix had become a major sporting event, with Alfa Romeo pitted against Mercedes-Benz. Throughout the late 1930s it was noticeable that the Germans kept winning.

The large British expat population in Cairo partied on as if nothing was happening. Anyone who was anyone had to be seen at the cocktail receptions at the imposing British Embassy in Garden City, hosted by the Ambassador Sir Miles Lampson. Garden City was also the location of the British military's General Headquarters Middle East. Life went on as normal at the Gezira Sporting Club and at the Turf Club, where polo ponies were put through their paces. The large terrace of Shepherd's Hotel, which was the city's second-most famous landmark after the pyramids, remained an epicentre for idle gossip among the European community. Outside of GHQ, no one really contemplated the prospect of fighting the Italians, let alone the Germans or the French. Only the latter were uneasy. Although they lived gaily in Algiers and Tunis, they had begun to build the Mareth Line to protect the Tunisian–Libyan border.

Hitler's escalating land grabs across Europe, culminating with the invasions of Poland and France, inevitably meant the Mediterranean would be dragged into the Second World War. The reason for this was that Mussolini, although alarmed at Germany's expansionism, decided he would throw his lot in with Hitler. This foolhardy opportunism would cost him dearly and condemn the Mediterranean to five long years of bloodshed.

Mussolini declared war on Britain and France on 10 June 1940, triggering the long-feared European conflict in the Mediterranean. His cowardly assault on a prostrate France would spark campaigns the length and breadth of the Sea. These commenced in the Balkans, spread across North Africa and into the Levant. He needed a swift and decisive victory, because his country was not prepared for prolonged large-scale war; Italian industry was simply incapable of meeting his armed forces' needs. Furthermore, Mussolini knew that the moment he attacked the British, they would close the Gibraltar Straits and Suez Canal. When that happened, he would be completely reliant on Hitler for the supply of raw materials. Mussolini therefore needed to take Egypt and force Churchill to sue for peace as quickly as possible.

Instead, Italian military ineptitude soon dragged Hitler into war in the Mediterranean whether he wanted it or not. Although Mussolini had a modern fleet, it lacked aircraft carriers, much of his large air force was obsolete and his plodding army relied on its boots, not mechanization. Luckily for Churchill, the Italians also proved nowhere near as aggressive as their British counterparts. On land and at sea, Mussolini's forces hesitated and this cost them dearly at Beda Fomm and Cape Matapan.

This affected Germany, too. In order to safeguard his southern flank in 1941, prior to invading the Soviet Union, Hitler was obliged to complete Mussolini's botched invasion of Greece. In addition, he felt compelled to attack Yugoslavia and Crete. Likewise, Mussolini's bungled attack on Egypt meant Hitler was forced to send troops to Libya under the command of General Erwin Rommel. This set the scene for the bitter struggle between the Axis and the British for control of the Mediterranean on land, in the air and at sea.

Rommel, always short of resources, remarkably by 1942 got as far as a place called El Alamein to the west of Alexandria. For a brief moment it looked as if Cairo might fall, but by that stage Rommel was outnumbered and outgunned by General Bernard Montgomery. Rommel was duly chased all the way back to Tripoli and his fate sealed by the Anglo-American landings in French North Africa. In a stroke, the Axis forces were surrounded in Tunisia.

While the dramatic fighting on land dominated the news, the conflict at sea was equally important and equally intense. This involved warships, submarines and aircraft. A fierce battle was fought over the vital shipping lanes, particularly in the Sicilian Channel between Sicily and Tunisia. This reached its height with the Battle for Malta and culminated with the surrender of the Axis forces trapped at Cap Bon. However, complete Allied dominance of the Mediterranean was not secured until the landings in the French Riviera in the summer of 1944. Even then, Hitler remained defiant in Italy, the Balkans and the Aegean. After he was forced to withdraw, he left behind garrisons in Crete and the Dodecanese.

Mussolini, Hitler, Pétain, Darlan and Franco were all painted as the villains of the story, although history is never really that black and white. Geopolitical and strategic interests were often trumped by national self-interest. Notably, France was left in a highly perplexing situation following its capitulation to Hitler. Divided in half, the unoccupied zone in the south was demilitarized, with the French Empire ruled by Marshal Pétain's Vichy government. Thanks to France's division, she found herself Britain's foe. Britain was thus left in the unenviable position of fighting the French, Italians and Germans. The arrival of the Americans in French North Africa in late 1942 finally tilted the balance in the Mediterranean in the favour of the Allies. The battles fought there made household names of Generals Eisenhower, Montgomery, O'Connor, Patton, Rommel and Wavell as well as Admirals Cunningham and Somerville, to name but a few. They oversaw some of the most dramatic campaigns of the entire Second World War.

*   *   *

The Mediterranean is very special to me. As a very young child, I spent four blissful years on the island of Malta. Scampering around the beaches and bathing in the blue sea was idyllic. Since then, I have revisited it many times. Its beautiful geography and climate seeps into your psyche, fuelling the urge to return. Like everywhere around the Mediterranean, it has become overdeveloped and congested. However, if you go off the beaten track you soon find old Malta, where life still chugs along to the rhythm of the sun. It is beguiling.

I recall as a teenager researching the 1565 Great Siege of Malta in the Valletta public library. The siege was an epic struggle between Christendom and Islam. The second siege was an epic struggle between democracy and Fascism. It felt as if history oozed from the very bedrock of this tiny, courageous island. I was hooked. Algeria, Egypt, Morocco, Tunisia – all hold a similar allure. Standing amid the dusty Atlas Mountains, you wonder how the European colonial powers ever thought they could exercise any lasting authority over such cultural diversity. Yet their presence plunged the region into decades of heartbreak and bloodshed.

Thanks to these experiences, I fully appreciated Malta's dramatic role in the Second World War, during which it earned the dubious accolade of being the most densely bombed place on the face of the planet. I have sat in the communal subterranean air raid shelter across the road from Mġarr's domed church. Hewn from the bedrock, it is surprisingly spacious, with a central corridor off which radiate individual rooms. It is cool, but also damp and not a place you would want to linger. It is not hard to imagine the tense atmosphere as the townsfolk gathered there to ride out yet another devastating attack. What I wanted to do was to understand why the island had become the centre of such a violent maelstrom. And in order to do that, you need to explore the wider battle for the Mediterranean and the impact it had on the nations clustered along its shores. Thus the idea for this book was conceived.

PART 1:

The Mediterranean and North African Theatre of War

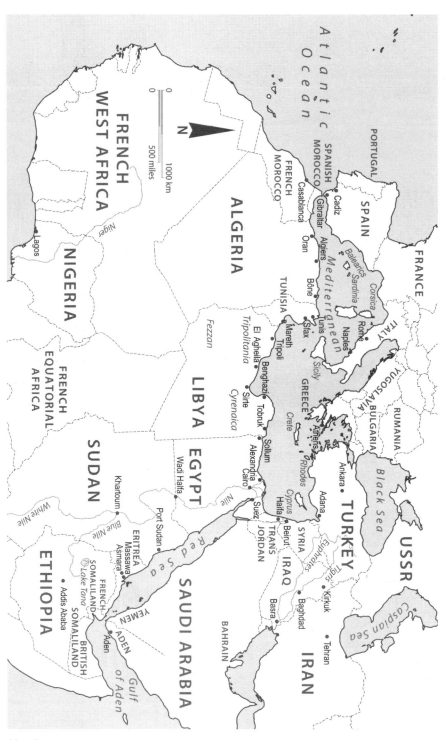

Map A

CHAPTER 1:
Rumblings in the Med

THE CROWD roared when the horseman and his retinue appeared. They rode down the wide boulevard, basking in the adoration and into the city square. A defeated chieftain stepped forwards and ceremoniously offered up his sword to the mighty Caesar. Triumphantly, the conqueror raised the jewel-encrusted weapon skywards, accepting the symbol of a fallen people. The rider was Il Duce, Benito Mussolini, the city was Tripoli and the year was 1937. At the time of Julius Caesar's death, Rome controlled an empire in North Africa that stretched from Numidia in the west to Cyrenaica in the east. History had now come full circle and Mussolini was reasserting Italy's ancient birthright. In doing so, he sowed the seeds for the Second World War spilling over into the Mediterranean.

Italy had taken much longer than many of its neighbours to forge itself into a unified state. As a result, it was slower than the other European powers in carving out a colonial empire; Italian expansion overseas had only really started just before the First World War. Across the Mediterranean, the Italians watched with intense interest as the French loosened the failing Turkish Ottoman Empire's grip on Algeria, Tunisia and then Morocco.

France and Spain came to a gentlemen's agreement, whereby the Spanish gained control of much of north-western Morocco. In particular, they occupied Ceuta opposite British-controlled Gibraltar. To the east, the British had long established themselves in Egypt. In between Tunisia and Egypt lay three Libyan provinces, Turkey's last possessions in North Africa, which Italy coveted. The Italians knew that the British, French and Spanish would not come to the Turks' aid if they attacked. The colonial powers already had their hands full. Besides, no one really wanted the desert wastes of Libya. It was just a case of waiting for the right moment to pounce.

POWER SHARING IN MOROCCO

During the early 1900s, the French resolutely expanded their North African Empire westwards into neighbouring Morocco. For many years, the Moroccans had avoided subjugation, but in 1906 the French persuaded the British and the Spanish to ignore France's military activities and that year, French soldiers moved into Oujda, just across the border from French Algeria – a move that was made in reprisal for the murder of a Frenchman. Their goal was the city of Fez, but an attack from this direction across the Atlas Mountains was not practical.

Then, in 1907, when the Moroccans rioted in Casablanca, French troops landed on the coast in order to restore order. In response, tribesmen came down from the hills to attack the coastal plain settlements. Fighting flared at Sidi Brahim, Taddert and Mediouna, although the French were subsequently distracted for a while by the unrest spreading into Algeria.

Riots in Fez in April 1911 gave General Moiner, at the head of 35,000 French troops, just the excuse he needed to occupy the city. At the same time, the Spanish moved to assert the Sultan of Morocco's authority over the rebellious tribes of the Ghomara and Yebala regions, adjacent to the Straits of Gibraltar, as well as the Rif mountains further east. The following year, Spain signed a joint protectorate treaty with France. The rest of Morocco became a French Protectorate under the Treaty of Fez, although resistance was not completely overcome until mid-1914. Nonetheless, these actions left France and Spain dominating both sides of the western Mediterranean.

THE ITALIAN BID FOR POWER

Italy was determined not to miss out on this North African land grab. Rome declared war on Turkey on 29 September 1911, with the intention of seizing control of Libya. Just as Rome had liberated Tripolitania and Cyrenaica from Carthage, now Italy was liberating them from despotic Ottoman rule. Or at least that was the public version of events. The Italians knew that the Turks, native Arabs and Berbers were not in a position to withstand an all-out attack.

In order to distract the Turks, the Italian Navy struck first in the Adriatic, attacking the Turkish base at Preveza in Epirus. For two days, Italian warships bombarded it, sinking a number of Turkish torpedo boats in the process. Then, on 3 October 1911, the Italians showed their true hand, launching a three-day bombardment of the Libyan port of Tripoli that saw Italian troops come ashore to secure the port of Tobruk on 4 October and the following day land at Tripoli.

Six days later, these operations developed into a fully fledged invasion, when General Carlo Caneva arrived at the head of an Italian expeditionary force. This proceeded to secure Benghazi and Derna, thereby giving the Italians control of Libya's coastline, in particular, the Gulf of Sirte. Although the Turks did not have the resources to launch a counter-attack, they inflamed the locals with a call to arms against the invading 'infidels'. Interestingly, former Italian soldier and political agitator Benito Mussolini was arrested for taking part in demonstrations against the war. He was sentenced to 12 months in jail, reduced to five on appeal. Mussolini therefore spent the winter of 1911–12 locked up in Forlì prison. When he emerged, he was an anti-war hero and a public figure.

To keep Turkey distracted, Italian warships appeared off the Dardanelles between 16 and 19 April 1912. They shelled Turkish defences, suggesting a threat to Constantinople. In reality, this was just a feint, as the Italians turned their attentions to the southern Aegean. There, they occupied Rhodes and the other Dodecanese islands without meeting any opposition from the Turks. From Rhodes, the Italians could intercept Turkish ships trying to ferry reinforcements and supplies to Libya.

In the summer of 1912, the Italians began to move into the Libyan interior. They deployed 100,000 troops to crush any resistance, 3,000 of whom were lost during the campaign. The Turks were defeated at Derna and Sidi Bilal, ending any hope they might have had of fending off the invaders. After years of feeling inferior, these victories created a new sense of national confidence in Italy. To safeguard Libyan waters, the Italian Navy created the Sicily-Libya command. Its naval bases included Palermo, Syracuse, Tobruk and Tripoli.

Turkey was unable to respond any further to this violation of its territory, because it faced a threat much closer to home. The Balkan

League, comprising Bulgaria, Greece and Serbia, were intent on driving the Turks from Macedonia and Thrace. These territories were vital for the defence of the northern reaches of the Ottoman Empire. On 15 October 1912, the Turks were obliged to sign a peace treaty with Italy. Just two days later, the Balkan League attacked.

Turkey was eventually defeated, losing all its European possessions. Ironically, the victors fell out, sparking the Second Balkan War. The Turks remained in no position to regain their lost lands, leaving Italy firmly in control of much of Libya. Not long after, Turkey, supporting Germany, became embroiled in the First World War. Following that, it found itself at war with Greece.

Italy sided with the Western Allies during the First World War, when it was promised a further share of the dismembered Ottoman Empire. Afterwards, the Italians were furious that they were not given the port of Fiume at the head of the Adriatic Sea. This had been ruled as part of the Austrian Empire until 1918. Instead, the Conference of Versailles wanted to give it to newly created Yugoslavia. In the Middle East, Britain and France shared out the remnants of the Ottoman Empire between themselves: Britain took control of mandates in Iraq, Jordan and Palestine; France gained Lebanon and Syria.

Once again, the Italians were made to feel inferior, which created a nationalist backlash. One thousand Italian war veterans, led by the poet Gabriele D'Annunzio, marched into Fiume in September 1919 and refused to leave. It was not until five years later that Italy was officially permitted to keep the port. In the aftermath of the First World War, the country was left in a state of political and economic chaos. This provided a highly fertile breeding ground for Mussolini's Fascist Party, which came to power in 1922.

THE NATIONALIZATION OF ITALY

Up until 1871, Italy was a country but not a nation. The great Italian nationalist Giuseppe Garibaldi started the process of nationalization in the mid-19th century and Mussolini's plan from the 1920s onwards was to complete it. Mussolini had every reason to resent his neighbours. After the Napoleonic wars, the various Italian kingdoms had been left in the hands of the Austrian and French royal families and the Pope. After the Congress of Vienna in 1815, Prince Metternich, the Austrian chancellor, said: '"Italy" is merely a geographical expression.'[1] That remark had rankled ever since. Between 1820 and 1845, Italy endured a series of rebellions. Garibaldi arrived in Genoa in 1848 for yet another one. Austria, Spain and France intervened and the independent kingdom of Italy was not declared until 1861. It was another five years before 80 per cent of Italian territory had been unified. This process was completed in 1870, with the inclusion of Venice and Rome. The Vatican, furious at the loss of its vast papal territories, refused to recognize Italian sovereignty until 1929.

MOROCCO FIGHTS BACK

In the meantime, the European powers remained largely indifferent to Italian colonial activities. While Italy slowly consolidated its hold on Libya, Spain struggled to retain Spanish Morocco. The Spanish Foreign Legion, although most of its recruits were actually Spanish, was formed in 1920 for just this purpose. Its second-in-command was a major by the name of Francisco Franco. He was already a veteran of the region, having previously commanded Moroccan troops. Promoted three years later to lieutenant-colonel, Franco took charge of the Legion. He was subsequently promoted to brigadier-general at the age of 33 on 3 February 1926, making him the youngest general in both Spain and Europe.

During the Rif War, Abd el-Krim led the Berbers against the Spanish at Annual in 1921 and annihilated 12,000 Spanish troops. This brought down the Spanish government and confined the Spanish to a few Moroccan coastal enclaves. These were later to provide Franco with a springboard for his Nationalist forces against the Republic. Franco and the Legion arrived at Melilla just in time to save the city from the Rifian forces.

This conflict showed up the inadequacy of the Spanish Navy. Spain's three battleships did not perform very well during the Rif War: the *España* ran aground on an uncharted reef off Morocco on 28 August 1923 and was abandoned after all salvage attempts failed and the *Jaime I* was damaged the following year by Rif artillery.

Abd el-Krim then foolishly tangled with the French military. His rebellion spread, but the French fought a determined and successful pacification campaign that lasted well into the early 1930s, by which time el-Krim had surrendered. Meanwhile, the strategically important Moroccan city of Tangier, with its large European population, was designated an international zone in 1924. This was administered by Britain, France and Spain, but not Italy.

ITALIAN RULE IN LIBYA

After Mussolini took charge in Rome in 1922, he saw Libya as a way of recapturing past imperial prestige. After all, it had once been a wealthy Roman province. Indeed, Mussolini had the ruins of the Roman cities, such as Cyrene and Leptis Magna, excavated and restored the ancient irrigation systems. He also built a triumphal arch between Tripoli and Benghazi and shipped in 300,000 settlers to create Italy's 'fourth shore'.

Mussolini's handling of the Libyans was brutal. When there was Libyan unrest between 1923 and 1931, Mussolini authorized the use of poison gas. Marshal Rodolfo Graziani next spent four years 'pacifying' the country. This gained him the nickname 'Breaker of Natives'. Despite these harsh methods, some Libyans fought back. One resistance leader who became a national hero was Omar al-Mukhtar, who waged a 20-year guerrilla campaign in Cyrenaica against the Italians. Mussolini eventually drained away his support by driving 100,000 people out of the Jebel Akhdar region into coastal concentration camps. There, many of them died from disease and starvation. Al-Mukhtar was captured in 1931 and Graziani had him tried and publicly executed.

Playboy Italo Balbo, governor-general of Libya. Italy's control of the country became a major threat to British interests in Egypt.

Mussolini subsequently appointed national hero and celebrity Air Marshal Italo Balbo as governor-general in 1933. He oversaw the merging of the provinces of Cyrenaica, Fezzan and Tripolitania under centralized rule, thereby creating Italian Libya. In addition to this work, the flamboyant Balbo was also a supporter of the paratrooper concept, establishing one of the very first parachute regiments in Tripoli.

Mussolini added yet more territory to Libya in early 1935. He did this by waiving Italian rights in Tunisia, where there were almost as many Italians as Frenchmen. In return, France granted Mussolini 114,000 sq miles (295,000 sq km) of territory in southern Libya. More importantly, France also surrendered a 21,000-mile (33,800-km) section of coast in French Somalia, which neighboured Eritrea. The latter had been an Italian colony since 1890. The French had moved to ensure that Mussolini had no say over affairs in Tunisia.

THE ALLIES TAKE DEFENSIVE ACTION

Behind the scenes, Pierre Laval, the French foreign minister, also told Mussolini that he could have a free hand with Ethiopia (Abyssinia). Laval did this because he was concerned about Germany and the future of Austria. It seemed a small price to pay if it meant an alliance with Fascist Italy. Laval was later to deny he ever made such a suggestion. France, though, was taking no chances with security in North Africa and was poised to start construction of the Mareth Line, designed to defend southern Tunisia against possible attack from Libya.

Mussolini gathered more than 500,000 men, under marshals Badoglio and Graziani, for the invasion of Ethiopia, to be launched from Eritrea and Italian Somaliland. Many of them were sent from Italy via the Suez Canal. The latter was owned by a consortium, with the British government as the majority shareholder. This military build-up could therefore hardly be missed. Sir John Maffey, the British permanent under-secretary at the Colonial Office, when asked to assess the threat reported: 'No vital British interest is concerned in Ethiopia except the head waters in Lake Tsana and the Nile basin'.[2]

Nonetheless, in response to Mussolini's preparations, Britain deployed its Mediterranean Fleet from Malta to the Levant. This was far weaker than the Italian Navy. Winston Churchill, in a state of some alarm, wrote to Sir Samuel Hoare, the foreign secretary, warning: 'It seems to me that you have not half the strength of Italy in modern cruisers and destroyers, and still less in modern submarines.',[3] He went on to point out that the Atlantic and Home fleets were 3,000 miles (4,830 km) away. Churchill was also concerned about rumours that in the event of war with Italy, Britain would withdraw from the Mediterranean and only defend the Strait of Gibraltar and the Red Sea. 'If we abandon the Mediterranean while in a state of war or quasi-war with Italy,' wrote Churchill, 'there is nothing to prevent Mussolini landing in Egypt in force and seizing the Canal. Nothing but France. Is the Admiralty sure of France in such a contingency?',[4] Part of the Home Fleet was therefore sent to reinforce the Mediterranean. The arrival of the battlecruisers *Hood* and *Renown*, along with the 2nd Cruiser Squadron and a destroyer flotilla, at Gibraltar seemed to indicate Britain's hardening resolve. Churchill was encouraged, noting: 'It was assumed on all sides that Britain would back her words with deeds.',[5]

Quite what the government hoped to achieve with this muscle flexing is unclear. British warships could hardly intercept Italian troopships without causing an international incident. Indeed, this deployment sparked an Anglo-Italian 'Cold War' that was to last five years before turning hot in 1940. Mussolini, however, was caught out by this 'Mediterranean Crisis' and ordered Marshal Pietro Badoglio to prepare plans for a possible conflict with Britain. After consulting his service chiefs, Badoglio replied: 'Your Excellency, with your inexhaustible resources of which you have given such evident proof, will surely be able to find an honourable solution to the current dreadful situation, and avoid a war with Britain.',[6] He pointedly provided no operational plans.

THE INVASION OF ETHIOPIA

Mussolini took no notice of the fact that the army and navy did not think he could win a war against Britain. His intelligence told him the British Home Fleet was short of ammunition, especially anti-aircraft rounds. 'Our battleships of course were old,' admitted Churchill, 'and it now appeared that we had no aircraft cover and very little anti-aircraft ammunition.',[7] The British could not afford to fight without the support of the French. Besides, the Royal Navy was having to counter the growing threat posed by the

Japanese in the Far East. Also, an Italian spy obtained a copy of the Maffey report from the British Embassy in Rome. Furthermore, the League of Nations would not sanction a war to stop a war. Mussolini therefore concluded that the British were simply bluffing. He guessed right: Britain had no intention of going to war and wanted to keep him as an ally against Hitler. Even if this meant sacrificing the Ethiopians.

MUSSOLINI AT WORK

The fortress-like Palazzo Venezia in Rome was where Mussolini maintained his office. In order to awe his visitors, he used the cavernous hall on the first floor. The imperial splendour, at odds with his socialist credentials, dwarfed his workspace, which consisted of a large table. Here, he insisted on absolute silence. Reportedly, his obsession for quiet was such that at the first sound of a fly he would summon a member of staff to swat it. The hall had a less savoury reputation, too, as it was where the Italian leader undertook many of his sexual assignations. Such were the trappings of this latter-day Caesar.

Mussolini duly appeared on the balcony of the Palazzo Venezia in Rome on the evening of 2 October 1935 to announce that Italy was poised to invade Ethiopia. Reporter Ward Price, with the *Daily Mail*, estimated that in excess of 400,000 people gathered for the occasion. Furthermore, Mussolini's speech was broadcast by radio throughout the country and was heralded by church bells. 'Then at 7.30, a sudden roar like a volcano eruption broke from the crowd,' recorded Price. 'Mussolini, in the grey uniform and round black cap of the Fascist militia, had stepped on to his floodlit balcony.'[8] He told the country they were at war. The following day, Italian troops poured into hapless Ethiopia, which had been so callously abandoned by Britain and France. Mussolini, and Hitler, took note that the Royal Navy did nothing. The British government had blinked and lost its nerve in the Mediterranean.

Churchill learned an important lesson. Britain had not acted soon enough, firmly enough or decisively enough in its dealings with Mussolini. 'The sensible course would have been gradually to strengthen the Fleet in the Mediterranean during the early summer,' Churchill noted, 'and so let him see how grave the situation was.'[9]

In his war of conquest, Mussolini relied on air power and gas to give him victory over the ill-equipped Ethiopians. To the outside world, this looked like a case of revenge for the Italian defeat at the hands of the Ethiopians at Adowa in 1896. Hitler had tried to dissuade Mussolini from his invasion, seeing it as an unnecessary diversion. The Italian leader took no heed and threw three army corps, supported by light tanks, artillery, aircraft and gas against the doomed Ethiopians. The latter bravely and futilely attacked the tanks with their bare hands.

An Ethiopian counter-offensive in December successfully drove Mussolini's forces back, ironically using German and Japanese-supplied weapons. Mussolini retaliated by bombarding their stronghold at Amba Aradam using 170 aircraft and 280 guns. What followed was little more than a massacre on an industrial scale. The Ethiopians were then finished off at Tembien and Maychew. Thus Mussolini annexed Ethiopia in 1936 and added it to his African empire.

He went on to employ the same repression techniques in Ethiopia that he had used to crush opposition in Libya. When a full-scale guerrilla war broke out, he summoned the 'Breaker of Natives'. 'I authorise Your Excellency once again,' he instructed Graziani, 'to begin conducting systematically the policy of terror and extermination against the rebels and the accomplice population.'[10]

In this way, Mussolini created Italian East Africa, comprising Ethiopia, Eritrea and Italian Somalia. His logic was hard to fathom. Libya was hardly an economic asset and these countries were little better. What this did do, though, was pose a direct threat to Britain's position in Aden, British Somaliland and access to the Red Sea. Lord Halifax, the British foreign secretary, lamented Mussolini's actions, observing: 'The general result has been, as we know, to produce a regrettable state of tension between our two countries, the effect of which was felt not only upon our mutual relations but over a much wider field. Particularly was this so in the Mediterranean…'[11] The French, meantime, continued building their 28-mile (45-km)-long Mareth Line – just to be on the safe side.

Churchill deeply regretted that Britain had missed an opportunity to teach Mussolini a lesson by taking military action:

How could Italy have fought this war? Apart from a limited advantage in modern light cruisers, her navy was but a fourth the size of the British. Her numerous conscript army, which was vaunted in millions, could not come into action. Her air power was in quantity and quality far below even our modest establishments. She would have been instantly blockaded.[12]

He made a mental note that Britain should never make the same mistake again.

CHAPTER 2:
Hemmed In

SPAIN FELL into a state of civil war in the summer of 1936, creating yet more security concerns in the Mediterranean. Mussolini immediately sided with the rebel Nationalists. This was hardly surprising as links between Italian Fascists and the Spanish right dated back to the creation of the Spanish Republic five years earlier. One of Mussolini's chief concerns was that communism be prevented from gaining a presence at the mouth of the Mediterranean, which as far as he was concerned was an 'Italian Sea'. His two senior generals, Balbo and Badoglio, did not support his desire for direct intervention.

Mussolini felt that a Republican victory would inevitably bring Spain and France together in an alliance against him. He complained to his wife: 'Bolshevism in Spain means Bolshevism in France, which means Bolshevism next door.'[1] Hitler agreed with him. 'If there hadn't been the danger of the Red peril's overwhelming Europe, I'd not have intervened in the revolution in Spain,'[2] he explained. However, Hitler had another motive: 'To distract the attention of the world powers to the Pyrenean Peninsula in order to complete the German re-armament without them intervening in Germany.'[3]

From the start, General Franco controlled Seville, Cádiz, Ceuta and Mellila as well as most of the Balearic Islands. This was largely thanks to Hitler and Mussolini. Franco and his other conspirators planned for the Spanish Navy to side with them, because it had a key role in the rising against the government. The warships were needed to ferry Nationalist colonial troops from Spanish Morocco to reinforce the mainland.

However, on most vessels, when the crews were tipped off, they overpowered the aristocratic officers. On the destroyers *Almirante Valdés* and *Sánchez Barcáiztegui*, for instance, the sailors swiftly took over. After shelling Ceuta and Melilla, they then sailed back to the naval base at Cartagena. The only operational battleship, the *Jaime I* (or *Jaime Primero*), the cruiser *Libertad* and the destroyer *Churruca* were all quickly secured for the Republic. In some cases, there was bloodshed. A case in point was the cruiser *Miguel de Cervantes*, aboard which the crew killed their officers after they resisted and hoisted the Republican flag. Again on the *Jaime I*, the sailors had to use force to subdue the officers, resulting in fatalities. When asked what to do with them, the Spanish Admiralty responded: 'Lower bodies overboard with respectful solemnity.'[4]

The loss of the fleet initially threatened to derail the rebels' plans. The Republicans possessed a battleship, three cruisers, 15 destroyers and about ten submarines. Some of them were gathered at Cartagena, from where they could easily menace Ceuta, Melilla and the Balearics. Fortunately for Franco, the ships were run by elected committees and the Republican fleet was soon in a state of utter confusion. The Royal Navy, alarmed at this mutiny by the lower decks, secretly permitted Franco to operate a signals section from Gibraltar.[5]

Taking advantage of the disarray in the Republican Navy, Franco crossed the Strait of Gibraltar from Ceuta with 3,000 men in early August 1936. His convoy was guarded by an ancient gunboat, which successfully fended off the Republican destroyer *Alcalá Galiano*. Two German battleships, the *Admiral Scheer* and *Deutschland*, then arrived to screen further Nationalist convoys. More significantly, Hitler secretly sent 30 Junkers 52 and Mussolini 11 Savoia 81 transport aircraft to Spanish Morocco.

Although painted with Nationalist Air Force markings, no one was fooled as to the origin of these aircraft or the nationality of their pilots. They airlifted 12,000 Nationalist troops to the mainland in the first two months of the conflict. By November 1936, almost double that number had been flown across the Straits. This was the very first massed airlift in the history of warfare. Hitler boasted: 'Franco ought to erect a monument to the glory of the Junkers 52.'[6] Certainly, without the aid of the Spanish

Foreign Legion and Moroccan forces, the Nationalists on the mainland could have lost the war in the opening stages.

In reality, Mussolini's contribution to this airlift was a farce from the start. Three aircraft from the first contingent flying from Sardinia got lost, one crashed in Algeria and two made forced landings in French Morocco. The French authorities found that the Italian Air Force markings had been recently painted out and that the crews were dressed as civilians. Not long after, a Spanish aircraft flew over Berkane, in French Morocco, and dropped a bundle containing Spanish Foreign Legion uniforms. They included a message written in Italian saying: 'Put on these and tell the French you belong to the Legion stationed at Nador.',[7] By then, a survivor had already admitted that they had been sent to help Franco.

In response, France sent the Republicans reconnaissance aircraft, bombers and fighters. For the French, the Spanish Civil War was a disaster. If Franco won, it meant they would have to contend with not two but three Fascist states on their borders. Instead of uniting France, though, the war in Spain splintered the French left- and right-wing political parties even further. The country already had a left-wing Popular Front government and many Frenchmen wanted to support Franco as a way of getting back at it.

Lord Halifax, the British foreign secretary, was adamant that 'the Spanish Civil War should not be permitted materially to affect the relations of Mediterranean Powers and their position in the Mediterranean.'[8] Both Britain and France wanted to encourage non-intervention by the international community, but this stance was undermined by Italy, Germany and Russia. Ulrich von Hassell, the German ambassador in Rome, astutely reported on 18 December 1936: 'The struggle for dominant political influence in Spain lays bare the natural opposition between Italy and France; at the same time the position of Italy as a power in the Western Mediterranean comes into competition with that of Britain.'[9]

Mussolini and Hitler, as the 'bulwarks of Western Christian civilization', grandly recognized Franco's regime on 8 November 1936 as the 'peak of life in the world'.[10] Hitler moved swiftly to reassure Mussolini that despite Germany's support for Franco, he had no ambitions in the Mediterranean. 'The Führer is anxious,' noted Count Galeazzo Ciano, the Italian foreign minister, 'that we should know that he regards the Mediterranean as a purely Italian sea. Italy has a right to positions of privilege and control in the Mediterranean. The interests of the Germans are turned towards the Baltic, which is their Mediterranean.'[11]

At the other end of the Mediterranean, the British were distracted by the Arab revolt in Palestine, which also broke out in 1936. The Arabs wanted independence and an end to Jewish immigration. It would take British forces until the summer of 1939 to quell the unrest. This required the commitment of up to 50,000 troops supported by the RAF and the Mediterranean Fleet. Among those involved were Generals Archibald Wavell and Bernard Montgomery. Even more worrying for the British, Egypt gained almost complete autonomy as well as a share in the control of the Suez Canal in 1936.

Mussolini sent 50,000 men, under General Mario Roatta, to Spain. They first saw action during the Málaga campaign in January–February 1937, when Italian forces supported the Nationalist offensive. Franco was clever, for he knew he could not lose, and anticipated Mussolini's position would harden in the face of international criticism, once his men tasted victory. Nothing could halt Roatta's light tanks, because a third of the Republican troops did not even have rifles and there was little ammunition for those who did. Thus Roatta cut through to the Mediterranean coast and Málaga fell. Mussolini was elated by the prowess of his troops.

MUSSOLINI WORKS ON HIS IMAGE

Despite his involvement in Spain, Mussolini had not forgotten Libya. In a piece of comic opera and grand propaganda he declared himself the 'Protector of Islam' in March 1937. Mussolini travelled to Tripoli to accept this accolade and to open the Via Balbia, a new, strategically important coastal road. Built by Balbo, it ran from the Egyptian border all the way to Tunisia, a distance of 1,132 miles (1,822 km). This was the first time Mussolini had been in the country in more than a decade. In that time, Balbo had modernized Tripoli to create a chic city by the sea. Gone were the slums, replaced with new civic buildings, gardens and wide tree-lined boulevards. There were also extravagant hotels built in neo-Moorish style, shops and a thriving tourist industry thanks to the grand prix.

Mussolini rode into Tripoli on horseback and received the Sword of Islam from Iusuf Kerisc, a pro-Italian Berber leader. Flanked by two mounted officers, with two Libyan foot soldiers stationed in front of him,

Mussolini posed for photographs with his new sword resting on his right shoulder. One of these showed him holding the sword aloft, with a groom holding the horse's bridle. This did not, however, fit Mussolini's image of machismo and the groom was subsequently airbrushed out. Heroic images of Mussolini were plastered all over Italy to promote his cult of Il Duce or 'The Leader'. To these, he now added the image of him as the successor to the Roman emperors.

He pompously declared his visit was: 'the consecration of the achievement of Fascist Italy in North Africa...'[12] Afterwards, there was a sumptuous banquet held in Balbo's headquarters, the former Turkish governor's palace. The whole event was like a badly orchestrated Hollywood epic with a cast of thousands. Most Muslim Libyans did not see Mussolini as anything other than a brutal conqueror. The sword he was so generously gifted had been crafted in Florence, on his orders.

Mussolini's actions naturally caused controversy in Jerusalem and Islam's other holy places. How, asked Mohammad Amin al-Husayni, the Grand

Benito Mussolini in Tripoli with the Sword of Islam. He dreamed of making himself the master of the Mediterranean.

Mufti of Jerusalem, could an Italian Roman Catholic be the 'Protector of Islam'? He was well aware of the brave exploits of Omar al-Mukhtar, who was also a Koranic scholar, against the Italians. However, al-Husayni was not in a position to cause trouble. Indeed, he was forced to flee Palestine in 1937 because of his support for the rising against British rule. Ironically, he would end up an ardent supporter of Mussolini and Hitler.

MUSSOLINI AND HITLER CEMENT THEIR RELATIONSHIP

Hitler sought to capitalize on Mussolini's ill-feeling towards Britain and France over how they had treated him in the Mediterranean, in Ethiopia and in Spain. He wanted Mussolini to side with him and knew the best way to impress the Italian leader was by a display of Germany's growing military strength. Mussolini duly arrived on a state visit on 25 September 1937. After a whirlwind three-day tour of Germany, the pair attended a massed rally in Berlin involving a million people. 'The greatest and most genuine democracies that the world knows today are Germany and Italy,' Mussolini told the rain-soaked crowd. 'I have a friend, I go with him through thick and thin to the very end.'[13] Mussolini went home suitably impressed and prepared to ignore Hitler's intended Anschluss with Austria. In return, Hitler would give him a free hand in the Mediterranean.

In Europe, Hitler's occupation of the demilitarized Rhineland, along the French border, was of much greater concern than the war in Spain. Britain and France, still hoping to stop Mussolini siding with the increasingly belligerent Hitler, therefore shamefully recognized his conquest of Abyssinia. Britain did this through the Easter Agreement signed in Rome on 16 April 1938. In return, Mussolini had to make some concessions: British recognition would only follow once Italian troops had ceased their involvement in Spain, and Mussolini had to promise that he had no territorial ambitions in Spain, in particular the Balearic Islands. Also, the Italians were to reduce their forces in Libya. Lord Halifax naively believed this agreement had: 'contributed to the cause of international peace...'[14]

British concern regarding the Balearics was understandable. Mussolini called them: 'our formidable new pawn on the Mediterranean chess board.'[15] He practically occupied the island of Majorca, where Palma hosted a joint Nationalist-Italian staff headquarters, overseeing the blockade against the Republic. The Italians were firmly the senior partners as they had greater resources. Furthermore, it was the main Italian bomber base for attacks on Republican shipping.

In addition to providing ground troops and aircraft, Mussolini meddled further in the war at sea by gifting Franco an old cruiser, four destroyers and two submarines to strengthen the Nationalist Mediterranean Fleet. However, this did not prevent the Republicans sinking the cruiser *Baleares* in the largest sea battle of the war. Other losses followed. Franco's only battleship, the *España* (previously the *Alfonso XIII*), was lost on 30 April 1937, after accidently hitting a Nationalist mine. The *Jaime I*, which fought with the Republicans, was damaged in an air attack on 13 August 1936. The following year, the vessel was destroyed by an internal explosion and the remains were scuttled. The Nationalists also lost a cruiser on 6 March 1938, when three Republican destroyers torpedoed the *Baleares*. The latter, and sister cruiser *Canarias*, had been responsible for sinking many Republican warships and merchant vessels.

Mussolini's Italian 'Legionary' submarines roamed the Mediterranean in support of the Nationalists from the summer of 1937. These sank Republican and neutral vessels at will, including the French merchant vessel *El Djem* off Valencia. One of them even fired a torpedo at the destroyer HMS *Havock*, but fortunately missed. The incident could have sparked a wider war.

British complaints about this and other torpedo attacks did nothing to deter Mussolini's support for Franco. In response, a maritime conference was held at Nyon, near Geneva, that deliberately excluded the Italians. The other Mediterranean powers agreed to establish naval patrols that would use force to protect non-Spanish shipping. If Mussolini stopped his submarine attacks, he could join the Nyon scheme. 'It is a fine victory,' noted Italian Foreign Minister Ciano with amusement. 'From suspected pirates to policemen of the Mediterranean – and the Russians, whose ships we were sinking, excluded!'[16] The Nyon Agreement did not stop the flow of weapons to the belligerents and ships continued to be sunk, but from the air rather than by submarine.

Hitler's warships were also involved in the Mediterranean. After a German cruiser was bombed by the Republicans off Ibiza, he ordered another cruiser to shell the Republican-held port of Almería in reprisal. All this made the British extremely nervous about the future of Gibraltar. If Franco prevailed, might he seek to take it with the help of his new-found allies?

Republican Barcelona, Spain's largest city and biggest Mediterranean port, also came under air attack. On the evening of 16 March 1938, Mussolini sent his bombers from Majorca to hit it 17 times over the space of two days. At first, it was thought they were targeting the port, but the bombs rained down indiscriminately. The city had no anti-aircraft guns and around 1,300 people were killed and 2,000 wounded. Mussolini authorized these attacks without Franco's permission. The latter, when he learned of them, ordered an immediate stop.

Mussolini was clearly grandstanding and was very pleased by the results. He said that his countrymen: 'should be horrifying the world by their aggressiveness for a change, instead of charming it by the guitar.'[17] His real intention, though, had been to impress Hitler. 'This will send up our stock in Germany too,' observed Ciano, 'where they love total ruthless war.'[18]

Barcelona fell to Franco's forces on 26 January 1939. The Republicans, who had already been cut off from the Bay of Biscay in the north, were now cut off from the Mediterranean. Willie Forest, a reporter with the *London News Chronicle*, was there and witnessed the Nationalist and Italian advance from Mount Tibidabo: 'We had a magnificent grandstand view of the battlefields. The city, choked with refugees, was being bombed by the Italians. It was wintry cold,' he wrote. 'What a contrast to those summer days of August 1936 when I'd seen the streets filled with laughing, cheering crowds of anarchists and communists…'[19]

In the wake of the Easter Agreement, Mussolini still felt hemmed in by the British and French. To him, this was a national affront. On 4 February 1939, he warned the Italian Grand Council: 'Italy is closed in the Mediterranean "prison". The bars of this prison are: Cyprus, Malta, Tunisia, Corsica; the gates: Suez and Gibraltar…'[20] He knew that he was not in a position to challenge the combined strength of the British and the French fleets. Not yet at least. Looking ahead, if he were to ally himself with Hitler's Nazi Germany and there was war in Europe, perhaps some spoils might fall his way. At the same time, though, Mussolini was alarmed by Hitler's steady expansion down the Danube and sought to block him in the Balkans. Shortly after, Mussolini felt compelled to send troops to Veneto to deter a German invasion of Croatia.

Mussolini and the Italian military then received a major morale boost on 28 March 1939, when Franco's army marched triumphantly into Madrid, heralding the end of the civil war. Italian troops came home as heroes and Mussolini rather surprisingly withdrew from the Balearics. This was because he was already planning his next military campaign. Meanwhile, Hitler had dismembered Czechoslovakia.

MUSSOLINI INVADES ALBANIA

Casting about to expand his empire and counter Hitler, rather ridiculously, Mussolini turned on Albania. Signalling trouble, Italian warships arrived off the Albanian coast on 6 April 1939 and evacuated Italian nationals. That night, his troopships sailed across the Adriatic from Bari and Brindisi. The following day, soldiers, backed by a naval bombardment and air attacks, landed at the coastal towns of Durazzo, San Giovanni di Medua, Santi Quaranta and Valona. From there, they advanced into Tirana, the Albanian capital, on 8 April.

Mussolini claimed he had been forced to act after King Ahmed Zog had shown hostile intentions against Italy and her citizens. These, he argued, were as a result of his refusal to provide Zog with troops for use against Yugoslavia. In reality, he had demanded extensive basing rights that Zog

Italian warships entering Durazzo harbour during the invasion of Albania.

simply could not agree to. There was little the 10,000-strong Albanian army could do and within a week the country was completely occupied. The Italian King, Victor Emmanuel III, took the Albanian throne and Zog fled into exile, eventually arriving in London. He took with him his queen, Hungarian Countess Géraldine Apponyi, all of Albania's gold reserves and 12 bodyguards. Royal official Abas Kupi tried unsuccessfully to lead a rebellion in Durazzo, after which the Albanians were largely resigned to their fate. They were subsequently recruited into the Italian armed forces, except for the army.

The British military were caught out by the invasion and were dismayed by Mussolini's hollow platitudes. They did not believe he would actually do it and refused to countenance the threat was real until too late. 'It would take weeks of preparation and we would be bound to know of it,' said General Lord Gort, the chief of the imperial general staff on 5 April. 'Besides, Mussolini had given the assurance that there was no intention on the part of Italy to interfere with Albania's integrity.'[21]

The irony was that Albania had been a de facto Italian protectorate ever since the First World War. Zog, who came from a bandit family, only remained Albania's first monarch thanks to Italian money. The League of Nations did nothing in response and Mussolini blandly reassured Britain that he would not attack Yugoslavia or Greece. He had not warned Hitler prior to his operations against Albania, but Hitler did not seem to care. Nor did the French. Britain, though, was thoroughly alarmed that this military adventure breached the Easter Agreement and threatened the balance of power in the Mediterranean. This the Italians denied. On the very day of the invasion, Count Ciano, the Italian foreign minister, claimed: 'The Italian Government fully intended to respect the independence and integrity of Albania and the status quo in the Mediterranean.'[22] Afterwards, Lord Halifax warned: 'Disquiet and uneasiness have been manifested not only in the adjacent areas but in other countries bordering on the Mediterranean...'[23]

Mussolini now had a springboard from which to attack Greece or Yugoslavia – both of which were much weaker militarily than Italy. British Prime Minister Neville Chamberlain was furious that he had been duped: 'Mussolini has behaved to me like a sneak and a cad.'[24] Chamberlain therefore felt obliged to add Greece and Romania to the list of countries Britain pledged to support.

Publicly, the successful occupation of Albania had been yet another demonstration of Mussolini's military prowess. Behind the scenes, though, the reality was somewhat different. Radio communication between Italy and Albania was so poor that it required a senior officer to fly between the two countries on a regular basis to deliver situation reports. Filippo Anfuso, Ciano's chief of staff, noted scathingly: 'If only the Albanians had possessed a well-armed fire brigade, they could have driven us back into the Adriatic.'[25] Taking Tirana was hardly comparable to Hitler's highly significant triumphs over Vienna and Prague.

Mussolini was not concerned by such trivia; it was the result that mattered. Flexing his military muscles even further, he rapidly expanded his number of divisions. He did this by the simple expedient of reducing divisional strength from three infantry regiments to just two. This meant the army could field an impressive 73 divisions, though 24 of these were deployed in Aegean and other overseas possessions. Albania alone tied up four divisions. Furthermore, all of them were infantry units, largely armed with First World War vintage weapons.

Britain had every reason to be nervous about Mussolini's intentions. The revitalized Italian fleet currently outnumbered the Royal Navy in the Mediterranean and had a plethora of bases. Those at Sardinia, Sicily and Libya posed a serious threat to the central Mediterranean. From the tiny island of Pantelleria, the Italians were able to regularly spy on shipping passing between Sicily and Tunisia. This area formed a choke point at which the Italian fleet could cut Alexandria off from Malta and Gibraltar.

Mussolini's greatly enhanced navy was impressive, comprising six battleships, 21 cruisers, 50 destroyers and 100 submarines. Against this, the British Mediterranean Fleet had seven battleships, eight cruisers, 37 destroyers and just eight submarines. Crucially, it also had two aircraft carriers, which extended its strike range. Mussolini was not unduly concerned about this, because the land-based Italian Air Force could pit 2,000 aircraft against the Fleet Air Arm and the RAF.

TIME TO PICK A SIDE

Just six weeks after the invasion of Albania, Mussolini committed himself to a military alliance with Hitler known as the Pact of Steel. Britain, scrabbling around for allies in the region, approached Turkey. The Turks, however, were much more concerned about events in the neighbouring Aegean and the Balkans. Nonetheless, the Turkish government agreed in principle that in the event of war in the Mediterranean, the two countries should co-operate and assist each other. That this never came to anything is hardly surprising in light of Turkey traditionally being pro-German.

Mussolini, meanwhile, was alarmed by the cynical Nazi-Soviet Pact, which enabled Hitler and Stalin to carve up Poland between them in September 1939. He knew this would have serious ramifications with Franco. The Spanish leader could hardly be happy that his former ally had sided with his former enemy, which had fought to save the Republic. 'You will not be surprised if I tell you that the German-Russian agreement has had painful repercussions in Spain,' Mussolini warned Hitler on 3 January 1940. 'The earth which covers the dead – yours and ours and Spanish – is still fresh.'(26) Hitler's duplicity signalled to Franco that he could not be trusted. Germany's attack on Poland now meant that it was at war with Britain and France. Mussolini and Franco had a decision to make: would they side with Hitler?

PART 2:
The Western Desert

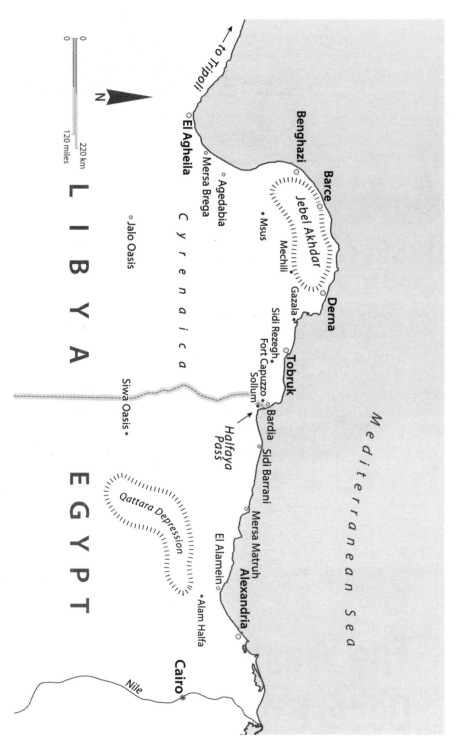

Map B

CHAPTER 3:
Desert Frontline

FROM THE Palazzo Venezia, on 10 June 1940, Mussolini informed the world that Italy was going to war with Britain and France. As far as he was concerned, their provocations over the last few years could no longer be tolerated. 'We want to break the territorial and military chains which hold us asphyxiated in our sea,' he declared, 'for a people of 45 million souls is only truly free if it has at its disposal free access to the ocean...', Dressed for the occasion, in his comic opera uniform of Corporal of Honour of the Fascist Militia, he looked like some Ruritanian general. Mussolini, though, was deadly serious.

The crowd gathered below were decidedly unenthusiastic at the prospect of yet another war. There seemed to be no end to them. While the young men may have been fired up at the thought of a fight, the police noted that none of the women clapped. Waving his arms with a flourish, Mussolini concluded: 'To arms and show your tenacity, your courage and your valiance.', His speech was broadcast live around Italy's piazzas and again was greeted with mixed emotions. People's reservations quickly proved well founded.

THINGS START TO GO WRONG FOR THE ITALIANS

That very day, just over a month after Hitler had invaded France, Marshal Graziani attacked westward against French defences high in the Alps.

Although he had an overwhelming numerical superiority his men were poorly equipped to cope with the cold and resupply proved a serious problem. Embarrassingly, they failed to break through. This hardly put Mussolini in a strong negotiating position with the French, who were already teetering on the brink of defeat thanks to Hitler. Mussolini was undoubtedly shaken by the poor performance of the Italian Army during the campaign against France from 10 to 25 June 1940. 'Mussolini is quite humiliated because our troops have not moved a step forward,' wrote Ciano on 21 June. 'Even today they have not succeeded in advancing and have halted in front of the first French fortifications which put up some resistance.',[3] Strategic planning by the Italian general staff was always focused on the Mediterranean. They had never really considered an Alpine offensive operation. In consequence, Mussolini's opportunist attack on the south of France was a shameful fiasco in the face of French resistance; the latter with just five demoralized divisions beat off 32 Italian divisions. Mussolini's pilots had done little better against their French counterparts. The Italians suffered 4,000 casualties, whereas the French lost just over 200 men.

In retaliation, the French very briefly attacked Italian soil in the Mediterranean. A French naval squadron sailed up the coast to Genoa, where it shelled factories, oil tanks and refineries. However, the French High Command, in a state of disarray after Hitler's invasion, refused to authorize offensive action against Mussolini. As a result, Admiral Jean François Darlan stopped any further naval attacks. What is more, when Churchill wanted the RAF to bomb Milan and Turin from Marseilles, the French prevented the British bombers from taking off. This was despite the RAF having already made a series of attacks on Genoa in support of the French.

Battered France signed an armistice with Hitler on 22 June 1940, followed by one with Mussolini two days later. These came into effect on 25 June and the war in France officially came to an end. Mussolini wanted the French naval bases at Toulon and Marseilles, as well as the disarmament of French Corsica, Djibouti and Tunisia. He received little except use of the port of Djibouti in French Somaliland. This was not much of a concession as he already controlled most of the Horn of Africa.

Mussolini was gambling on Hitler next invading Britain, which would give him an opportunity in North Africa and the Balkans. However, things there did not go any better. Marshal Italo Balbo, the Italian commander in chief in Libya, was under no illusions about the capability of his forces. He had no way of emulating Hitler's Blitzkrieg because he had no way of speedily moving his large army up the coast road. Although his 250,000 men easily outnumbered the 36,000 troops in Egypt, many of his divisions were poorly equipped and far from mechanized. Notably, they were deficient in transport and tanks.

A LACK OF MILITARY MIGHT

The bulk of Balbo's forces, consisting of the 5th Army's nine divisions divided into three corps, were deployed in Tripolitania facing the French in Tunisia; 10th Army's five divisions organized in two corps were in Cyrenaica, poised to threaten Egypt. Following Hitler's invasion of Poland, Balbo was instructed by Marshal Graziani, Army chief of staff, to prepare plans for attacks on both Egypt and Tunisia. Balbo was not optimistic about implementing these when war broke out. Being between the British in Egypt and the French in Tunisia made his position feel 'like a slice of ham in a sandwich'.[4] Once France had been knocked out of the war, however, Balbo was able to redeploy some of the Tripolitania forces. At this stage, Balbo pointed out to the Italian High Command in Rome that he anticipated an attack on Egypt would require at least 13 divisions, two of which should be armoured and two airborne.

Balbo's infantry divisions were equipped with the L3 tankette, which was no match for the British cruiser tanks, and most of his artillery was decades old. Although the Italian Air Force and Navy were powerful, only the army could seize and hold Egypt. The Libyan Tank Group, consisting of two battalions of M11/39 medium tanks, was forming. However, these tanks were poorly designed and the unit lacked the flexibility and strength of a proper armoured division. Nor was the air force in a position to assert full control over sea and land in North Africa. Although it had 84 modern bombers, 144 obsolescent fighters and 113 other aircraft, the air force was unable to conduct sustained operations against the British.

Furthermore, most of Italy's colonial troops were untrained for modern warfare and were poorly armed. The Italians had good cause to restrict their colonial forces, for fear they might one day turn on their masters. Generally, their role was to keep the tribes of the interior in check. The Royal Corps of Colonial Troops included infantry and cavalry. At the outbreak of war,

Balbo amalgamated these into two motorized infantry divisions. By far the best desert warfare forces were the motorized Saharan units, but they only consisted of six companies plus two companies of camel-mounted troops.

THE BRITISH AND ITALIANS COME TO BLOWS

War in North Africa was exactly a development that Churchill feared. General Sir Archibald Wavell's position in Egypt was extremely weak and he knew that while he assembled more troops he needed to keep the Italians off balance. He had been appointed in August 1939 and his command covered a vast area: he was responsible for all British forces in Aden, British Somaliland, Cyprus, Egypt, Iraq, Palestine, Transjordan and Sudan. Not only had he to contend with the Italians in Libya, but there were also those in East Africa. At the same time, he had to be alert to Russian intentions in the Persian Gulf after Stalin had so treacherously supported Hitler's destruction of Poland.

Wavell's forces in Egypt comprised the incomplete 7th Armoured Division, the 4th Indian Division plus two infantry brigades; one of the latter was deployed on permanent internal security duties. The 6th Australian Division was in the process of assembling in Palestine, but even when that arrived Wavell would only have a corps with which to fend off the entire Italian Army. On 8 June 1940, this task fell to General Richard O'Connor, who took charge of all the British forces in the Western Desert. With the outbreak of war two days later, Wavell, encouraged by Balbo's inactivity, instructed elements of 7th Armoured to raid the Italian frontier.

Mussolini's declaration seemed to have little impact on the Italian garrisons at Capuzzo, Maddalena and Sidi Omar. The next day, Rolls-Royce armoured cars of the 11th Hussars ambushed an Italian convoy on the way to Sidi Omar and captured two bewildered Italian officers along with 50 Libyan soldiers. At the same time, the RAF launched raids against Italian targets in Libya. It also took the war to the Italian Navy by disabling the cruiser *San Giorgio* moored at Tobruk. By midday on 12 June, some 70 Italian and Libyan prisoners were being herded back to Egypt. When the British reconnoitred the two forts at Sidi Omar on 13 June, they found them abandoned and partly gutted. Simultaneously, a British patrol probed the defences at Fort Maddalena. This time, they were greeted by machine-gun fire and attacked by the Italian Air Force.

The following day, the British struck again, supported by a squadron of bombers. After some token resistance, Maddalena was quickly taken. The fort included 'a high class barracks, an electric light plant and a refrigerator, a garage, an underground water tank, an 80-foot observation tower'.[5] At the same time, the British 4th Armoured Brigade attacked Fort Capuzzo and the fortified camp at Sidi Azeiz. Although the former was taken, the Italians held on to the latter.

On 15 June, O'Connor and Wavell had a bit of luck when they captured a staff car containing an Italian general and his two lady friends. The general just happened to be carrying detailed plans of the defences at Bardia.

The Italians were annoyed by these constant small border incursions. In response, Colonel D'Avanzo was given instructions by the commander of the 1st Libyan Division that said: 'You will destroy enemy elements which have infiltrated across the frontier, and give the British the impression of our decision, ability and will to resist.'[6]

D'Avanzo's strike force consisted of two columns of lorried infantry, supported by four guns and a company of tankettes. They promptly ran into British armoured cars and light tanks, sparking the Battle of Nezuet Ghirba on 16 June. Foolishly, D'Avanzo's men formed a square with their

The Italian cruiser San Giorgio *at Tobruk. Its fate was to be used as an anti-aircraft barge.*

vehicles, while their tiny tanks roared forwards to counter-attack. When the dust settled, the British had suffered no casualties, whereas just a third of the Italian force survived, with seven officers and 94 men captured. The British also seized their guns and 17 light tanks. Among the dead bodies was the unfortunate D'Avanzo. While these victories were modest, they did wonders for British morale. In contrast, the Italians were alarmed by just how aggressive the British were.

Frustratingly for Mussolini, when pressured to attack, Balbo came up with numerous excuses for not doing so. 'It is not the number of men,' he signalled Mussolini, 'which causes me anxiety, but their weapons.',[7] He pointed out that his artillery was ancient and that he lacked anti-tank and anti-aircraft guns. Without these, he would be unable to protect his lines of communication from Tripoli, through Benghazi to Tobruk and Bardia. 'To have fortified works without adequate weapons is an absurdity,' concluded Balbo.[8] The logic of this argument was hard to fathom when he was supposed to be taking the war into Egypt, not worrying about defending Libya.

Balbo's list of demands went on. To get his men over the frontier he would need armoured divisions, 1,000 lorries and 100 water-tankers. He was promised that he would get what he needed. Balbo knew, though, that Italian military resources were stretched to the limit. Even if he got everything, on the Egyptian side of the border the road between Sollum and Sidi Barrani was not surfaced. How was he supposed to rush headlong towards Suez when there was not even a proper road?

There was another reason for Balbo's reluctance to act. While the British saw themselves surrounded and outnumbered, faulty Italian intelligence assessed that the enemy was stronger than it really was; Italian reports spoke of a 100,000-strong Anglo-Egyptian Army. Even the Italian Navy, which was the most modern of the Italian armed forces, feared the firepower of the Royal Navy. The Italian chief of the general staff warned:

The British battleships, escorted by a considerable number of destroyers, could cruise at will in the Mediterranean inflicting all the damage they wanted on our ill-defended coasts. Nor can we make much use of the air force which finds itself in a state of crisis and whose older material, which is the bulk of it, would be out of action after a few days...[9]

Then the Italians suffered yet another mishap. On 28 June, Balbo was accidently shot down over Tobruk while flying from Derna to Sidi Azeiz to review the troops. Unfortunately for Balbo, the British had just been bombing Tobruk, so the nervous gunners were extra alert. When Balbo's three-engine Sparrowhawk bomber appeared not only did the anti-aircraft batteries open fire, but the cruiser *San Giorgio* added to the deadly barrage. The plane fell from the sky, instantly killing Balbo and his crew. Tellingly, Mussolini did not seem unduly distressed by the loss of Balbo, who had been with him since the start of Fascism. This led to rumours that Mussolini had plotted Balbo's death. He was replaced by Marshal Graziani, whom many Libyans despised as a butcher.

Despite their blunders, the Italians did learn from their early brushes with the British and had some success. For example, a British patrol sent to raid the Bardia–Tobruk road on 25 July was caught by the Italian Air Force and the survivors were successfully surrounded by Italian tanks. Then on 5 August, the 8th Hussars clashed with a battalion of Italian medium tanks between Capuzzo and Sidi Azeiz. This action, though, proved inconclusive and the frontier lapsed into a period of inactivity.

These probing attacks confirmed to Wavell and O'Connor that although the Italians might have superior numbers they were poorly equipped. Also, there was a very noticeable distance between Italian officers and their men. While most officers were capable, they lived privileged and separate lives from the rank and file. On the whole, most Italians were reluctant soldiers who had little respect for their commanders. Additionally, in the first three months of the war, Italian morale had taken a pummelling. They had suffered 3,500 casualties; the British just 150. Large quantities of equipment had likewise been lost. It was not a promising start.

Meanwhile, in Rome, Mussolini was continually exasperated by the army's apparent inactivity in Libya. Graziani, like Balbo before him, seemed to have unending reasons for not striking Egypt. He had promised to start an offensive on 4 August 1940 and then promptly cancelled it. Losing patience, Mussolini told him that unless he attacked immediately he would be relieved. While in Rome on 8 August, Graziani told Count Ciano: 'The water supply is entirely insufficient. We move towards defeat which, in the desert, must inevitably develop into a total disaster.'[10]

Shortly after, Mussolini sent instructions stating: 'It is not a question of aiming for Alexandria, nor even for Sollum. I am only asking you to

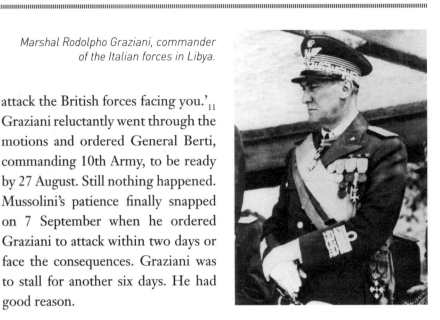

Marshal Rodolpho Graziani, commander of the Italian forces in Libya.

attack the British forces facing you.'[11] Graziani reluctantly went through the motions and ordered General Berti, commanding 10th Army, to be ready by 27 August. Still nothing happened. Mussolini's patience finally snapped on 7 September when he ordered Graziani to attack within two days or face the consequences. Graziani was to stall for another six days. He had good reason.

OPENING FORAYS IN LIBYA

Along the eastern coast of Libya, the Italians were learning to fear the power of Admiral Andrew Browne Cunningham's heavy guns. He sent his battleships HMS *Warspite*, *Malaya*, *Ramillies* and the cruiser HMS *Kent*, with a destroyer escort, to pound Italian positions around Bardia and Fort Capuzzo. At 0700 hours on 17 August 1940, *Warspite* opened up with her massive 15-in guns. Behind her, the *Kent* joined in with a salvo from her 8-in guns. The latter alone fired 94 rounds before being ordered to cease fire. A spotter plane reported that both ships were right on target, though there was no sign of life.

The force then turned back for Alexandria, but this was a deliberate ploy to draw out the Italian Air Force. It had the desired effect when Italian bombers appeared. British fighters gave chase and three planes were brought down near the *Kent*. These harassing operations by the navy continued. The gunboat HMS *Ladybird* on the night of 23/24 August 1940 sailed unopposed right into Bardia harbour and shelled everything in sight. Such attacks greatly hampered Graziani's preparations.

Graziani's generals told him that to take Sollum and secure the coast road they would first have to take the pass to the west and Halfaya Pass to the south. He planned to march eastwards using the 21st Metropolitan Corps. This would oversee the two divisions committed to the main attack, with a third held as reserve near Tobruk. To shield their flank, the two motorized Libyan divisions, plus a mobile group under General Maletti, would push over the escarpment in the south. This plan was swiftly thwarted by poor co-ordination and mobility. The Libyan divisions took ages to gather near Fort Capuzzo and the Maletti Group, due to rendezvous near Sidi Omar, got lost. The Italian Air Force, which was supposed to be attacking British outposts, had to divert planes to find the wayward Maletti.

Graziani was forced to rethink his plans, especially after he received intelligence indicating British armour was poised to strike his southern flank. The Libyan divisions were instructed to head the advance, with the 1st Blackshirt Division ready to come forwards if they suffered heavy casualties. The 4th Blackshirt and 64th Catanzaro divisions would be on call near Tobruk. Maletti was ordered to move further north to screen the advance. This was hardly the 13 divisions envisaged by the late Balbo.

To oppose them, O'Connor had three infantry battalions, with armoured car, artillery and tank support. He had established his main defensive position at Mersa Matruh 120 miles (193 km) from the frontier. Held in reserve were the tanks of the 7th Armoured Division. Wavell and O'Connor had no intention of sacrificing their screening force. Its job was simply to harass the Italians as much as possible, then retreat to the next position so the process could start all over again.

BATTLE BEGINS

Graziani's attack on Egypt opened on 13 September 1940, when his artillery shelled the abandoned Egyptian barracks at Musaid. The battle for the Mediterranean had finally started, much to Mussolini's relief. He had been waiting three long months for this day. The Italian columns rolled through the gaps in the frontier wire left by the 11th Hussars. From Musaid, the Italian guns then bombarded the barracks at Sollum. Another column, stretching back towards Capuzzo, moved up the pass and then down towards the little port of Sollum. Graziani's advance was very old-school: his artillery first pounded the open desert before his men advanced cautiously, fearful of a British armoured counter-attack. Although the cavalcade was protected by the Italian Air Force, it still presented an easy target.

The Italians took Sollum, which was only held by a platoon, and Halfaya Pass. Men from the 3rd Coldstream Guards were almost amused to find

Italian troops in Libya taking Holy Communion in September 1940. Mussolini was incensed that his attack on Egypt took so long to prepare.

themselves the target of the entire 1st Libyan Division. The congested Italian lorries, motorcycles and light tanks negotiating the sharp hairpin bends in the passes soon came under fire from British artillery and were bombed by the RAF. Moving east, the Italian vehicles threw up great clouds of choking dust that attracted yet more shell fire. They then pressed on towards Buq Buq with the waters of the Gulf of Sollum to their north.

Up on the plateau above Halfaya, the Italian units that had moved up from Sidi Omar baked in the sun and the engines of their vehicles boiled in the heat. To add to their misery, they were subjected to continual air attack and shelling. By nightfall, when they got to the pass, they found an enormous traffic jam involving thousands of Italian and Libyan troops. Fearful of attack, they formed leaguers (encampments) like old-fashioned wagon trains. Their searchlights, intended to detect enemy aircraft, simply acted as aiming points for a detachment of British guns.

This pattern of fighting was exactly the same on 14 September, with the British artillery regularly firing and then redeploying. Overhead, the RAF's fighters fought their Italian counterparts, while its bombers broke through to attack the columns. When the Italian column coming down from Halfaya Pass met the one from Sollum, they combined into a swirling mass of vehicles, presenting an even greater target. The tempo of British shelling was such that by early afternoon the next day the gunners had run out of ammunition.

On 16 September, some 50 Italian tanks turned from the road and moved a few miles inland in the Alam el Dab area. For an instant it looked as if they might cut off the British rearguard. Instead, the 11th Hussars swiftly intervened, enabling the 3rd Coldstreams to get clear. That night, the British rearguard slipped away from Sidi Barrani to Mersa Matruh. They were replaced by advance elements of the 1st Blackshirt Division. It took Graziani four days to cover the 60 miles (97 km) to Sidi Barrani, which was only halfway to the main British defences. Italian radio grandly announced the successful capture of an Egyptian town. In reality, it was little more than a coastal village. 'All is now quiet in Sidi Barrani,' claimed the broadcast, 'the shops are open and the trams running again.'[12] This was news to the locals, as they did not have any tramlines.

It was such a small victory. Graziani's troops were covered in dust, exhausted and parched. They had suffered 120 dead and 410 wounded. Their tanks and what lorries they had kept breaking down. Ammunition and fuel were running low. Graziani ordered an advance post to be established at Maktila, just 10 miles (16 km) east of Sidi Barrani and refused to go any further. He signalled Rome that he needed substantial reinforcements and until he got them that he would hold the British by building defensive positions stretching south-west towards the escarpment. Graziani intended to deploy his two Libyan divisions in forward positions, backed by the 4th Blackshirt Division holding Sidi Barrani. Behind them would be another five divisions.

In the meantime, the Italians set about resurfacing the road between Sollum and Sidi Barrani. They also began to lay water pipes and stockpile supplies. Graziani, in an act of self-inflated ego, ordered the construction of a monument at the roadside in Sidi Barrani to celebrate the Italian Army's achievement.

General O'Connor was deeply disappointed that Graziani had halted, noting: 'We had hoped he would try and advance to the neighbourhood of Matruh, as we had prepared a full-scale counter-stroke with all our armour … he never came far enough to put it into execution.'[13] The loss of

Sidi Barrani was, however, a blow to Wavell, because he lost the advanced airfields there. This deprived his bombers of a refuelling stop and reduced his aircrafts' range; the RAF's Hurricanes could no longer reach Malta and ships intending to attack Bardia could no longer expect fighter cover.

CHAPTER 4:
Fallen Allies

AT SEA, Churchill enjoyed a number of significant technological advantages. First, he had aircraft carriers, which Mussolini did not. Perhaps even more critical was the fact that the Italian warships had no radar, so they were forced to fight visually by day and blind by night. They were therefore largely reliant on maritime reconnaissance squadrons based along the Italian coast and in Sardinia and Sicily, some of which were equipped with long-range seaplanes. To make matters worse, the bulk of these units were operated by the Italian Air Force, not the Italian Navy, which invariably led to co-ordination and communication problems.

At the start of the war, superficially, Britain's carrier force looked formidable. However, half the fleet was in fact obsolete. HMS *Courageous*, dating from 1916, had been sunk in 1939, only a fortnight after the conflict commenced. In response, her sister ship *Glorious* was recalled home from the Mediterranean, only to be lost during the evacuation of Norway in June 1940. She was replaced in the Mediterranean by HMS *Eagle*, which dated from the 1920s.

Luckily, in light of the increasing threat of war, in the 1930s five new British carriers were laid down. *Ark Royal* was completed in 1938 and was the first 'modern' carrier to join the fleet since the remodelled *Glorious* in 1930. She was able to carry more aircraft and was faster than the earlier types. *Ark Royal* was deployed to the Mediterranean. In addition, four Illustrious class carriers were laid down in 1937, with *Illustrious*, *Victorious* and *Formidable* launched two years later. The last of the class, *Indomitable*, was launched in 1940. *Argus* was also recalled to active service. Two more carriers, in the Implacable class, were started in 1939, but changing priorities meant they were not completed until 1944.

While the Royal Navy were planning their operations against the Italians, they also had to consider the uncertain fate of the sizeable French Mediterranean fleet. There was every prospect that *Ark Royal* might have to act against its former allies. Churchill and the Admiralty were particularly alarmed at the prospect of the French Navy falling into Hitler and Mussolini's hands.

In the end, Hitler, after the fall of France, decided not to demand the French fleet. It was better to leave it dispersed across the Mediterranean than force it together in response to orders it surrender to Germany. The reason for this was that such a move might also force it into the arms of the British. Instead, under the terms of the Franco-German Armistice, French warships were to assemble at specified ports and disarm under German or Italian supervision. The French naval bases at Ajaccio, Bizerte, Oran and Toulon were to be demilitarized.

Stationed at Mers-el-Kébir, the French naval base at Oran, were two powerful battleships, four cruisers, six heavy destroyers, a seaplane tender and various smaller vessels and submarines. Two other incomplete battleships had taken refuge at Casablanca and Dakar. There were six cruisers at Algiers, while moored at the naval base at Toulon were more than 70 vessels. At British-controlled Alexandria, there was a French battleship and four cruisers. Sheltering in British waters after Dunkirk were two French battleships, four light cruisers, eight destroyers and several submarines, including the giant *Surcouf*, and 200 smaller vessels. The authorities removed 8,000 men, mostly refugees, from these vessels and they were interned near Liverpool ready to be transported to Casablanca.

In the wake of France's capitulation, the German and Italian dictators gained an altogether unexpected ally. This was in the guise of the Vichy government, in unoccupied southern France, under Marshal Henri-Philippe Pétain. Instead of instructing the French Navy and Empire to fight on, the Vichy regime was more concerned with protecting its colonial possessions. This effectively meant that French interests in North Africa and the Levant posed a potential threat to Britain's vulnerable position in Egypt. French-administered, and potentially pro-Nazi, Algeria, Morocco,

Syria and Tunisia were now a severe headache for Churchill as he attempted to contain initially Italian and then joint Italian-German attacks on Egypt.

Churchill had every right to be anxious about the fate of France's powerful warships. Ideally, they should have joined the Royal Navy and continued the struggle against Hitler and Mussolini in the Atlantic and Mediterranean, but it was not to be. The diminutive Admiral Jean François Darlan, Vichy's minister of marine, was in overall command of the French Navy. However, he left its day-to-day running to Vice-Admiral Paul Auphan. Darlan's main concerns were to secure the release of sailors captured by the Germans, keep the navy intact and defend the empire. In his mind, the latter two meant from everyone, not just the Axis.

Darlan knew that if his warships went over to the British then Hitler would almost certainly retaliate by invading Vichy. If Hitler did that then there would be nothing to stop him taking the ships berthed at Toulon. Similarly, if Franco assisted Hitler to capture Gibraltar, Darlan's warships might side with the Axis on Pétain's orders. The best Darlan could do was instruct his captains to make for America if they were threatened by a foreign power. This was a plan that pleased no one.

Admiral Darlan, commander of the French fleet, found himself caught between the Germans and the British after France's surrender.

THE FRENCH UNDER FIRE

Churchill had the options of letting things slide or taking action. It was an appalling choice in light of the fact he had just stood shoulder to shoulder with the French trying to fight off Hitler's overwhelming Blitzkrieg. Nonetheless, his hard-line view was that the French fleet must either join the Royal Navy or perish. 'There was no security for us at all,' wrote Churchill. 'At all costs, at all risks, in one way or another, we [had to] make sure that the Navy of France did not fall into the wrong hands, and then perhaps bring us and others to ruin … There was one step to take. It was obvious, and it was dire.'[1]

Admiral Cunningham, at Alexandria, and Admiral James Somerville, at Gibraltar, were instructed to give the French four choices: continue the fight; sail to British ports and be interned; sail to the French West Indies and be demilitarized; or be scuttled. There was an unspoken fifth option: 'or be sunk'. Cunningham managed to secure French co-operation, but Somerville had a greater problem on his hands. Under Operation *Catapult*, Somerville and his Force H arrived off Oran on 3 July 1940. The ships included the battlecruiser *Hood*, battleships *Resolution* and *Valiant*, two light cruisers and 11 destroyers, as well as *Ark Royal*.

The man tasked with personally taking British demands to the French commander, Admiral Marcel-Bruno Gensoul, was Captain Cedric 'Hookey' Holland. He was an ideal choice: having served as the British Naval attaché in Paris, he was known to Gensoul. Holland arrived at Mers-el-Kébir on the destroyer *Foxhound*. The admiral aboard his flagship *Dunkerque* refused to meet him, but sent Lieutenant Bernard Dufay to parley. If Gensoul co-operated, Darlan would still have the remains of the fleet at Toulon as leverage with Hitler. Instead, the dice were thrown.

A defiant Gensoul signalled the French Admiralty at Nérac, south-east of Bordeaux, at 1250 hours: 'An English force comprising three battleships, one aircraft carrier, cruisers and destroyers off Oran. Ultimatum sent, sink your ships in six hours or we will compel you to do so by force. Answer: French ships will reply to force with force.'[2] Unfortunately for Gensoul, neither Darlan nor Auphan were contactable. Darlan's chief of staff, Vice-Admiral Le Luc, had been left in charge in their absence.

Gensoul sent a second message to clarify the negotiations: 'Initial English ultimatum was either to sail with the English fleet or destroy ships … to avoid them falling into German or Italian hands.'[3] The French Admiralty responded firmly: 'Tell the British intermediary that the Admiral of the Fleet has given orders for all French forces in the Mediterranean to rally to you immediately.'[4] These were to include warships from Algiers and Toulon.

This show of force was simply designed to persuade the British to back off and to buy time. Vice-Admiral Le Luc was left in a jam because his boss was in the Clermont-Ferrand region scoping out a new headquarters and Auphan was in his car on the road to the town of Vichy. Unfortunately, Le

Luc's reply did not reach Gensoul until the afternoon, by which time it was too late.

In the meantime, *Ark Royal*'s aircraft were in the air keeping an eye on things. They were now tasked with sealing the entrance to Mers-el-Kébir to stop the French putting to sea. Five Swordfish carrying mines, escorted by six Skua fighters, were tasked with this mission.

THE 'STRINGBAG'

Affectionately known as the 'Stringbag', the Swordfsh was first delivered to the Fleet Air Arm in the mid-1930s. Although its cumbersome shape and twin wings made it look an anachronism, it could carry a deadly 457-mm torpedo slung beneath the fuselage, designed to hole warships. The crews liked the Swordfish because it was rugged, versatile and could be flown in most weather conditions from vessels ranging from the largest fleet carriers to the smallest escort carriers.

The French were quickly alerted to what was happening. Gensoul reported: 'At 1330 English aircraft dropped four or five mines – probably magnetic – in the channel and the approaches at Mers-el-Kébir.' He knew that the British meant business and that he needed to evacuate the fleet as quickly as possible. 'I ordered the Marine Oran to clear the buoys and nets from the southern part of the fairway,' he said, 'sinking the buoys by machine-gun fire, and this was immediately begun.'[5] At 1525 hours, two Swordfish were sent to mine the inner harbour at Oran. Had the French been at sea, the firepower of both sides would have been largely even. As it was, they were now hemmed in.

Somerville made his position perfectly clear: 'If none of the British proposals are accepted by 1730 BST I repeat 1730 BST it will be necessary to sink your ships.'[6] The French did not respond well to threats and Holland's negotiating team left the *Dunkerque* empty handed. The French ordered action stations. Bugles were sounded and battle flags run up on the warships. The shore battery gun crews ran to their weapons at Forts Mers-el-Kébir, de Santa Cruz and Santon. Still the talks dragged on, with both sides extremely reluctant to start shooting.

Somerville's patience finally ran out at 1754 hours and his Force H, spearheaded by HMS *Hood*, opened fire on the French warships. The initial salvo of 15-in shells, each carrying over a ton of high explosive, fell short in the sea to the north of the harbour. Lieutenant-Commander Davies, who had been with Holland, observed: 'The effect of those shells bursting on the breakwater was far more devastating than a direct hit. The jagged stones they hurled up in all directions cut like scythes through the men crowding the upper decks of the ships, killing scores of them and maiming hundreds more.'[7]

This was followed by more salvos that enfiladed the five ships along the mole. They tried to flee but largely to no avail. The battleship *Bretagne* was hit before she could escape the breakwater. Her magazine exploded, ripping her apart, and she capsized, taking nearly 1,000 of her crew with her. 'I felt certain they hadn't the slightest idea what was going on,' recalled Lieutenant-Commander Davies. 'I clearly remember too the Officer of the Watch on board the *Bretagne* saluting us smartly as we passed. Ten minutes later, the shells from our battle wagons blew her to pieces!'[8]

The battleship *Provence*, although immediately returning fire and successfully slipping her moorings, was also struck and caught fire. Her crew beached her opposite Roseville. Ordinary Seaman Vernon Coles,

The French fleet under fire by the Royal Navy on 3 July 1940 at Mers-el-Kébir.

aboard HMS *Faulknor*, witnessed the shelling: 'The French battleship *Dunkerque* was right under a dockyard crane and the *Hood* had to destroy it before she could get at the *Dunkerque*. Her first broadside hit the crane … The second salvo hit the *Dunkerque*.'[9] The vessel was quickly crippled, and drifted into the centre of the harbour near Saint-André. The crew fired around 40 shells at the *Hood* and her anti-aircraft guns fired on the circling British spotter planes. An electrical systems failure then silenced her guns. French shore batteries also returned fire. These scored no hits apart from splinter damage to the *Hood*.

Only the *Strasbourg* and a handful of destroyers escaped their berths in time to make a run for the safety of Toulon. Somehow, they successfully managed to avoid the magnetic mines dropped by the *Ark Royal*'s Swordfish. The *Strasbourg* was last out and turned to engage her tormentors, but found the British vessels shrouded in a smokescreen. Hugging the eastern shore, she made a break for it. The destroyer *Mogador* was struck and her depth charges exploded, blowing off her stern. The seaplane carrier *Commandant Teste*, moored south of the *Bretagne*, miraculously remained untouched. She later sneaked away under the cover of darkness and headed for Algiers. The British bombardment of the harbour area lasted just ten minutes. Gensoul, who had watched the unfolding mayhem, exclaimed: 'You're murdering us.'[10]

The battle now moved out to sea. Six Swordfish and three escorting Skuas were sent in hot pursuit of the *Strasbourg*. Their bombs missed with the loss of three aircraft brought down by French anti-aircraft fire. A second attack by six Swordfish also failed to sink the battleship. However, a French cruiser from Oran was hit after being engaged by four British warships and tried to limp to Algiers. The vessel was sunk by a British submarine the following day.

Away from the action, tension mounted in Alexandria when the French admiral there heard what had happened. Fortunately, though, both sides were distracted by a well-timed Italian air raid. Eventually, the French refused to hand over their ships, but agreed to disarm rather than fight.

At the same time as Operation *Catapult* was being conducted, all those French warships in British harbours were stormed by armed boarding parties. In the case of the *Surcouf*, the crew resisted and a British lieutenant-commander was killed and three men injured when the French opened fire. None of the French sailors taken during the raids wanted to join General

The French battleship Provence *blowing up at Mers-el-Kébir.*

Charles de Gaulle's Free French and 100 sailed from Southampton on the French passenger ship *Meknes* bound for unoccupied France. However, a German torpedo boat sank her, with the loss of 400 lives, and Churchill was blamed. Nevertheless, when Churchill addressed the House of Commons on the matter, he was greeted with cheering.

Subsequent action involved a British submarine sinking a French sloop trying to reach Algiers, and aircraft from the *Ark Royal* returning on 6 July and attacking the *Dunkerque*. During that raid, a trawler and tug were sunk, with the former suffering 154 casualties. These attacks were followed on 8 July by a British naval torpedo bomber attack on the incomplete *Richelieu* at Dakar, leaving her immobilized.

ANGLO-FRENCH RELATIONS BREAK DOWN

Somerville and Gensoul were dismayed by what had happened, but there was no going back. The French suffered 1,297 dead and 351 wounded. Later, salvage crews discovered that some of the *Bretagne*'s crew had survived in watertight compartments, only to suffocate before they could be rescued. Darlan was furious and at 2000 hours on 3 July he issued orders for the French fleet to attack all British ships on sight. Two days later he adopted a more defensive posture, warning: 'All British ships approaching to within less than 20 sea miles of the French coast are open to attack.'[11]

Pétain's Vichy regime immediately closed ranks, determined never to co-operate with Churchill or de Gaulle. After Mers-el-Kébir, Pétain was more determined than ever to adhere to the conditions of the Armistice with Hitler. Any opposition to this would not be tolerated. France, he said, had a 'duty to defend her soil, to extinguish divergences of opinion, to put down dissidence in her colonies" This was a clear warning to the British and the Free French. To many, it sounded like a Fascist regime in the making. Pétain then added: 'This policy is mine ... It is I alone who will be judged by history.'[12]

Darlan, meanwhile, not only survived the political fallout, but also greatly benefitted from it. In February 1941, he was appointed vice-president of the Council and foreign minister. This was in addition to his naval responsibilities. Shortly after, he was granted the ministerial posts of the Interior, of War and of Information. No French politician had ever enjoyed such powers.

Churchill accepted the Anglo-French alliance was completely in tatters when the bulk of the 120,000 French troops who had been evacuated to Britain chose repatriation rather than to join the Free French. Although war was not formally declared, Vichy France's neutrality had been decisively violated and Britain now found itself having to wage a series of campaigns against French interests around the world.

ENEMIES IN MULTIPLE THEATRES

Mussolini was absolutely delighted by the news. Any threat from Tunisia against Tripoli was now completely removed. In contrast, his naval commanders braced themselves for the inevitable clash of arms. Just six days after the British attack on Mers-el-Kébir, the Royal Navy fought with the Italian fleet for the very first time. Cunningham found himself up against none other than Admiral Inigo Campioni, the commander-in-chief of the Italian fleet. The engagement occurred 30 miles (48 km) east of Punta Stilo and became known as the Battle of Calabria.

Campioni's force consisted of three groups escorting four merchant ships bound for Libya. At the same time, the British were protecting supplies sent from Alexandria to Malta. Cunningham's force was also rendezvousing with Somerville's. Although vessels on both sides were damaged, the battle proved inconclusive. However, the Italian convoy did get to Benghazi, so in that respect the Royal Navy failed.

Within a month, Britain attacked the battleship *Richelieu* again with Operation *Menace*. On 23 September 1940, de Gaulle, supported by the Royal Navy, tried to secure Dakar, which had strategic importance because it sat astride the vital Atlantic shipping routes. Negotiations between the Free French and Vichy garrison failed and HMS *Cumberland* was damaged by accurate fire from French shore batteries. In response, a French submarine was sunk and a French destroyer disabled and beached. The following day, aircraft from *Ark Royal* attacked the *Richelieu* and another French submarine was sunk. The *Richelieu* was then torpedoed on 25 September. The Anglo-French operation was subsequently abandoned and British and Free French troops were not put ashore, to avoid further bloodshed.

HITLER SEEKS NEW ALLIANCES

In the meantime, Hitler sought a way to close off the western Mediterranean by taking Gibraltar. Under Operation *Felix*, he hoped to secure not only Gibraltar, but also the Spanish Canary Islands and the Portuguese Cape Verde Islands. In addition, he ideally wanted the Azores as they could act as a potential base against America. To achieve this, he was even prepared to occupy Portugal under Operation *Isabella*. All these plans required the full co-operation of Franco.

Initially, Franco had shown some enthusiasm for joining Hitler in June 1940, when it seemed as if the war was about to end and he could share in the spoils. After meeting with Ramón Serrano Súner, the Spanish minister of the interior, Hitler wrote to Franco saying: 'Spain's entry into the war on the side of the Axis Powers, must begin with the expulsion of the English Fleet from Gibraltar and immediately thereafter the seizure of the fortified rock.'[13] He suggested they discuss his plans face to face. Rather prematurely, Joachim von Ribbentrop, the German foreign minister, assured Mussolini in Rome on 19 September that Spain would soon enter the war on their side.

By the end of the summer, Britain clearly remained undefeated, so Franco began to place unacceptable conditions on Spain's intervention. In return, he wanted part of French Algeria, all of French Morocco and an increase in other existing Spanish territories. Hitler was not keen on this, as he did not want the Vichy authorities in North Africa siding with the British. His hope was that if the French status quo was guaranteed then they would protect their colonies from any further British incursions. Franco was understandably uneasy about widening the war. To secure the Azores and the Cape Verde Islands would almost certainly mean invading Portugal, otherwise the Portuguese would side with Britain. For Franco, this could potentially result in a two-front war.

Hitler met Franco at the French frontier town of Hendaye on 23 October 1940. His intention was to flatter and seduce Franco as he had Mussolini. On the way, he stopped off at Montoire-sur-le-Loire, to see Pierre Laval, the Vichy deputy premier. Hitler also wanted to enlist Vichy and French North Africa in the war against Britain and planned to see Pétain on his return. His hope was that the French would be so enraged by the British attack on Mers-el-Kébir and Dakar that they would now side with him.

At Hendaye, Hitler explained that if Franco entered the war in the New Year, German airborne forces would seize Gibraltar on 10 January 1941 and hand it back to Spain. Franco responded by saying his country would first need considerable economic and military assistance, as it had been exhausted by the civil war. In particular, he needed heavy guns to defend Spain's coast from the Royal Navy and anti-aircraft guns to fend off the RAF. He also warned that even if Britain were defeated, the British government would continue to fight from Canada with American help. Franco proved very evasive about allowing Hitler to move an army group through Spain to attack Gibraltar or Algeria and Tunisia, which could have sealed off the western Mediterranean from British domination. At one point, Hitler lost his temper and said there was no point in continuing the talks.

Hitler was furious that no agreement had been reached that day. In the evening, after a state dinner on board his train, he remained frustrated by Franco's deliberate dithering. 'Franco is a little major!' fumed Hitler privately to his staff. 'In Germany, that man would never rise higher than a sergeant!'[14] Franco, while he may have wanted Gibraltar back, was completely deterred from siding with Hitler after Mussolini's subsequent defeat in North Africa. Hitler was later to state quite categorically that: 'I shall never go to Spain.'[15] His failure to woo Franco was to prove a major strategic blunder in the Mediterranean.

The very day after the Hendaye meeting, Hitler returned to Montoire-sur-le-Loire. There, as scheduled, he met with Pétain. In return for assistance against the British, Hitler promised that France would be compensated for any territorial losses and would retain an empire the same size as it currently held. 'Once this struggle is ended,' he told the old marshal, 'it is evident that either France or England will have to bear the territorial and material costs of the conflict.'[16] Pétain made all the right noises, convincing Hitler that Vichy was prepared to collaborate. Still smarting from the British attacks, he agreed that the French government within the limits of its ability would support Axis efforts to defeat Britain. When news of this leaked out, President Franklin Roosevelt sent Pétain a message warning him of the dire consequences of betraying Churchill.

HITLER OFFERS LIMITED HELP TO THE ITALIANS

Hitler briefly contemplated taking Gibraltar solely by air assault, thereby bypassing Franco. General Kurt Student, commander of the German airborne forces, was ordered to assess the feasibility of seizing it using paratroops. He rapidly concluded: 'Gibraltar cannot be taken if the neutrality of Spain is to be observed by us.'[17] Hitler uncharacteristically heeded his advice. Besides, he had to shelve his plans for Gibraltar once he was forced to help out Mussolini in Greece and Libya. All of these were unwanted distractions from his ultimate goal of invading the Soviet Union.

He decided that German attacks into the Balkans would offer him an opportunity to neutralize Greece and Turkey, and threaten the British position in the eastern Mediterranean. Hitler also looked to Sicily as a useful choke point with which to throttle British operations through the central Mediterranean. He therefore moved Luftwaffe units to the island to support the Italian Air Force, increasing local air superiority over the narrow waters between Sicily and Tunisia. He also supplemented the Italians' rather inaccurate high-level bombing of British convoys with dive-bombing by Stukas. This, though, was not as effective as closing the Strait of Gibraltar.

Elsewhere, Hitler considered helping Mussolini out in North Africa. That October, General von Thoma flew to Tripoli to assess whether German troops should be committed. Thoma reported back that due to British dominance of the Mediterranean it would be impossible to maintain two large German and Italian armies in theatre at the same time. He therefore recommended sending at least four Panzer divisions and conducting the attack towards the Nile purely with German troops. Understandably, however, Badoglio and Graziani did not want their men replaced by Germans.

According to Thoma, at this stage, Hitler was not greatly interested in driving the British from Egypt. Instead, having postponed the invasion of Britain, Hitler was now focused on Russia. He therefore told Thoma he could only spare one Panzer division, to which Thoma responded it would be better not to help at all. Mussolini's inadequate armoured forces were thus left on their own and a military disaster of epic proportions followed.

ITALY GOES IT ALONE IN GREECE

Despite all previous assurances, on 28 October 1940, Mussolini attacked Greece. This marked a further step towards dominating the eastern Mediterranean. When he met Hitler in Florence, he exclaimed: 'Führer, we are on the march! Victorious Italian troops crossed the Greco-Albanian frontier at dawn today.'[18] Mussolini, fed up with Hitler taking unilateral action, had deliberately not informed him of his intentions until the last minute. 'Hitler keeps confronting me with accomplished facts!' he had moaned to Count Ciano beforehand. 'This time I shall pay him back in his own coin: when I have marched against Greece he will only learn about it from the newspapers!'[19]

Mussolini's actions were extremely foolhardy, as was his timing. Earlier, when he and Hitler met at the Brenner Pass on 4 October, Hitler admitted that he was not going to invade Britain. If this threat was not maintained then this meant that the British would be able to reinforce their positions in North Africa and the Middle East. By attacking Greece, Mussolini was stretching his resources even further, at a point when he could not afford to do so. The Italian leader, however, seeing his modest gains in Egypt as a 'victory', declined any offers of help to take Mersa Matruh. Then, in a U-turn, he almost admitted the shortcomings of his army when he agreed that German armoured vehicles and dive-bombers might be needed if stiffer resistance was met between Matruh and Alexandria. Hitler's stalling response was that his Panzers were not designed for tropical use.

Tensions between Italy and Greece began to mount after the Greek Navy suffered its first casualty on 15 August 1940. The minelaying cruiser *Helle* sank near Tinos, with the loss of nine crew, after being torpedoed by an Italian submarine. The latter then attempted unsuccessfully to torpedo two passenger vessels before escaping. The submarine had been deployed from Rhodes by Governor Cesare Maria De Vecchi, who hated the Greeks with a passion. Trying to downplay the attack, the Greek authorities claimed they did not know the nationality of the culprits.

Mussolini was encouraged by Greece being a deeply divided nation. It was ruled by a military dictatorship under General Ioannis Metaxas, supported by right-wing royalists, who were opposed by radical republicans and communists. The Italian governor in Albania, Francesco Jacomoni, and military commander General Sebastiano Visconti Prasca, were both convinced that the Greek military would crumble when attacked. In the event, Mussolini's act of aggression temporarily united Greece behind the government.

News of Mussolini's latest Balkan aggression was a mixed blessing for Churchill. Although it signalled that Mussolini was slackening the pressure on Egypt, it also compelled him to go to the aid of the Greeks. 'We will give you all the help in our power!' he informed the Greek government. General Metaxas was of the view that he would need six divisions to make the offer worthwhile, but at the same time he worried that this might provoke Hitler. Nonetheless, Churchill ordered the Royal Navy into Greek waters, sent the RAF to Greece and the Army to Crete. This was bad news for Wavell, but where Cunningham was concerned it very much focused his plans on trying to bring the Italian Navy to battle.

On the Italian side, General Badoglio informed Ciano that the service chiefs were opposed to a campaign against Greece, but none of them was prepared to stand up to Mussolini. At the beginning of October, Mussolini had ordered more than half a million men be demobilized and allowed home. That now seemed a foolish decision. His generals tried to warn him that their attacking force, of about a dozen divisions, needed to be double in number if they were to overrun the whole of Greece. Furthermore, Albania's infrastructure could not support a large-scale military operation.

Logistically, getting men, arms and equipment from Italy across the Adriatic, through Albania's ports and to the front would be a time-consuming process.

General Prasca, in Albania, deliberately chose to ignore intelligence reports from the Italian military attaché in Athens on Greek preparedness. Instead, he relied on Albanian sources, many of whom had little incentive to assist their occupiers. The result of this was that he grossly underestimated Greek military capabilities. Prasca's 70,000 troops were soon driven back into Albania by the Greek frontier forces. The Greeks then proceeded to capture a quarter of Albania.

Although this situation was of Mussolini's own making, he called his generals together on 10 November 1940 and demanded to know what had gone wrong. Badoglio spoke his mind, making it clear whom he held responsible: 'Neither the General High Command nor the army High Command had anything to do with the organizing, which was done in a way completely contrary to our system based on the principle of planning thoroughly beforehand and then showing daring ... when I think of the Greek affair I feel the blood rushing to my face.'[20]

Although Mussolini was offended by this impertinence, he had no option but to continue the war, which meant denying Libya reinforcements.

Italian troops in Greece. Just like Mussolini's attack on Egypt, this invasion proved ill-fated.

Rather than recall those troops who had just been demobbed, 100,000 men therefore had to be deployed from elsewhere and sent to Albania. Likewise, at the meeting it was agreed, rather bizarrely, to ship thousands of vehicles to Albania. The mountainous terrain there was hardly conducive to mobile warfare and the vehicles would have been of far greater value in North Africa.

Hitler was soon aghast at Italian ineptitude in Greece. The British presence on Crete meant that their bombers could reach Romania's oilfields, which were vital to his war effort. Their presence greatly enhanced Britain's strategic position in the eastern Mediterranean. To counter this, Hitler was now forced to draw up plans to attack Greece through Bulgaria. Much to his annoyance, and thanks to Mussolini, he was facing mission creep.

CHAPTER 5:
Second Blood

CHURCHILL SOUGHT to reinforce Admiral Cunningham's Mediterranean Fleet at the end of August 1940. The brand new carrier *Illustrious*, the battleship *Valiant*, the anti-aircraft cruisers *Calcutta* and *Coventry*, and other supporting vessels arrived at Gibraltar ready for action. They were escorted as far as Malta by Admiral Somerville's Force H, which also took men and supplies to the island. War correspondent Alan Moorehead sailed from Alexandria, on Cunningham's flagship *Warspite*, to meet them. 'No ship like *Illustrious* had ever been seen in the Mediterranean before,' wrote Moorehead in awe, 'nothing of its kind, so fast, so modern, so reassuring.'[1] In addition to *Warspite*, Cunningham's force included the 20-year-old carrier *Eagle*, protected by cruisers and destroyers.

This was fortunate, for on the return journey, Cunningham's ships were attacked by continual small waves of Italian bombers operating from Sicily and shadowed by Italian submarines. In response, when it got dark, Cunningham split his fleet, sending one half back to Alexandria while the other half embarked on a daring new mission. Early in the morning on 4 September 1940, Cunningham showed Mussolini just what his carriers were capable of, by attacking Rhodes.

THE 'MALTA OF THE AEGEAN'

During the 1930s, the Italians had turned the Dodecanese Islands into fortresses, building roads, airfields and naval facilities. Their intention was that these bases would help gain Italy dominance of the eastern Mediterranean. Under Governor De Vecchi's rule, Rhodes was grandly dubbed the 'Malta of the Aegean'.[2] At the outbreak of war, Italian aircraft from the island had made a few daring raids against Alexandria and Haifa. De Vecchi, however, was soon more interested in attacking Greek ships, as he was a keen advocate of the invasion of Greece. He detested the Greeks and had done everything he could to alienate the Greek population in the Dodecanese.

Cunningham's daring raid involved Swordfish from the *Illustrious* dive-bombing the airfields at Calato and Maritsa. The cruisers *Orion* and *Sydney*, supported by two destroyers, would also shell the airfield on the island of Scarpento to the south-west of Rhodes. 'This take-off in the half-dark was dangerous,' observed Moorehead, 'and one aircraft, its engine failing at the crucial moment, poised for a second on the lip of *Illustrious'* flight-deck, then plunged sickeningly into the sea to be cut to pieces by the warship's bows.'[3] At Calato and Maritsa, the attackers managed to destroy aircraft on the ground, barracks, fuel dumps and hangars.

Governor De Vecchi was awoken to be informed that Rhodes was under air attack. He was widely considered 'a complete buffoon'[4] and had previously been the governor of Italian Somaliland and minister of education. Cunningham had made him look even more foolish with his surprise assault. Near the island of Kasos, the *Sydney* was attacked by four Italian motor torpedo boats. She quickly claimed one before it could fire and the destroyer *Ilex* claimed another. The rest fled back to the island. Moorehead noted with some satisfaction that: 'the pirates' nest at Rhodes had been badly shaken up'.[5] Italian pilots, recovering from the shock, took to their fighters and shot down four Swordfish on the way back to the carrier. It was little compensation for De Vecchi, who was later replaced by Admiral Campioni.

In the aftermath, the Italian Air Force was scrambled to exact an even greater revenge. When Cunningham's force withdrew towards Alexandria, bombers gave chase and spent about two hours launching attacks. They first tried hitting the *Warspite*, but were met by a wall of anti-aircraft fire. 'I was caught typing behind one of the four-inch guns,' recalled Moorehead, 'and the typewriter flew from my hands...'[6] The Italian pilots, however, proved unwilling to press home their attacks and their bombing proved inaccurate. Between the naval gunners and *Illustrious*' fighters, the British claimed 20 Italian planes during this action. Cunningham's ships went unscathed.

Admiral Andrew Browne Cunningham, commander of the British Mediterranean Fleet.

Mussolini was too preoccupied with his plans to attack Egypt and Greece to be worried about an isolated air raid on Rhodes. However, he should have taken note of the threat posed by Britain's carrier-borne aircraft. Cunningham had signalled he could strike anywhere at any time. He had enjoyed a good week.

Reinforcements were duly brought through the Straits of Gibraltar to both Malta and Alexandria, without having to go round the Cape of Good Hope. The Italian torpedo boats had not proved to be as much of a threat as first expected. Furthermore, the Italian Air Force insisted on operating at high altitude, which made it difficult for them to hit anything, and the Italian's submarines had been chased off using depth charges. Cunningham was thus greatly encouraged to be even more aggressive towards his Mediterranean foe.

THE ACTION HOTS UP IN THE ADRIATIC

Throughout October and early November 1940, it was increasingly clear that war had come to the Mediterranean. Italian ships were busy ferrying men and equipment to Albania and Libya. On the whole, these were safe from British interference. The British, on the other hand, were equally busy shipping reinforcements from Gibraltar to Malta and from Alexandria to both Crete and Malta. The former were protected by British cruisers and destroyers and the latter were safeguarded by Cunningham's Mediterranean

Fleet, comprising the carrier *Illustrious*, four battleships, two cruisers and 13 destroyers.

In early October, Cunningham ran a convoy from the east to Malta and escorted some empty ships back to Alexandria, during which operation the Royal Navy bumped into an Italian destroyer force. The Italians came off worst, with two ships sunk and a third damaged. The latter was taken under tow and limped away. Despite this, Cunningham was genuinely impressed by his enemy's gallantry, noting: 'On this occasion the Italian destroyers had fought well.',[7] He signalled this sentiment to the Admiralty and Churchill was cross when he heard. 'This kind of kid glove stuff,' he said, 'infuriates the people who are going through their present ordeal at home [i.e. the Blitz] and this aspect should be put to the admiral.',[8] Cunningham, however, remained unrepentant.

TARANTO UNDER ATTACK

After the Royal Navy's blatant attack on the French fleet, the main Italian battle fleet largely kept out of harm's way. 'The Italian Navy suffered deeply from inexperience,' wrote Alan Moorehead, 'and the Italian high command knew it.',[9] Cunningham appreciated that Admiral Campioni was waiting for him to stray too close to the Italian mainland. Considerable numbers of Italian warships were sheltering in the two anchorages of Mar Grande and Mar Piccolo at Taranto, which made them a very tempting target. However, the port, in the northern corner of the Gulf of Taranto and surrounded by land on three sides, would not be easy to attack. For Mussolini, it was hard to comprehend that the British would even contemplate such an audacious move. For a start, they would have to transit the Ionian Sea, which was not only patrolled by the Italian Navy, but also the Italian Air Force.

There was no way the British could shell the Italian warships at anchor as they had done with the French, because of the presence of the Italian Air Force – now increasingly backed by the Luftwaffe. Aerial reconnaissance showed that the harbour was protected by an array of torpedo nets. This meant submarine attack was unlikely to be successful. The only option was air attack. The port was well out of range of the RAF's bombers, which meant the task fell to the Fleet Air Arm.

Cunningham initially planned the attack on Taranto for the night of 21 October employing the *Eagle* and *Illustrious*, but fate took a hand.

The latter suffered a hangar fire, which according to Cunningham's report:'destroyed and damaged a number of aircraft'.[10] As a result, the operation was postponed for ten days, but by that point there was no moon to aid a night attack and the crews had not had time to train using flares. In the meantime, *Eagle*, following air strikes against Italian shipping at Tobruk, was damaged during the action off Calabria. Just two days before the fleet sailed for Taranto, the carrier developed engine troubles and had to be left behind.

Nonetheless, undeterred on leaving Alexandria, Cunningham signalled: 'I intend to act offensively.'[11] During early November, he manoeuvred his

Warships at Taranto in 1940. Mussolini never thought the Royal Navy would dare attack the Italian fleet at anchor.

fleet to within 200 miles (320 km) of Taranto. Intelligence showed that six Italian battleships along with some cruisers and destroyers were anchored in the Mar Grande. To the north-east, the Mar Piccolo was sheltering more cruisers and was surrounded by vital shore installations. Campioni had not only made his fleet a very tempting target, but he also assumed the Royal Navy after its run to Malta was heading back to Alexandria and Gibraltar.

On 9 November, Swordfish from the carrier *Ark Royal* conducted a small raid on Cagliari in Sardinia. Land-based Italian aircraft retaliated by attacking both the Alexandria and Gibraltar naval forces. They hit nothing but achieved some near misses, especially in the vicinity of the battleship *Barham*. After landing troops on Malta, those ships due to return to Gibraltar headed west while others rendezvoused with Cunningham.

Just before 2100 hours on 11 November 1940, the first wave of 12 Swordfish took off from *Illustrious* heading for Taranto. Fighter cover was provided by the carrier's new Fairey Fulmar two-seat fighter. This aircraft had only joined the Fleet Air Arm earlier in the year. It did not have a very good performance because of its second cockpit, something that the navy had felt necessary in order to carry a navigator and thus prevent the pilot from getting lost on the way back to the carrier.

Swordfish torpedo bomber banking over the Ark Royal. *The Fleet Air Arm gave the Royal Navy a much greater and deadlier reach.*

Under the command of Lieutenant-Commander Kenneth Williamson, half the Swordfish were carrying torpedoes, the other half bombs, slung under their bellies. Four had six 250-lb bombs, while the other two had four bombs and illumination flares to highlight the targets. After flying through cloud at some 4,500 ft (1,370 m), when Williamson emerged another 3,000 ft (915 m) higher, he discovered one torpedo plane and three of the bombers were missing. He decided they would have to make their way to the target on their own.

Williamson looped in from the south-west, flying between the island of San Paulo and the Diga di San Vito, a mole extending from Cape San Vito. His targets were the warships sheltering behind another mole, the Diga Taranto. These vessels were protected by barrage balloons and torpedo nets. At 2250 hours, Taranto's air raid sirens went off and the sky lit up with a barrage of flak. Taranto's air defences included a formidable 21 batteries of 4-in guns, almost 200 machine guns and searchlights.

Six minutes later, two of the Swordfish dropped flares that outlined the battleship *Conte di Cavour*. Williamson released his torpedo and was then shot down. He and his observer survived and were taken prisoner by the Italians. Two other aircraft launched their torpedoes at the battleship. At the same time, the battleships *Littorio* and *Vittorio Veneto* were attacked, with successful strikes on the *Littorio*.

It was now that the second wave of nine Swordfish, commanded by Lieutenant-Commander 'Ginger' Hale, attacked from the north-west, flying in over the breakwater between Cape Rondinella and the island of San Pietro. Considerable anti-aircraft fire rose from the latter to greet them. Two more torpedoes hit the *Littorio*, one of which failed to explode. South of the channel leading into the Mar Piccolo, the battleship *Caio Duilio* was hit amidships by a torpedo. Once again, the *Vittorio Veneto* was spared when a torpedo either missed its hull or failed to detonate. The last Swordfish to carry out its attack run was hit and went down in the Mar Grande along with its pilot and observer.

'Taranto, and the night of November 11-12, 1940,' wrote Cunningham, 'should be remembered for ever as having shown once and for all that in the Fleet Air Arm the Navy has its most devastating weapon.'[12] For the cost of two lives and two aircraft, his surprise raid successfully put three Italian battleships out of action: the *Cavour* was beyond repair and it took many months to get *Caio Duilio* and *Littorio* back in service. Although the former two were First World War-vintage dreadnoughts, they had been completely rebuilt in the 1930s and were therefore almost new ships. The cruiser *Trento* had been hit by a bomb but it had failed to go off.

That night, the Italian Navy suffered another setback in the Adriatic. Cunningham had sent three cruisers and two destroyers north through the Strait of Otranto. There, the British caught a convoy of four merchant ships and two escorts headed for Brindisi. In the moonlight, the British sank all the merchantmen while the escorts fled.

Mussolini was livid that the British had so successfully crept up on his fleet. 'A black day,' noted Ciano in his diary on 12 November. 'The British, without warning, have sunk the dreadnought *Cavour* and seriously damaged the battleships *Littorio* and *Duilio*.'[13] The Italian intelligence failure at Taranto did nothing to encourage the Germans. Admiral Erich Raeder, in command of the German Navy, was dismayed at Italy's performance in the Mediterranean. He was of the view that Britain must be defeated before contemplating an attack on the Soviet Union. 'Italy will never carry out the Egyptian offensive. The Italian leadership is wretched,' Raeder warned Hitler on 14 November. 'They have no understanding of the situation. The Italian armed forces have neither the leadership nor the military efficiency to carry out the required operations in the Mediterranean area to a successful conclusion with the necessary speed and decision.'[14] Hitler sought to reassure Raeder that he would gain Franco's assistance to take Gibraltar.

VITTORIO VENETO

From the British perspective, the only real blot on the remarkable Taranto raid was failing to damage the battleship *Vittorio Veneto*. She was the pride of the Italian Navy having only just been commissioned. Although laid down in 1934, the ship had not been completed until the end of April 1940. At 45,000 tons, she took a complement of almost 2,000 men and her armament included nine 15-in and twelve 6-in guns. Her sister ship *Littorio* had also only come into service in May 1940. Although well armoured, this class of battleship was not as well protected as its foreign contemporaries. The Italians preferred to rely on speed and manoeuvrability and this came at a cost. The same policy had been applied to Italy's newer cruisers.

THE BATTLE OF CAPE SPARTIVENTO

Fearing further such attacks, the Italians sent their fleet to Naples, where it could be better protected in the Tyrrhenian Sea, bordered by airbases in Sardinia and Sicily. From here, the Italian Navy, led by the *Vittorio Veneto*, ventured out to sea again just six days later in a vain effort to intercept a British convoy bound for Malta, which turned tail and headed back to Gibraltar.

The Italians tried again on 27 November, when the battleships *Vittorio Veneto* and *Giulio Cesare*, with six cruisers and 14 destroyers, attempted to stop the British. These forces were divided into two under Admiral Campioni and Admiral Angelo Iachino. Their actions sparked the Battle of Cape Spartivento south of Sardinia, when they tangled with a British escort fleet under Admiral Somerville that included the carrier *Ark Royal*, the battleship *Ramillies* and the battlecruiser *Renown*, plus numerous light cruisers and destroyers. The two sides engaged each other for just under an hour, inflicting little damage before the Italians withdrew. The *Vittorio Veneto* was once again lucky and successfully eluded the *Ark Royal*'s Swordfish.

Somerville decided not to give chase and broke off the engagement. He felt that preliminary air reconnaissance by land-based aircraft to locate the Italian fleet had been poor. This was then compounded by the inexperience of the *Ark Royal*'s pilots and observers. Somerville struggled to hide his frustration, noting: 'Skilful, unobserved approaches were made in each case and the attacks were pressed home with courage and resolution, but the results obtained were disappointing.'[15] Subsequent battle damage assessments suggested that the *Vittorio Veneto* had been hit and that a cruiser had been damaged, but this remained unsubstantiated.

For a brief moment, Campioni and Iachino were offered a chance of revenge for Taranto, but they had been instructed only to give battle if they had decisive superiority. Campioni took the blame for Taranto and Spartivento and was eventually packed off to become governor of the Dodecanese. He was replaced as commander-in-chief of the Italian fleet by Iachino on 9 December 1940.

DIVISION AND DISTRUST

Admiral Iachino served as the Italian naval attaché in China during the late 1920s and then in London through the early 1930s. This meant that he was well versed in the ways of the Royal Navy. However, his knowledge and experience were wasted, because the Italian Institute of Warfare ignored the potential for conflict with the British. In addition, Iachino commanded naval forces supporting the invasion of Albania and had been promoted to admiral.

Iachino was unhappy that the Italian Navy and Air Force had not acted more aggressively against the British at the start of the war, with an all-out air and sea assault on Malta. He felt this would have established and maintained local naval superiority in the central Mediterranean. The British attack on Taranto highlighted to Iachino just how poor Italian long-range reconnaissance was.

Behind his back, the Italian Navy did not have much confidence in Mussolini, who as an ex-soldier did not understand sea power. Mussolini had failed to employ the Dodecanese islands as forward naval bases and had failed to take Malta in the opening rounds of the war. He had dismissed the value of aircraft carriers and favoured the air force as the protector of Italy. Mussolini in turn distrusted his navy, viewing it as dangerously Anglophile and too conservative. It was becoming rapidly apparent that despite his constant rhetoric about the Mediterranean, he did not know how to conduct naval warfare. At home, the police began to report a 'very widespread lack of confidence and rising discontent'.[16]

HALYCON DAYS FOR THE BRITISH

Although Spartivento was inconclusive, there was no doubt that Taranto was a massive morale booster for the British. It shifted the balance of power in the Mediterranean in favour of Britain for several months. During the winter, Cunningham was able to get his ships close to the Libyan coast and shell the Italian Army and Air Force largely with impunity. It also made getting reinforcements to North Africa and the Middle East slightly easier for a time.

The Royal Navy continued to ensure that the Italian fleet did not feel safe in its home ports. Somerville, with Force H – consisting of the *Renown*, *Malaya* and *Sheffield* – arrived off Genoa on 9 February 1941. For 30 minutes, they shelled the port and shipping. At the same time, Leghorn (Livorno) and Pisa were attacked by aircraft from the *Ark Royal*. These also dropped mines off La Spezia. Somerville then successfully withdrew without loss, eluding the Italian Navy to the west of Sardinia.

These were halcyon days for the Royal Navy, for soon the Luftwaffe would make life much more dangerous and costly. Losses would mount, especially during the disastrous Battle for Crete.

In the meantime, General Wavell was alert to the growing German threat to the Balkans. On 17 November 1940, he wrote: 'I am quite sure Germany cannot afford to see Italy defeated – or even held – in Greece, and must intervene ... As in the last war, Germany is on interior lines and can move more quickly to attack Greece or Turkey than we can to support them.'[17] However, Wavell was doubtful that Hitler would push Bulgaria into war or invade Yugoslavia. He was to be proved horribly wrong.

CHAPTER 6:
Fox is Killed

CHIEF OF the Imperial General Staff General Sir John Dill had asked Wavell as early as 11 September 1940 when he would be able to go over to the offensive against the Italians. The objective would be the port of Tobruk. Much to Wavell's displeasure, Churchill was pushing the pace for action against Mussolini as soon as possible. Wavell, quite rightly in his role as commander-in-chief in the Middle East, was of the view they should not act rashly until reinforcements were in place. Two days later, Mussolini pre-empted him.

In the meantime, Graziani was planning to renew his stalled advance in mid-December 1940. Once again, Mussolini was angry at his continual dithering. On 26 October, he had signalled Graziani: 'Forty days after the capture of Sidi Barrani I ask myself the question, to whom has this long halt been any use – to us or to the enemy?' Mussolini concluded, quite rightly, it had helped the British. 'It is time,' he added, 'to ask whether you feel you wish to continue in command.'[1]

Wavell and O'Connor had started to receive much-needed reinforcements in early October. These consisted of three armoured regiments shipped round the Cape of Good Hope. The most significant of these were the 50 Matilda infantry tanks of 7th Royal Tank Regiment (7RTR). These were much more powerful than the feeble British A13 cruiser tank. Frontal armour was almost three times that of the cruiser, rendering it invulnerable to every Italian anti-tank gun, field gun and tank.

This made the Matilda the most potent weapon in the British armoury and understandably Wavell did not want the Italians learning of its presence in Egypt before they had to. He therefore decided to hold these back for an attack on Sidi Barrani.

OPERATION *COMPASS*

The plan was for the light, cruiser and infantry tanks of 7th Armoured Division to cut off Sidi Barrani, while the 4th Indian Division stormed the Italian fortified camps at Nibeiwa and Tummar to the south. Although Wavell only had 30,000 men available, he had superior armour and air power. During November, 7RTR began training with the Indians using dummy camps representing Italian defensive positions. These were based on aerial photographs and patrol reports. The men were told that this training was a rehearsal for a bigger corps-level exercise. In reality, it was to be the attack on Sidi Barrani dubbed Operation *Compass*.

Although this was limited in scope, the plan needed to be flexible. Ultimately, there was no way of really knowing how the Italians would react. 'I hoped our raid would be successful and that if it was so we might be able to exploit it. But it was a complicated affair,' said O'Connor, 'and I couldn't be certain what use we could make of the success we gained. But I was fully prepared, that if we did get a success that we would make full use of it.'[2]

His raid opened just after 0700 hours on 9 December 1940 when 200 guns supporting the 4th Indian Division began to pound Nibeiwa. The Italians were also pinned down by sustained heavy machine-gun fire. The garrison were tired and edgy after being bombarded intermittently during the night. On the coast, the Royal Navy began to shell Maktila and Sidi Barrani. Meanwhile, on the British left flank, 7th Armoured Brigade rolled forwards to screen 4th Division from attack from the Rabia and Sofafi chain of camps. Further south in the Enba Gap, the 4th Armoured Brigade swung north to cut the road west from Sidi Barrani.

General Sebastiano Gallina, commander of the Libyan Group, had his headquarters at Sidi Barrani. His forward defences at Maktila were manned by the 1st Libyan Division. To the south-west, the Italians had done all they could to fortify Nibeiwa. It was held by a divisional-size force, called Group Maletti after its commander, that included a battalion of tanks. The place was ringed by artillery positions and machine-gun posts, made from stacked dry stone walls. Between Nibeiwa and Sidi Barrani were the three Tummar positions. General Piscatori's 2nd Libyan Division was responsible for Tummar West.

At 0715 hours, A Squadron, led by Major Henry Rew, spearheaded the attack on Nibeiwa by 7RTR. To counter the anti-tank ditch, the Matildas carried small fascines with which to create a causeway. The only unmined approach to Nibeiwa was protected by 23 Italian M11/39 medium tanks. More should have been available but the M11/39 was so unreliable that the rest were being refitted in Tobruk. A Squadron caught the Italian crews by surprise as they emerged from their beds. They were all gunned down before they could reach their tanks, which were swiftly knocked out. The Italian artillery and infantry fought bravely but found the Matildas were impervious to their fire. Resistance was fierce and fighting lasted all morning, but once the Italian artillery had been silenced, the infantry began to give up. Around 4,000 men surrendered.

At Nibeiwa the 4th Indian Division reported:

Frightened, dazed or desperate Italians erupted from tents and slit trenches, some to surrender supinely, others to leap gallantly into battle, hurling grenades or blazing machine guns in futile belabour of the impregnable intruders … General Maletti, the Italian commander, sprang from his dug-out, machine gun in hand. He fell from an answering burst; his son beside him was struck down and captured.[3]

The Italians valiantly resisted for another two-and-a-half hours and one British tank crewman was struck by their bravery: 'The Italians may have been a push-over afterwards, but they fought like hell at Nibeiwa.'[4]

Once Nibeiwa had been taken, 7RTR and the 5th Indian Infantry Brigade headed for Tummar West. Once again, the tanks easily broke through the Italian defences. The fight lasted for two hours, but the garrison was overcome with the loss of a further 2,000 prisoners. Tummar Central then surrendered and Tummar East was taken, after much of its garrison had been killed in the open attempting to counter-attack Tummar West.

At Sidi Barrani, General Gallina was in a state of panic. The desert seemed to be swarming with British tanks. His communications and water

Italian gunners shelling British positions in North Africa.

supply to the west had been cut by yet more tanks. He had lost all contact with 2nd Division, and 1st Division retreating from Maktila had been intercepted by the British. His Blackshirt garrison soon succumbed once the perimeter was penetrated and he withdrew.

Wavell was delighted that Sidi Barrani had been liberated, but on the night of 10/11 December the 4th Indian Division was redeployed to Sudan, leaving O'Connor just 7th Armoured with which to pursue the dazed Italians.

The unfortunate Graziani signalled Rome admitting: 'four divisions can be considered destroyed'.₅ He was so despondent that he contemplated withdrawing all the way back to Tripoli – a distance of some 600 miles (965 km). Graziani blamed the Matilda tank for his defeat, remarking: 'one cannot break steel armour with finger nails alone'.₆ His poor performance was derided in Rome. 'This man has lost his mind or at least his senses,' cursed Mussolini. 'Here is another man with whom I cannot get angry, because I despise him.'₇

O'Connor pressed on to Buq Buq, which was held at divisional strength by the Italians. Here, the light tanks of the 3rd Hussars became stranded on the soft salt flats and were sitting ducks. Cruiser tanks then arrived on the scene and overran the Italian gun line. To the south-east, B Squadron 2RTR entered the Italian defences and the garrison soon gave up. Some 14,000 men and 68 guns were taken.

By this stage, Operation *Compass* and the follow-up had captured 38,000 prisoners, including four generals, 237 guns as well as 73 light and medium tanks. The 1st and 2nd Libyan divisions, 4th Blackshirt Division and Group Maletti ceased to exist. Two days after the liberation of Buq Buq, the 3rd Hussars crossed the border and occupied Fort Capuzzo. There, they captured an officer and 30 men. An attempt on Bardia, however, was repulsed. On 16 December, 4th Armoured Brigade set about Sidi Omar with the 7th Hussars and 2RTR leading the charge. The demoralized garrison of 900 men surrendered. The following day, HMS *Aphis* attacked Bardia harbour, sinking three Italian freighters.

O'Connor was not pleased that one of his divisions had been suddenly taken to spearhead an attack on Italian East Africa. 'As a result the Indian Division was replaced by the 6th Australian Division who had never been trained in desert war…' he observed unhappily. This also greatly hampered his operation: 'The net result was that the removal of the 4th Indian Division led to a serious delay before we could attack Bardia and by doing so we lost surprise completely.'[8]

Early in the New Year, O'Connor, reinforced by the Australians, finally attacked Bardia again. It was defended by a formidable force of 45,000 men under General Bergonzoli. They were from the 62nd Marmarica, 63rd Cirene and 64th divisions as well as including survivors from the 1st and 2nd Blackshirt divisions. Their 17-mile (27-km) defensive perimeter consisted of a continuous anti-tank ditch, barbed wire, concrete gun emplacements and blockhouses. Mussolini ordered Bergonzoli to fight to the last. O'Connor's preparations were meticulous: Australian engineers constructed a full-size replica in order to rehearse the attack.

An hour before dawn on 3 January 1941, the Australians effected a breech at Bardia and constructed six tank bridging points over the anti-tank ditch. At 0640 hours, two troops of Matildas supported by two battalions of infantry crossed, turning left and right. Two more troops of Matildas followed them, pushing deeper into Bergonzoli's defences. Off the coast, three British warships, using their 15-in guns, bombarded targets within the Italian perimeter, aimed at a garrison already rattled by the previous actions of the Royal Navy.

By late afternoon on 3 January, the Italian defences had been cut in half. The following day, the Australians renewed their assault and by 1600 hours the port had been secured. Bergonzoli, however, escaped to Tobruk.

The Australian attack in the southern sector lacked armour support and it was not until the arrival of the Matildas on 5 January that the last Italian resistance collapsed. The Italians lost all their equipment at Bardia, including 462 guns, 127 tanks and 700 vehicles.

On 10 January 1941, O'Connor's Western Desert Force was redesignated XIII Corps. On the same day, the Luftwaffe's Stuka dive-bombers made their debut in the Mediterranean. This had repercussions: on 10 and 11 January they put the aircraft carrier *Illustrious* out of commission off Crete, and damaged the cruisers *Gloucester* and *Southampton* off Malta. The *Southampton* caught fire and had to be torpedoed. That the *Illustrious* survived was testament to her modern design, as the damage would have sunk any other carrier in service. In the first attack, she was hit by eight bombs, followed by several more in Malta harbour six days later.

ATTENTION TURNS TO TOBRUK AND DERNA

The dive-bombers then turned their attentions on Malta for the next two months. Despite this development, there was now nothing to stop the British attacking Tobruk, which lay 70 miles (113 km) to the west. It was held by the 61st Sirte Division, plus 9,000 stragglers and 2,000 sailors, in total some 25,000 men. Their heavy equipment included 200 guns and 90 tanks. Inside the 30-mile (48-km) perimeter the key forts were Pilastrino and Solaro to the south-west of Tobruk. Morale, though, was not good. The men were afraid because they knew they had no way of stopping the Matilda tank. Graziani and his corps commander, General Patessi Mannella, had little hope of holding on to Tobruk with a force half that of Bardia covering twice the perimeter.

The Italian Navy did what it could to help, which was not much, but the Italian Air Force soon lost all its airbases in the Tobruk area and was forced back to Tripoli. The *San Giorgio*, a grounded cruiser in Tobruk harbour, was able to provide some fire support for the army since it had been turned into a flak ship with the installation of additional anti-aircraft guns. Three Australians destroyers were deployed offshore just in case the damaged cruiser attempted to escape.

The Australians, using the same Bardia tactics, at 0630 hours on 21 January 1941 penetrated the port's defensive perimeter. Once again, despite their best efforts, the Italian artillery could not stop the combination of

Matilda tanks and Australian infantry. By nightfall, they had got to the edge of the escarpment overlooking Tobruk. Overnight, the shelling was relentless. The following day, the Australians, using captured Italian tanks, reached the waterfront, where they were confronted by a beached freighter and liner, as well as the scuttled *San Giorgio*. Most of the garrison was captured.

Derna was next in the firing line. It was held by the 60th Sabratha Division, with the incomplete Babini Armoured Brigade protecting its flank at Mechili. The light tanks of the 7th Hussars moved to cut the Mechili–Derna road on the morning of 24 January. Just after 1000 hours, they bumped into 14 Italian M13 tanks. The British light tanks were only supported by three cruiser tanks and had to beat a hasty retreat. A request for help was signalled to 4th Armoured Brigade headquarters, but in the meantime several light tanks were lost, along with a cruiser. The gun on a second cruiser also jammed.

The Italians were counter-attacked from the south at 1155 hours by the cruisers of C Squadron, 2RTR. A squadron attacked from the east five minutes later. When the firing stopped and the smoke and dust cleared it was evident that the Italians had lost nine tanks. They decided to abandon Derna, and the Babini Armoured Brigade moved to cover the withdrawal towards Benghazi.

BRUTE FORCE AT BEDA FOMM

O'Connor was now presented with a golden opportunity of trapping the retreating Italians. He ordered 6th Australian Division to chase the fleeing enemy westwards along the coastal road. At the same time, 7th Armoured would strike south-west behind the mountainous Djebel Akhdar region. They were to travel from Mechili, through Msus to reach the coast near Beda Fomm south of Benghazi. Bergonzoli never imagined that the British would conduct a left hook and assumed it would take them about two days to reach Benghazi using the coastal road. On 4 February, Combeforce, numbering less than 2,000 men from 7th Armoured, set off. The going was extremely tough across the boulder-strewn desert, but the following day they set up their blocking positions on the coast road at Beda Fomm.

A long, unsuspecting convoy, consisting largely of Italian administrative staff from Benghazi, came down the road at 1430 hours on 5 February.

They first ran into British mines and then 25-pounder shells. The Italians, lacking artillery and tank support, counter-attacked, but were unable to dislodge Combeforce. At 1700 hours, 4th Armoured Brigade arrived and moved into position on a series of ridges just to the east of the road.

Bergonzoli, realizing he was trapped, spent the night devising a plan to break out. He decided the Babini Armoured Brigade would drive the British from a high point, known as The Pimple, south-west of Beda Fomm. Once this was done, his tanks were to sweep south behind Combeforce. At the same time, a diversionary attack from Benghazi along the coast road would pin down Combeforce.

On 6 February, the Babini attack did not go well. Only company commanders' tanks had radios, which meant co-ordinating the advance was almost impossible. The cruiser tanks of 2RTR were expecting attack and had deployed in hull-down positions on the ridges. To the north-east, 7th Armoured's support group drove the Italians out of Sceleidima and to the north the Australians entered Benghazi. The latter were somewhat bemused when they were welcomed by the civilian authorities as 'gallant allies'.

Trooper 'Topper' Brown with 2RTR was in the thick of it: 'Practically all morning we never stopped firing, at wagon loads of infantry or tanks. I haven't a clue how many enemy I killed, but it must have run into hundreds. We definitely had a score of twenty M13s at the end of the day…' He took out the last of these with his final shells: 'We had started out with 112 rounds of 2-pounder, 97 in the racks and 15 extra. Hughes had let us get down to the last two … so you can understand the amount of firing I had done.'[9]

By now, the Italian column trapped along the coast was 11 miles (18 km) long and under attack by the 3rd and 7th Hussars. Although Babini managed to drive 2RTR from The Pimple and the Italians pushed against Combeforce, British reinforcements stabilized the situation. Bergonzoli was desperate and at dawn on 7 February threw the last of his tanks against Combeforce. Backed by artillery, for a moment it looked as if they might break through. Instead, they were all knocked out. The Italians lost the last of their offensive strength and it was not long before white flags began to appear all along the column. Bergonzoli surrendered to Colonel Combe. A triumphant O'Connor signalled Wavell in Cairo – his message was short and to the point: 'Fox killed in the open.'[10]

When O'Connor toured the battlefield he remarked: 'I have seldom seen such a scene of wreckage and confusion as existed on the main Benghazi road.'[11] The area between Benghazi and Beda Fomm looked like some giant scrapyard. As far as the eye could see were abandoned guns, lorries and tanks. At the roadside were dead bodies, ammunition boxes, helmets and other personal effects. General Tellera, the commander of the Italian 10th Army, was found mortally wounded in one of the tanks. He died that day.

When the British did a head count at Beda Fomm they found they had taken more than 25,000 prisoners, 216 guns, 100 tanks and 1,500 vehicles. The Italian officers were rounded up and gathered at the village of Soluch. They included General Cona, who had taken over from Tellera, as well as Generals Bardini, Bignani, Giuliano, Negroni and Villanis. Bergonzoli, when asked about his defeat, shrugged and simply replied: 'You were here too soon, that is all.'[12]

Reporter Alan Moorehead who interviewed Bergonzoli recalled: 'He was a soft-spoken little man with a pinched swarthy face that had aged unbelievably since his great days in Spain. His famous "barba elettrica" was a neat, bristly beard parted in the centre.'[13] Moorhead was rather impressed by how Bergonzoli had eluded the British since December: 'One could not help perversely wishing that after so many risks and chances he had got away in the end.'[14] Instead, he was flown to Cairo with the others.

In a single battle, Mussolini's army in Cyrenaica ceased to exist. O'Connor destroyed ten divisions, capturing in excess of 130,000 men, along with 845 guns and 380 tanks. What made this victory so remarkable was that it had been achieved at the cost of just 500 dead, 1,373 wounded and 55 missing. The RAF, who covered O'Connor's daring dash behind Djebel Akhdar, destroyed about 150 aircraft. Although in places the Italians had fought bravely, they were outmatched and outmanoeuvred. After Taranto and Beda Fomm, the British had reduced Mussolini's armed forces to a laughing stock. O'Connor's decisive victory at Beda Fomm was the defining moment of the first round of the war in North Africa.

NEXT STEPS

Wavell, understandably, was full of praise for his troops' efforts: 'The Army of the Nile, as our Prime Minister has called us, has in two months advanced over 400 miles, has destroyed the large army that had gathered to invade Egypt … These achievements will always be remembered.' In Britain, newspaper headlines proclaimed: 'Wavell's Wave Sweeps over Libya.' Churchill was ecstatic about Mussolini's humiliating defeat and declared during a radio broadcast: 'Operation Compass will long be studied as a model of the military art.'[15]

In private, he signalled Wavell, warning of changing strategic requirements:

> Accept my heartfelt congratulations on this latest admirable victory and on the unexpected speed with which Cyrenaica has been conquered … Greece and/or Turkey must have priority … You should therefore make yourself secure in Benghazi and concentrate all available forces in the [Nile] Delta in preparation for movement to Europe.[16]

Wavell now wavered. Tripoli beckoned, but he was distracted by orders to send troops to help the Greeks. Besides, the Italian threat to Egypt had been completely removed.

O'Connor's men stopped at El Agheila and went no further. He wanted to press on, but it was not his decision to make. 'We completely liquidated the enemy and there were no other troops in the way,' recalled O'Connor, '– nothing to stop us really.'[17] He wanted to drive on Sirte and Tripoli and his boss seemed to agree with him. 'Extent of Italian defeat at Benghazi makes it seem possible that Tripoli might yield to small force if despatched without undue delay,' Wavell signalled to London. 'Am working out commitment involved but hesitate to advance further in view of Balkan situation unless you think capture of Tripoli might have favourable effect on attitude of French North Africa.'[18] He then went on to outline how he doubted the navy and air force would be keen to support a move on Tripoli.

O'Connor sent Brigadier Eric Dorman-Smith, his chief staff officer, back to Cairo to lobby Wavell to advance. At 1000 hours on the morning of 12 February he found himself in Wavell's office staring at a very large map of Greece. 'You see Eric,' explained Wavell, 'I am planning my spring campaign.'[19] O'Connor's XIII Corps was destined to stay put in Cyrenaica. That very day General Erwin Rommel arrived in Tripoli tasked with helping the Italians recover Cyrenaica. Rommel, though, had no intention of following such limited orders; he had set his sights on Cairo.

HITLER ASSESSES HIS OPTIONS

The Battle of Britain in the summer of 1940 showed that Churchill and the British people were ready to do everything in their power to defend the British Isles from invasion. In the Mediterranean, the battle of Beda Fomm clearly signalled that the British were prepared to strike back in order to protect Egypt. General Franco in Madrid took note of Mussolini's humiliation and saw little point in shackling his country to the Italians or the Germans. Hitler, in contrast, knew he now had little choice but to prop up his ally in the Mediterranean.

During November 1940, Hitler had continued to lobby Franco to join his war effort. The Spanish leader declined to give any definite commitment. In early December, the Germans submitted their proposals for the 10 January 1941 attack on Gibraltar. Franco flatly refused, alarmed at the prospect of a British or American occupation of the islands in the Atlantic. Hitler and Mussolini were both to make one last effort to persuade Franco in the New Year.

'The battle which Germany and Italy are fighting will determine the destiny of Spain as well,' Hitler wrote in a threatening letter to Franco on 6 February 1941. 'Only in the case of our victory will your present regime continue to exist.'[20] He went on to warn: 'Spain will never get other friends than those given her in the Germany and Italy of today, unless it becomes a different Spain. This different Spain, however, could only be the Spain of decline and final collapse … a bold heart can save nations.'[21] This reached Madrid the very day that Marshal Graziani's forces were being crushed.

Mussolini next tried to persuade Franco on 12 February 1941, when they met at Bordighera on the Italian Riviera. When Franco finally replied to Hitler at the end of the month, he pointed out that the situation had changed dramatically since last October. Clearly, Taranto and Beda Fomm weighed heavily on his mind and he continued to refuse to commit his country to the Axis cause.

Spain was exhausted after three years of internal conflict and Franco had no real desire to take his country to war again. If he helped Hitler secure Gibraltar, he knew that the Royal Navy and RAF would not sit idly by. The

Mussolini with General Franco (centre). Hitler and Mussolini hoped Spain would join the Axis and help secure Gibraltar.

Spanish fleet was in no condition to tangle with the British Mediterranean Fleet. Ultimately, there was no way of knowing how Churchill would retaliate. Securing Gibraltar would also inevitably mean a permanent German garrison.

'I fear,' Hitler wrote to Mussolini, 'that Franco is making the greatest mistake of his life.'[22] He had failed Mussolini twice. If Franco would not assist in the Mediterranean and Hitler did not conduct his threatened invasion of Britain, then Mussolini would have to face the British largely on his own. Hitler was loath to invade Britain if it meant derailing his timetable for the assault on Stalin. 'The long and short of the tedious Spanish rigmarole, is that Spain does not want to enter the war and will not enter it,' Hitler confessed to his Italian counterpart. 'This is extremely tiresome since it means that for the moment the possibility of striking Britain in the simplest manner, in her Mediterranean possessions, is eliminated.'[23]

Hitler appreciated that he could not let Italy be defeated again and that he must prevent Mussolini from losing Libya. He therefore decided to send some Luftwaffe and anti-tank units to North Africa to help out. Some two-and-a-half divisions were also to be sent to bolster the Italians. Hitler admitted that he might also have to act in the western Mediterranean, even if Franco would not help. He was angry that Pétain had not upheld his promise, made at Montoire-sur-le-Loire, to co-operate against the British. The reality was that the wily Marshal had been playing for time to protect the integrity of the French Empire.

General Maxime Weygand in charge of the French colonial empire did not act following Mussolini's defeat in North Africa. In southern France, Pétain's Vichy government arrested Foreign Minister Pierre Laval, a key advocate of collaboration. The Germans demanded his release but could not get him reinstated. 'If France becomes troublesome,' Hitler told his staff, 'she will have to be crushed completely.'[24] He put in place plans that envisaged occupying the rest of France and seizing Toulon along with the remains of the French fleet. Although Hitler threatened Admiral Darlan with Operation *Attila*, the occupation of Vichy was not carried out.

CHAPTER 7:
Back at Sea

IN EARLY January 1941, the British Mediterranean Fleet successfully pushed a convoy through from the west, but at some cost. Four merchant ships arrived, three of which were carrying urgent supplies for the Greeks and the fourth supplies for Malta. They were greeted in the narrows north-west of Malta by the battleships *Warspite* and *Valiant*, along with the carrier *Illustrious*. Shortly after, the Luftwaffe's Stukas damaged the *Illustrious*, which made it to Malta only to be bombed again. The carrier managed to reach Alexandria, but was unable to operate aircraft.

The *Formidable* was sent from the Atlantic as a replacement. She took the long route, sailing round Africa and through the Suez Canal, arriving at Alexandria on 10 March 1941. There, the crew found moored in the harbour the damaged *Illustrious*, the old carrier *Eagle* desperately in need of a refit, the battleships *Barham*, *Warspite* and *Valiant*, along with the submarine parent ship *Medway*. There were also numerous other ships of varying sizes, including the still-immobilized French warships.

Following the air attack on Taranto, the Italian Navy was risk averse. Their ships had been withdrawn north, where they could enjoy the protection of much better air cover. This was not an act of cowardice, rather one of pragmatism. In addition, the bureaucratic and centralized nature of the Italian Navy's command structure made it very difficult for commanders, even at flotilla level, to exercise any initiative. This meant that the Italian fleet had little option but to cling to its bases. By early 1941,

Mussolini's oil stocks were dangerously low, which meant the navy simply did not have the supplies to put to sea as often as it would like.

OPERATION *LUSTRE*

Just after the British victory at Beda Fomm, the Royal Navy gained another victory over the Italian fleet. This occurred near Cape Matapan off southern Greece. Britain commenced Operation *Lustre* in early March to ferry forces to support the Greeks. This requirement had become more urgent with the southward movement of German troops in February, as well as the accession to the Axis by Bulgaria on 1 March 1941. German troops entered the country that day and the Bulgarian Army deployed along the Greek frontier. In an operation that was anticipated to last two months, from 5 March, British convoys were run from Egypt to Greece every three days. It was therefore vital that Cunningham, whose ships were screening the troop shipments to Crete and Greece, be kept informed of any Italian naval movements.

Churchill noted: 'Admiral Cunningham left us in no doubt as to the considerable naval risks in the Mediterranean which were involved in the move of the Army and Royal Air Force to Greece.'[1] There was a very real danger that Hitler might launch air strikes from Bulgaria against the convoys while at sea and against their disembarkation ports. In addition, the Italian fleet might try to intervene. 'This could be met by our battleships based on Suda Bay in Crete,' said Churchill, 'but only at the expense of weakening the destroyer escort for the convoys and leaving the supply line to Cyrenaica practically unprotected.'[2] British plans to capture Rhodes had to be shelved. To complicate matters, the Suez Canal had been temporarily blocked by mines.

Mussolini, meanwhile, was desperate for a victory after the destruction of his army in North Africa. He now ordered his timid fleet to venture from their sanctuaries and intercept the British troop convoys. This would cow Greece and might encourage Yugoslavia to join the Axis. Admiral Iachino, on 16 March 1941, was therefore instructed to take offensive action as soon as possible. It was decided this would consist of a double sweep, with one in the western Aegean and another south of the island of Gavdos.

These operations were influenced by German intelligence. Just three days later, the German liaison officer in Rome advised his Italian colleagues that: 'the situation in the Mediterranean is at the moment more favourable for the Italian fleet than ever before'.[3] This was based on a German Naval Staff report that there was only one British battleship operational in the eastern Mediterranean – namely HMS *Valiant*. The Germans also reassured the Italians that the British convoys were 'inadequately protected' and they had no reinforcements to hand. 'Intensive traffic from Alexandria to the Greek ports,' added the report, 'whereby the Greek forces are receiving constant reinforcements in men and equipment, presents a particularly worthwhile target for Italian Naval forces.'[4]

The Italian Navy, quite rightly, were not prepared to take this intelligence at face value. From 25 March, Italian reconnaissance flights were stepped up in an effort to track the Mediterranean Fleet's movements. Regular reconnaissance over Alexandria soon tipped Cunningham off that the Italians were planning something. The question was, what? Logically, if they were trying to detect whether the British Fleet had left harbour, it indicated a potential attack on the lightly escorted convoys. Looking at the wider war in the Mediterranean, there was also the possibility the Italians were preparing a naval diversion. Such an operation might be designed to mask landings in Cyrenaica or Greece, or worse, a major assault on Malta.

At this very point, Bletchley Park's cryptographers cracked the Italian Naval Enigma communications on 25–6 March 1941. Matapan was to be the first victory achieved thanks to Enigma-derived intelligence. Mavis Batey, who worked for Alfred Dillwyn 'Dilly' Knox's team recalled: 'It was the Italians' errors that gave the game away.'[5] She managed to decipher a message to an Italian naval commander. 'Today 25 March is X-3,' which she noted, 'If you get a message saying "today minus three", then you know that something pretty big is afoot.'[6] More messages came in and Mavis worked late. 'It was eleven o'clock at night,' she recalled, 'and it was pouring with rain when I rushed, ran, absolutely tore down to take it to Intelligence, to get it across to Admiral Cunningham.'[7]

THE BATTLE OF MATAPAN

In the early hours of 27 March, Iachino and the battleship *Vittorio Veneto* sailed from Naples. He then rendezvoused with the cruisers *Fiume*, *Pola* and *Zara* in the Strait of Messina. The latter vessels were under the command of Admiral Luigi Sansonetti. Three other cruisers – the *Bolzano*, *Trento* and

Trieste – under Admiral Carlo Cattaneo, sailed from Taranto. They were supported by four destroyers. Two light cruisers also came from Brindisi. These vessels were instructed to gather off the island of Gavdos, south of Crete, and then move north-east into the Aegean.

Cunningham, at his headquarters in Alexandria, was immediately notified of the Italian battle groups' departure. His challenge was to intercept them without making it apparent their codes had been broken. Ironically, this meant he had to deliberately lose the element of surprise. This was done by sending a Sunderland flying boat from Crete on a 'routine' patrol. Not only did it have to spot the Italians, but it was also vital that the Italians saw the aircraft.

He was 'officially' made aware of the situation by the flying boat at 1220 hours. This reported seeing three Italian cruisers and a destroyer some 80 miles (130 km) east of south-eastern Sicily. They were sailing south-eastwards in the direction of Crete. Fortunately, there was only one British convoy at sea but it was south of Crete heading for Piraeus in southern Greece. The convoy commander was instructed when it got dark to turn about. Another convoy due south from Piraeus was ordered not to sail.

Keeping his cool, Cunningham stuck to his routine that day and went off to his country club to play golf. There, he bumped into the Japanese consul and made a point of being overheard discussing a dinner party he was going to that night. All this was subterfuge designed to give the impression that it was business as usual. Although Cunningham planned to deploy the fleet to the west of Crete, he felt: 'It was important to maintain an appearance of normality … lest the enemy should "smell a rat."'[8] The Italians, still keen to confirm the British Fleet was not at sea, sent a reconnaissance plane from Rhodes to see what was going on at Alexandria. It flew over the port at 1400 hours and reported the presence of three battleships, two aircraft carriers and a number of cruisers. All was as it should be.

Cunningham did not go to the party. Instead, he hopped into his car and headed for the docks. By 1900 hours on 27 March, Cunningham aboard the *Warspite*, supported by the *Barham*, *Valiant*, *Formidable* and two flotillas of destroyers, departed Alexandria. At the same time, Admiral Sir Henry Pridham-Wippell, with a second force consisting of four light cruisers and three destroyers, set sail from Piraeus. Other vessels escorting the convoys from Alexandria and in the waters off northern Crete were also put on alert.

The *Formidable* was not only carrying four Swordfish, but also ten of its successor, the new Fairey Albacore three-seat biplane torpedo-bomber. Dubbed the 'Applecore', it had a much longer range, although only half were fitted with the long-range tanks. They were supported by 13 of the ungainly Fulmar fighters. 'I was serving in an Albacore Squadron belonging to *Formidable*, which was disembarked at the Naval Air Station at Dekheila, about three miles outside Alexandria,' recalled Lieutenant Mike Haworth, 'when about noon on the 27th we received the order for a rushed embarkation.'[9]

The Italians were soon spooked by intelligence that HMS *Formidable* was on the move. The Italian naval command considered cancelling the operation, unaware that the bulk of the British Mediterranean Fleet was steaming towards Admiral Iachino's forces. Instead, he was told to stay in the Ionian Sea, but his captains had no intention of getting caught out. The cruisers carried two seaplanes in a hangar under the foredeck. These were launched from a fixed catapult and retrieved from the sea by a crane. Likewise, the *Vittorio Veneto* carried three aircraft. It was not long before Italian pilots were buzzing around desperately trying to locate the enemy.

At dawn, an Italian seaplane from the *Vittorio Veneto* spotted Pridham-Wippell on HMS *Ajax* and the rest of his group. Iachino ordered the *Bolzano*, *Trento*, *Trieste* and the destroyers *Ascari*, *Carabiniere* and *Corazziere* to attack. Fire was exchanged without damage to either side and the Italians headed back to their main fleet. Pridham-Wippell impetuously gave chase and nearly ran into a trap.

Cunningham and his force was still 80 miles (130 km) away, so he decided to launch six torpedo-armed Albacores, two Fulmar fighters and a single Swordfish flying observation from *Formidable* to assist Pridham-Wippell. Like the Swordfish, the wings of the Albacore folded back either side of the fuselage for storage in the armoured hangar. Once brought up on deck in the elevator, the ground crews worked to lock the wings forward in their flying position.

The Fleet Air Arm pilots, much to their displeasure, when they flew over Pridham-Wippell's ships came under friendly fire until they had passed out of range. Lieutenant F. Hopkins, an observer in one of the Albacores, recalled: 'We sighted one large warship, escorted by four destroyers, steaming towards our cruisers, and shortly after this the large warship, which turned out to be a battleship of the Littorio class, opened fire on our cruisers.'[10] He realized these were in trouble because the main fleet would not reach them quickly enough. In the meantime, the *Vittorio Veneto* would be able to pick them off one by one with its longer-range guns. Suddenly, two German Ju 88 fighter-bombers appeared out of the sun to attack the Albacores. The Fulmars, piloted by Lieutenant Donald Gibson and Petty Officer Theobold, intercepted them, shooting down one and chasing off the other. 'Later we strafed the *Vittorio Veneto*,' said Gibson, 'but quite out of phase with the torpedo attack.'[11]

Iachino was not unduly alarmed at the sight of the approaching aircraft. It was assumed they were Italian CR42 biplanes from Rhodes, until the air liaison officer pointed out that they were British. The battleship and her four destroyers suddenly opened up with their anti-aircraft guns. Iachino watched as six torpedoes missed the *Vittorio Veneto*. Lieutenant Hopkins thought one stuck home because the vessel circled and then stopped. This was actually just evasive action. 'She also ceased fire on the cruisers,'[12] he noted with satisfaction. Although undamaged, Iachino was forced to break off his attack.

Afterwards, it was the turn of the *Formidable* to have a scare. The anti-aircraft gunners were caught napping by a solitary Italian SM.79 torpedo-bomber. This swooped in and dropped a torpedo on the starboard bow at 1,000 yards (914 m), but the carrier lurched hard to starboard and it missed. A second torpedo-bomber appeared and dropped its weapon at 1,500 yards (1,372 m). Again, the *Illustrious* turned hard and the torpedo passed harmlessly by.

Cunningham sent his Albacores and Swordfish, plus land-based RAF Blenheim bombers, from Crete in pursuit of Iachino. At 1440 hours, three Blenheims tried unsuccessfully to bomb the *Vittorio Veneto*. Around 30 minutes later, a further six Blenheims attacked ineffectively from high altitude. Iachino zigzagged his ships and *Vittorio Veneto* avoided being hit. Iachino could only fume over the absence of the Italian Air Force and the Luftwaffe.

The *Formidable*'s second torpedo strike, employing three Albacores and two Swordfish, found the *Vittorio Veneto* at 1519 hours. This coincided with a high-altitude bombing raid by the RAF, which served to distract the Italian gunners. 'Whilst everyone was busy with the high level bombers,' said Iachino, 'three torpedo aircraft approached without being sighted until very close.'[13]

'The attack was delivered in two waves because the Albacores ...

climbed at a higher rate than the Swordfish,' said Captain Haworth flying observation. 'Diving out of the sun, the leading sub-flight appeared to achieve a degree of surprise and the enemy made a turn of 180 degrees to avoid.'[14] They then turned back, a manoeuvre that greatly reduced their speed. The escorting Fulmars strafed the battleship's bridge and anti-aircraft guns, enabling the Albacores to press home their attack. One aircraft was shot down by the hail of fire, but a torpedo hit the *Vittorio Veneto*. It holed the hull 15 ft (4.6 m) below the waterline and damaged the propeller. However, within a few hours, she was underway again.

At 1930 hours, *Pola* was hit amidships on the starboard side by a torpedo during an air strike. The vessel lost all power and was left adrift. Iachino assumed warnings that British ships were in the area referred to Pridham-Wippell's force. He had no clue that Cunningham was almost on him. 'I had not the slightest idea that we were being pursued so closely,' he said.[15]

At 2100 hours, Iachino foolishly sent the cruisers *Fiume* and *Zara*, as well as three destroyers, to help the stricken *Pola*. When it got dark, the Italian Navy had to operate blind, whereas for the Royal Navy with their radar it made no difference. Cunningham stated that he got a visual sighting from his new chief of staff: 'He calmly reported that he saw two large cruisers with a smaller one ahead of them crossing the bows of the battlefleet from starboard to port.'[16] Cunningham's three battleships were able to approach to within 2 miles (3.2 km) of the Italians at 2230 hours. He watched as the *Warspite* traversed her 15-in guns to target the Italian cruisers. 'The enemy was at a range of no more than 3,800 yards,' noted Cunningham, 'point-blank.'[17]

The Italians warships abruptly found themselves illuminated by British searchlights and being shelled at close range. *Fiume* was hit by *Warspite*, caught fire from stern to bow and sank. *Zara* was then struck by either the *Barham* or *Valiant* and also sank. *Pola*, still without power, was a sitting duck. She was torpedoed and despatched by the British destroyers. Each of the cruisers had more than 800 men on board. Other British vessels joined the battle, engaging the Italian destroyers. *Vittorio Alfieri* was hit, as was the *Giosuè Carducci*, causing fatal damage. Both were relatively new vessels. Iachino and the *Vittorio Veneto* had little choice but to withdraw. Cunningham did not give chase for fear of air attack. His sailors did what they could to help the defeated Italians, hauling about a thousand survivors from the water.

'The results of the action cannot be viewed with entire satisfaction,' wrote Cunningham afterwards, 'since the damaged *Vittorio Veneto* was allowed to escape.'[18] Embarrassingly, the *Formidable* had a close shave with the *Warspite*. The carrier was 5 miles (8 km) away when the battleship's searchlight spotted her. The officer in charge of the *Warspite*'s 6-in starboard battery swung his guns on to the *Formidable*. Luckily, the error was spotted just in time, before he opened fire.

By sunrise, the Italian Navy had lost five ships along with 2,400 men. Only three British lives were lost, when a torpedo-bomber was brought down. Cunningham's ships were largely unscathed and the Royal Navy was ecstatic. Admiral John Godfrey, director of Naval Intelligence, rang Bletchley and left a congratulatory message: 'Tell Dilly [Knox] that we have won a great victory in the Mediterranean and it is entirely due to him and his girls.'[19] Not long after, Cunningham travelled to Bletchley to personally thank the code breakers for their exceptional work.

'This timely and welcome victory off Cape Matapan,' wrote Churchill, 'disposed of all challenge to British naval mastery of the Eastern Mediterranean at this critical time.'[20] Although a stunning victory, however, the Battle of Matapan was quickly forgotten, in part because of the losses that were to follow. For Cunningham's triumph was not conclusive. Although the Italian Navy had been mauled again, it was not completely out of the fight. Neither side was able to gain complete mastery of the sea from the other. To make matters worse, Hitler's Luftwaffe was waiting in the wings ready to pounce.

That said, thanks to Matapan, Operation *Lustre* was a great success. More than 60,300 men were ferried across the eastern Mediterranean, despite being subjected to air attack launched from the Dodecanese islands and Rhodes. Total losses during this operation amounted to 25 ships of 115,000 gross registered tons. Luckily, all but seven of these occurred in port after the troops had been landed.

THE UNDERWATER WAR

The war in the Mediterranean rapidly spread beneath the waves. Throughout the 1930s, Mussolini had conducted an ongoing submarine-building programme. At the start, he had a large fleet of around 115 submarines consisting of numerous different types. Not all were operational and the active ones were divided up among the navy's seven regional commands, which included the Red Sea. These forces were further weakened when Mussolini sent 32 submarines into the Atlantic to support Hitler's U-boats at the beginning of 1941.

In the Mediterranean, the British were most concerned about the Sicily-Libya Command, which included 26 submarines. These posed a direct threat to shipping in the Sicilian Channel between Sicily and Tunisia. Likewise, the Naples Command, with less than a dozen subs, could venture across the Tyrrhenian Sea and menace the Channel. However, many of the Italian subs, with slow surface speeds and large conning towers, were unsuitable for surface attacks. Crucially, the Italians lacked radar and sonar, so they had to rely on reconnaissance aircraft and hydrophones to detect submerged British submarines.

Most notably, Commander George Simpson's British 10th Submarine Flotilla, operating from Malta, played havoc with the Axis shipping lanes. Cunningham warned Simpson, while in Alexandria, in early 1941: 'If you don't get results and don't dispose your forces to suit me I will very soon let you know.'[21] Simpson, who was given 'a free hand', did not disappoint. Based at Manoel Island, in Marsamxett Harbour just north of Valletta, his exposed subs when not on patrol had to ride out Axis air raids by submerging. 'His Majesty's submarines would creep in and out in such sinister silence that we seldom knew of their presence,' recalled fighter pilot Tom Neil, 'until the familiar, cheerful and bearded faces of their commanders turned up in the hotels and bars in Valletta.'[22]

Initially, the big older-class submarines were often spotted on patrol by Axis aircraft and attacked. The smaller and more manoeuvrable U-class first arrived at Malta in the spring of 1941. The larger mine-laying submarines based at Alexandria also ran supplies to Malta, before heading for their hunting grounds in Sicilian waters. Lieutenant-Commander Malcolm Wanklyn, commander of the *Upholder*, between April 1941 and March 1942 sank ten merchant ships, one destroyer and two U-boats. He also single-handedly prevented 5,000 Axis troops from reaching Tripoli on 18 September 1941 when he sank two troop ships.

The latter operation actually involved four U-class subs, deployed in a staggered ambush, but it fell to Wanklyn to make the kill shots. He caught them with a surface attack, in the moonlight and at 5,000 yards (4,572 ft). This was despite the convoy being escorted by five destroyers. Captain

'Sammy' Raw, who commanded the 1st Submarine Flotilla at Alexandria, informed Cunningham that Wanklyn's 'devastating accuracy ... was almost unbelievable and shows the highest skill...'[23] This was a blow to Rommel and to the morale of the Italian merchant fleet. It showed that the Italian Navy were incapable of protecting convoys at night-time.

Ciano, the Italian foreign minister, was furious: 'The supplies for North Africa are becoming more and more difficult. Only 20 per cent of the material set aside for September has been shipped and delivered.'[24] At the end of that month though, much to Rommel's relief, a convoy reached Benghazi. 'With things as they are in the Mediterranean it's not easy to get anything across,' he complained. 'For the moment we're only stepchildren and must make the best of it.'[25]

The *Upholder*'s run of luck finally ended when Wanklyn and his crew were lost off Tripoli in April 1942. A distraught Simpson wrote to inform Wanklyn's wife: 'I have lost a friend and advisor whom I believe I knew better than my brother ... His record of brilliant leadership will never be equalled.'[26] She did not receive her husband's personal effects as the ship carrying them was sunk.

Eventually, the lack of minesweepers and resulting losses forced Simpson to withdraw from Malta in early May 1942. He returned in the summer and departed again at the end of the year, having helped to greatly reduce Italian shipping. U-class scalps included the cruisers *Diaz* and *Banda Nere*, with serious damage inflicted on the *Trieste*. Over a two-year period, his subs were to sink five cruisers, eight destroyers, eight submarines, eight liners, eight tankers, 65 merchant ships and 27 other vessels. This amounted to a staggering 390,660 tons of shipping. It was a quite remarkable achievement.

Both sides also deployed manned torpedoes with varying degrees of success. Lieutenant Eric Newby, serving with the Special Boat Section, was approached in Tobruk in 1941 to test a prototype. The plan was to attack the cruiser *Raimondo Montecuccoli*, which, operating from Palermo, had been laying mines off Cap Bon and conducting convoy escort duties. 'The snag so far as I was concerned,' observed Newby, 'was that the apparatus was constructed in such a manner that its detonation required the operator to go up with it.'[27] He politely declined the task. The naval commander in charge of the project was annoyed by his candour. 'He never spoke to me again,'[28] recalled Newby with relief. The *Raimondo Montecuccoli* was to survive the war.

In contrast, on the night of 18/19 December 1941, three Italian two-man torpedoes snuck into Alexandria harbour. Italian planning was meticulous and involved aerial reconnaissance of the moorings and defensive measures. They managed to severely damage the battleships *Queen Elizabeth* and *Valiant*, as well as a destroyer and a tanker. The *Queen Elizabeth* was Admiral Cunningham's flagship and he was on board at the time of the attack. The blast was such that he was thrown 5 ft (1.5 m) into the air. All the Italian divers were captured and the attack was quickly hushed up, but the loss of the two battleships gave Mussolini temporary naval supremacy.

Count Junio Valerio Borghese, captain of the Italian submarine that transported the attackers, noted: 'The most important requirement was maintenance of absolute secrecy.'[29] The British, though, were alert to the threat as there had already been unsuccessful attempts at attacking Alexandria, Gibraltar and Grand Harbour using these weapons. Embarrassingly for Cunningham, British intelligence had warned him of such an attack. Unfortunately, his efforts to improve security at Alexandria were not quick enough. There was no denying the audacity of the raid and Cunningham was compelled to commend the 'cold-blooded bravery and enterprise of these Italians'.[30]

CHAPTER 8:
Unwanted Distractions

FOLLOWING MUSSOLINI'S mauling at Beda Fomm, Hitler reluctantly decided to come to his assistance. General Erwin Rommel therefore duly landed in Libya on 12 February 1941 ready to take command of the assembling Deutsches Afrika Korps. For the sake of diplomacy, he was formally placed under Italian command. This seemed reasonable as there were still 150,000 Italian troops in Libya, whereas Rommel only deployed with 40,000 men. That same day at Bordighera, Mussolini met Franco and vainly attempted to persuade him to join the war against Britain.

Wavell, faced by a host of other operational priorities, assumed that Mussolini and Hitler would bide their time while they built up their strength. He was increasingly distracted by the requirement to help defend Greece. This would put a terrible strain on British resources in North Africa and the Middle East; sending large numbers of men to Greece would be a major logistical undertaking.

Just as Rommel's forces were arriving in Tripoli, the British 7th Armoured Division withdrew to Egypt for a much-needed refit. Its replacement, the 2nd Armoured Division, consisted of the divisional Support Group and 3rd Armoured Brigade. The latter was a wholly improvised formation with a regiment of light tanks, a regiment of cruiser tanks and a regiment with captured Italian tanks. Notably, the 6th Royal Tank Regiment, issued with Italian M13s, lacked radios. In total, this weak brigade had just 86 of its authorized 156 tanks.

It would fall to this wholly inadequate division to confront Rommel's Panzers and Mussolini's new medium tanks. Mussolini's first armoured division, called Ariete, deployed to Libya in January 1941 – and was eventually destroyed at the Second Battle of El Alamein. The Italians made their only attempt to create a true mechanized corps in the summer of 1941: they assembled their armoured forces, nominally independent of Rommel, under the 20th Manoeuvre Corps, with the Ariete Armoured and Trieste Motorised divisions, commanded by General Gastone Gambara.

It is worth noting that much of the Axis armoured striking force during the rest of desert war belonged to Mussolini: both the Ariete and Littorio divisions were to play an important part at El Alamein. He eventually had three armoured divisions in North Africa, as well as two motorized divisions. All these forces ended up subordinate to German command and served Hitler's cause with mixed results. The Littorio, after deploying in Yugoslavia, arrived in North Africa in January 1942 and was also destroyed at El Alamein. The Centauro served in Greece and Yugoslavia before belatedly being sent to Tripoli in November 1942 and finally surrendered in Tunisia in 1943.

ROMMEL TAKES THE BATTLE TO THE ENEMY

Rommel, with a reputation for seizing the initiative, did not waste time and was soon probing Wavell's defences. Hitler and General Gariboldi urged caution but Rommel took no notice. When he attacked El Agheila on 24 March 1941, the understrength 2nd Armoured Division was forced to conduct a fighting withdrawal. While combat losses were not serious, the mechanical reliability of its tanks was a major concern and there were numerous breakdowns. Then, on 2 April, Rommel's Panzers forced the Support Group from Agedabia and most of the division was overrun. The 3rd Armoured Brigade was sent to Mechili to cover the retreat. In the chaos, a Free French Battalion at Msus, the brigade's main supply depot, took what they needed and burned the rest of the fuel supplies. By the time Rommel reached Mechili, the 3rd Armoured Brigade had lost all offensive capability. The survivors, short of petrol and with just a dozen tanks, drove north to Derna, only to be ambushed on 6 April.

Now that Rommel was in command, Mussolini's troops showed a marked improvement. Units of the Ariete captured 2,000 men from an

Indian brigade on 7 April, while at Halfaya Pass the Italian gunners gave a good account of themselves, knocking out seven British tanks. Rommel had quickly taken the battle to the enemy and rapidly reached the Egyptian frontier at Halfaya, with just Tobruk holding out in his rear. Everything O'Connor achieved against the Italians was swept away.

General Rommel's arrival in Libya significantly bolstered the Italian war effort and ensured the Axis forces reached Egypt.

A NEAR MISS

In their moment of triumph, the Axis almost suffered a catastrophe. Rommel's captured British Dorchester command vehicle was nearly the end of him, when late on 19 April two British Hurricane fighters spotted his column just short of Gambut. They strafed the exposed Germans three times. Rommel's driver failed to close the armoured shutter quickly enough and a bullet passed through him, narrowly missing Rommel's head. When the strafing was over, the wounded driver was moved to the back and Rommel drove.

Back in London, Churchill was understandably angry at the bad news and cabled Wavell, demanding to know what had gone wrong. Wavell responded that the units involved were simply not ready for action and that the cruiser tanks were constantly unreliable. '3rd Armoured Brigade practically melted away from mechanical and administrative breakdowns during the retreat,' he reported, 'without much fighting, while the unpractised headquarters of the 2nd Armoured Division seems to have lost control.'[1] Wavell had much greater concerns than this initial setback with Rommel: the situation in the Balkans was deteriorating very rapidly.

BATTLE FOR THE BALKANS

Anthony Eden, the newly appointed British Foreign Secretary, was determined to keep Hitler and Mussolini out of Greece. Eden felt that his country had broken too many promises over the years, and that now was the time to make a stand. Although Wavell had his hands full in North Africa, he embraced the possibility of an operation in Greece. Eden and Wavell were in Khartoum when Mussolini first attacked the Greeks. In response, Wavell was ordered to send very limited forces to Athens and Crete in a show of solidarity. 'All this meant a considerable drain on my resources,' grumbled Wavell, 'and led to my disclosing to Eden my plans for an early attack on the Italians.'[2] At the time, the Greek prime minister, General Metaxas, did not want a large British military presence, lest it antagonize Hitler.

When Eden arrived in Cairo on 20 February 1941, Wavell told him: 'I have begun the concentration for the move of troops to Greece.'[3] These included Australian, Cypriot, New Zealander and Palestinian units. Churchill, in contrast, was mindful of the risks and did not share their enthusiasm. 'Do not consider yourself obligated to a Greek enterprise if in your hearts you feel it will be only another Norwegian fiasco,' he cautioned. 'If no good plan can be made, please say so.'[4] It was too late: Eden and Wavell were committed to their course of action. Besides, Churchill had made it clear what he wanted: 'But of course you know how valuable success would be.'[5]

Eden and Wavell flew to Athens and promised the Greeks they would send 100,000 men. The general consensus was that in the event of invasion from Yugoslavia a combined force of nine divisions would be needed to hold the Aliakmon Line. There was also some discussion over whether Turkey and Yugoslavia might side with Greece. Colonel 'Freddie' de Guingand, who was part of the British delegation, recalled: 'from the purely military point of view, the whole thing looked terribly unsound.'[6]

Mussolini was nervous about Hitler's intentions in the Balkans. He was well aware that German troops had begun to move into Bulgaria, ready to head off any British intervention in Greece. Mussolini foolishly hoped that he could defeat the Greeks before Hitler felt obliged to secure his southern flank. He decided to launch a spring offensive in Albania to pre-empt the Germans. Mussolini duly flew to Tirana on 2 March, but his presence made little difference to the performance of his men and the offensive quickly came to a stop.

For Hitler, this and Yugoslavia were the final straw. He had successfully signed a treaty with the Yugoslav government, only to have the pro-British military stage a coup and renege on the deal. Hitler therefore invaded both Greece and Yugoslavia on 6 April 1941, supported by Bulgaria, Hungary and Italy.

Churchill began to have second thoughts about the Balkans and signalled Eden in Cairo: 'We must be careful not to urge Greece against her better judgement into hopeless resistance alone when we have only handfuls of troops which can reach a scene in time.',[7] The first British convoy from Alexandria was due in Piraeus the following day. 'In the existing situation we are all agreed that the best course advocated,' replied Eden firmly, 'should be followed and help given to Greece.'[8] In reality, in the face of such widespread attack, Greece was indefensible.

In theory, the Yugoslav Army, consisting of 28 infantry divisions, should have put up a good fight. Instead, Hitler's Panzers and dive-bombers just sliced through it. In Croatia, some local units even refused to resist. Only further south in Montenegro were the Yugoslavs able to launch a successful counter-attack. It was not enough. Mussolini's forces in Albania played their part. Four divisions from the Italian 11th Army marched north. At the same time, the 2nd Army with 14 divisions advanced from Trieste and Fiume into Slovenia towards Ljubljana and south down the Adriatic coast. Another Italian division moved south from Italy's enclave at Zara on the Dalmatian coast. The Italian Navy, operating from its bases in the Adriatic, supported these operations. The small Yugoslav Navy under Vice-Admiral Marijan Polić was swiftly overwhelmed. Just a single submarine and a few smaller craft managed to escape and join the Allies. Anything left afloat was grabbed by the Italians.

The Luftwaffe mercilessly pounded Belgrade, killing 17,000 civilians, and German and Hungarian troops entered the city on 13 April. By this stage, the Yugoslav Air Force had almost ceased to exist. Four days later, the Yugoslav Army surrendered at Sarajevo. Some 6,028 Yugoslav officers and 337,684 other ranks were captured. Hitler then proceeded to dismember Yugoslavia as he had Czechoslovakia and Poland. Mussolini shared in the spoils: he annexed Dalmatia and western Slovenia, established a puppet state in Montenegro and incorporated Kosovo into Albania. Two Italian armies were deployed on occupation duties in western Yugoslavia.

The Greek Army, under General Alexander Papagos, had 14 divisions facing the Italians in Albania, with just seven-and-a-half on the borders with Yugoslavia, Bulgaria and Turkey. Three-and-a-half of these were defending the so-called Metaxas Line between the Struma Valley and the Turkish frontier. Two were between the Struma and the Vardar and the rest were west of the Vardar trying to screen the British forces gathering on the Aliakmon river. Under General Sir Henry Maitland Wilson, they included the 2nd New Zealand Division, 6th Australian Division and the British 1st Armoured Brigade. Ultimately, they were too little, too late. The deployment of these forces, numbering over 60,000, deprived Wavell of his chance to reach Tripoli.

Papagos requested up to nine British divisions. Wavell planned on sending just four, but the 7th Australian Division and a Polish brigade were held back because of Rommel's advance in Cyrenaica. The Greeks had been greatly weakened by the fighting during the winter with the Italians. Their army suffered some 60,000 casualties and only 41 combat aircraft were available to support it. This meant the Greeks were not in a position to resist a full-scale offensive by the German armed forces and their allies.

THE GERMAN ADVANCE IN GREECE

Elements of Mussolini's 9th and 11th armies supporting the Germans moved south against the Greek 1st Army. The collapse of the Yugoslav forces in southern Macedonia opened the path for a rapid German advance. The German 12th Army crossed the frontier with ten divisions on 6 April. The following day, the Metaxas Line was breached and on 9 April the Panzers took Salonika, cutting off all Greek units east of the Struma. Thessaloniki fell on 9 April and Yannina on 20 April.

Once the Germans had overrun southern Yugoslavia they crossed the border and advanced through Florina towards the Pindus mountains. This posed an immediate threat to those Greek divisions on the Albanian front. They were forced to retreat, but were not quick enough. The British, meantime, withdrew on the Thermopylae Line with a view to evacuating. From the very start, the 1st Armoured Brigade's cruiser tanks proved to be a disaster and kept breaking down. Brigadier Harold Charrington was furious: 'They were quite hopeless rotten metal and not up to specification in any way.'[9]

The trapped Greek Army surrendered on 23 April and four days later the Germans were in Athens. Hitler's victory was achieved at modest cost with 1,685 killed and 3,750 wounded. Greek losses in a six-month campaign, which included the war with Italy in Albania, consisted of 15,700 dead and 218,000 prisoners. The bulk of the Greek Navy was lost, with 29 warships and auxiliary vessels sunk. A Greek cruiser, six destroyers and four submarines managed to reach Alexandria. In contrast, the British lost just over 2,150 killed and wounded and about 14,000 captured. Thanks to British rearguards in the Mount Olympus area and then Thermopylae, many of Wilson's troops managed to escape.

The Royal Navy delivered the expeditionary force, now it had to retrieve it. At Dunkirk, the British had at least been able to contest control of the air. Over Greece, the Germans had complete air supremacy. Nonetheless, Admiral Cunningham despatched six cruisers, 19 destroyers, 11 transport ships and numerous smaller craft to southern Greece on 24 April. That night and the following night, under the direction of Vice-Admiral Pridham-Wippell, some 17,000 men were taken aboard, though two transports were lost. Another 19,500 were rescued on 26 April, including 8,650 from Kalamata. At this point, German airborne troops grabbed the bridge over the Corinth Canal, giving them access to the Peloponnese and the remaining ports in Allied hands.

The Luftwaffe now did all it could to stop Cunningham's evacuation and sank a transport ship as well as the destroyers *Diamond* and *Wryneck*. The loss of these three vessels resulted in 700 deaths. On the night of 28/29 April, the navy tried to rescue 8,000 men still stranded at Kalamata, but the Germans had already overrun the town and controlled the quay. To the east, four destroyers managed to retrieve only 450 men. However, at Monemvasia, *Ajax* and three destroyers saved 4,300 personnel. Warships also retrieved another 4,527 men from Navplion.

More than 50,200 men of all nationalities were ferried to safety, half of whom went to Crete. Those evacuated there were surprised by their reception, for far from being treated as a defeated army they were warmly welcomed. 'Snow' Nicholas, who landed at Glyphisia, recalled: 'The Cretans came out and showered us with food and wine.'[10] During the evacuation, the Luftwaffe destroyed 26 ships, most of which were Greek. Churchill tried to put a brave face on what had essentially been a terrible waste of time and lives. He signalled Wavell to say: 'We have paid our debt of honour with far less loss than I feared.'[11]

Wavell was hard pressed to agree; not only had he lost around 16,000 men, but he had also lost a considerable amount of equipment: 8,000 vehicles, 1,812 machine guns, 209 aircraft, 192 field guns, 164 anti-tank guns and 104 tanks. They would have been far better deployed fending off Rommel. 'If Greece had asked for assistance then we were in honour bound to do our best,' Colonel Guingand later wrote, 'but I contend we misled her as to our ability to help.'[12]

Mussolini was highly delighted that the British had been unceremoniously shoved out of Greece, although it was little recompense for the loss of an entire army in Libya. His six-month involvement in Greece cost his army 13,755 dead, 50,875 wounded, 25,000 missing and 12,370 cases of frostbite. It was yet another major drain on his resources. Nonetheless, Mussolini could not help himself and declared: 'The just God, who lives in the souls of young nations, has decided: we shall win.'[13]

THE PRICE OF VICTORY

Once again, Hitler's allies shared the spoils of war. While the Germans occupied Salonika, Athens and key islands in the Aegean, the Bulgarians gained Thrace and Mussolini got the rest of Greece. To patrol Greece's southern waters, the Italian Navy operated under the Dodecanese Command based on the island of Leros. Mussolini's Balkan empire had grown considerably, but it also stretched his military and his finances to breaking point.

Hitler's invasion of the Balkans contributed to him postponing his invasion of the Soviet Union by one vital month. In fact, he was so anxious to redeploy his forces eastwards that the task of disarming and demobilizing the Yugoslav Army was not completed. Around 300,000 soldiers escaped, many of whom joined the increasingly powerful resistance lurking in the mountains. General Ambrosio's Italian 2nd Army was hardly up to the job of keeping the peace; his junior officers were inadequately trained, most of the infantry was of a poor quality, apart from the Alpini divisions, and their arms and equipment were obsolete. Italian troops were held in contempt by the Balkan nations. Ambrosio's men were treated no differently by the locals.

If Mussolini's strategy had been to prevent Hitler invading the Balkans, his actions completely misfired. The failure of his army in Libya and Greece had made him look weak and foolish. His plans for dominating the Mediterranean were not going smoothly. He now had to pay for most of the security in the Balkans, which absorbed almost half of the Italian Army for the rest of the war. More than 30 Italian divisions were tied up needlessly policing Albania, Greece and Yugoslavia. In the face of an escalating guerrilla war, his men would suffer more casualties in the mountains of the Balkans than in the deserts of North Africa. Furthermore, the Italian Navy would have to patrol the Dalmatian coast, thereby diverting warships that could have been used to fight the British in the Mediterranean.

THE BRITISH RESPONSE

Churchill, quickly recovering from the shock of Wavell's unwelcome expulsion from Libya, considered the defence of Egypt and the Suez Canal a priority. He therefore gathered every aircraft and tank that could be spared at a time when Britain's factories were having to cope with the Luftwaffe's Blitz. Enthusiastically, he wrote to Wavell on 22 April:

> You will, I am sure, be glad to know that we are sending 307 of our best tanks through the Mediterranean, hoping they will reach you around 10 May. Of these 99 are cruisers, Mark IV and Mark VI [Crusader I], with necessary spare parts for the latter, and 180 'I' tanks [Matildas].[14]

Upon reading this, Wavell must have shaken his head when he thought of what was occurring in Greece.

Protected by the Royal Navy, the five ships of Churchill's 'Tiger' Convoy passed Gibraltar on 6 May. One vessel was sunk, along with 57 tanks and ten Hurricanes, after striking mines in the waters south of Malta, though no one was killed. The rest reached Malta and pressed on to Alexandria unscathed on 12 May, delivering much-needed tanks and 43 Hurricanes. Conscious of the growing German threat to Crete, Churchill ordered a dozen tanks to be diverted there, but Wavell had already arranged for six infantry tanks and 15 light tanks to be sent.

By mid-May, Wavell's tank force was increased by 135 Matildas, 82 cruisers – 50 of which were the brand new Crusader Is, enough to re-equip a whole tank regiment – and 21 light tanks. All, with the exception of the Crusader, were slow.

THE CRUSADER I

While the Germans and Italians respected the Matilda, the Crusader, which came with the 'Tiger' Convoy, carried the same inadequate 2-lb gun and its superior cross-country handling was hampered by serious engine problems. It had exactly the same defects as its predecessors, particularly mechanical unreliability and thin armour. The Crusader was hurried into service before these could be ironed out. Although it was fast and could manage up to 40 mph (64 km/h) in the desert, the engine design was old and suffered cooling problems, especially with the fan's drive shafts and with clogged air filters.

Churchill wanted Wavell to attack Rommel immediately, but to his immense irritation, once in Egypt, his 'Cubs' had to be worked up and the crews and mechanics trained. Vital sand filters had to be installed and cooling systems modified. Despite the Crusaders' and Mark IV's shortcomings, these tanks were issued to Major-General Michael O'Moore Creagh's 7th Armoured Division. This unit had been without tanks for four months, so needed time to familiarize themselves with the vehicles, especially the new Crusader.

Rommel's 15th Panzer Division was ready for action by the end of May, which meant that most of the Axis armoured forces facing Churchill's 'Tiger Cubs' would be German rather than Italian. The German 5th Light Division (which became the 21st Panzer Division) was south of Tobruk and the Italian Ariete Division's tanks were on the perimeter, along with two Italian infantry divisions. This gave the impending battle an entirely new complexion. British tanks could take on the first two models of Panzer but not the subsequent two.

MIGHTY PANZERS

The Panzer III, armed with a 50-mm gun, was superior to every British tank until 1942. The early Panzer IV, with its short 75-mm gun, although it had limitations, was able to fire armour piercing, high explosive and smoke – so could easily outshoot British cruisers and shell 25-pounder gun crews. While Germans tanks using high explosive could start shooting from 3,000 yards (2,743 m), their British counterparts had to wait for them to close to within at least a third of this distance to engage with their solid shot. In the meantime, the British artillery had to withdraw, leaving the tanks on their own.

While the 'Tiger Cubs' were prepared for action, the British attempted to drive Rommel away from the frontier before his Panzers were ready to attack. Operation *Brevity* thus commenced on 15 May 1941 and saw the British lose yet more tanks to Rommel. The 22nd Guards Brigade, with 26 Matildas, was instructed to take Fort Capuzzo via Halfaya, while to the south, 2nd Armoured's Support Group, with 29 old cruiser tanks, was to screen the attack with a push on Sidi Azeiz. The Guards made little headway, losing five Matildas and suffering 13 damaged. Many of the cruiser tanks broke down on the way to Sidi Azeiz and more broke down on the way back. At Halfaya Pass, the 15th Panzer Division captured seven Matilda tanks, three of which were still operational.

ATTENTION SHIFTS TO THE EASTERN FRONT

In the Italian capital, Mussolini's generals struggled to follow his strategic logic. In one breath, he made it clear that he did not trust Hitler, in another he was shackling the Italian military to Hitler's anti-Bolshevik crusade. On the first anniversary of the war he had said: 'We must put thousands of guns along the rivers of the Veneto, because it will be from there that the Germans will launch the invasion of Italy…'[15]

Yet, on 26 June 1941, just four days after Hitler invaded the Soviet

Union, the first of 62,000 Italian troops headed east to fight alongside the Germans, Hungarians, Romanians and Slovaks. They formed an Italian expeditionary corps in Russia consisting of three divisions. Like Mussolini's other forces in the Balkans and North Africa, they were poorly armed and equipped. They took with them 5,500 vehicles and 4,000 pack animals, but no tanks. The following year, this force was expanded to create the 227,000-strong Italian 8th Army. This was vastly more troops than Hitler ever committed to North Africa.

Hitler's attack on the Soviet Union clearly indicated in the short term that he had no intention of committing sufficient forces to take Egypt and Suez. German intelligence estimated that the Red Army would be unable to last much more than six weeks. Despite this highly optimistic assessment, it still meant that Rommel was unlikely to receive significant reinforcements until 1942. The Italian corps, and indeed the army, sent to Russia would have been of greater use in North Africa. Likewise, their commander General Giovanni Messe, who was a good soldier, would have been of much greater help in Libya. Ironically, though, to the Italians a war against the communist Russians was much more popular than the one against the capitalist British. Messe would end up in North Africa – overseeing the Italian surrender in Tunisia.

CHAPTER 9:
Falling from the Skies

AFTER THE fall of Athens, Hitler sought to challenge the British dominance of the eastern Mediterranean even more. In the most audacious airborne attack in history, at 0715 hours on 20 May 1941 he invaded Crete. From the moment Mussolini attacked Greece, Hitler assessed that it was potentially vital to secure Crete. If the British established themselves on the island then their air force would be able to roam the Aegean and Ionian seas and threaten the vital Romanian oilfields at Ploeşti. In German hands, it would provide a springboard for attacks in the Mediterranean as well as against North Africa and Suez. Wavell was therefore expecting the invasion.

INADEQUATE GARRISON

Following the occupation of Greece, the Allies had withdrawn most of their forces to the island. Under New Zealander Major-General Sir Bernard Freyberg, the garrison numbered 42,500 Australian, British, Greek and New Zealander troops. They had occupied the hills around Crete's three main airfields at Maleme, Heraklion and Rethymnon (Retimo) along the north coast. They had no artillery, few aircraft and were short of ammunition. Most of the Greek troops were unarmed and untrained. Freyberg was discouraged from arming the local Cretans because they were strongly anti-royalist. In some quarters, it was felt this might constitute a threat to the Greek king, who had also fled to Crete.

General Kurt Student, the founder of Hitler's airborne and airlanding forces, had shown Hitler what could be achieved during the invasion of the Low Countries the previous year. According to him, Hitler 'wanted to break off the Balkan campaign after reaching the south of Greece'. Hitler was understandably reluctant to tackle the Royal Navy and doubted Mussolini's fleet would be much help. This meant a seaborne assault was out of the question. Student then prevailed upon him that they could take Crete using just airborne forces. 'When I first explained the project,' recalled Student, 'Hitler said: "It sounds all right, but I don't think it's practicable," but I managed to convince him.'[1]

Student's intelligence on Crete's garrison was woefully inadequate. It assessed that there were no more than 5,000 troops on the island, of which none were deployed at Rethymnon and only 400 were defending Heraklion. The Germans also believed that all the Australians and New Zealanders who evacuated from Greece had been shipped to Egypt. Likewise, it was thought that there were no Greek troops on the island. An assessment that the Cretans were unlikely to co-operate with German occupation was simply ignored.

Hitler authorized the invasion, code named Operation *Mercury*, with Führer Directive No. 28 on 25 April 1941 and Student's men deployed to the Athens area. In the process, they had become entangled with forces moving north ready for Hitler's attack against the Soviet Union. More than 490 Ju 52 transport aircraft and 65,000 gallons of petrol were gathered. Student's assault forces comprised Brigadier Eugen Meindl's glider-borne Airlanding Assault Regiment, Major-General Wilhelm Süssmann's 7th Parachute Division and Major-General Julius Ringel's 5th Mountain Division (trained for airlanding operations). They were divided into three groups that would capture Maleme, Canea, Suda, Rethymnon and Heraklion. It would take two airlifts to get them there.

There was no role for Mussolini's parachute regiments, even though an Italian battalion had been dropped on to the Greek island of Cephalonia at the end of April. This operation was not repeated with neighbouring Zante; instead, the Italian paratroopers had simply invaded by boat. They were then followed by an Italian infantry division. Mussolini had at least three or four parachute battalions available. There had even been a Libyan parachute unit, but it was disbanded after serious accidents during training. What Mussolini lacked, even if he had wanted to take part in the invasion of Crete, was an airlift capability. He had few transport aircraft, and unlike the Germans, had no assault gliders.

Student's build-up in Greece could hardly go unmissed. 'It seems clear from our information that a heavy airborne attack by German troops and bombers will soon be made on Crete,' Churchill warned Wavell on 28 April. 'Let me know what forces you have on the island and what your plans are.'[2] Wavell responded the following day: 'Crete was warned of possibility of airborne attack on 18 April.'[3] Despite this intelligence, Freyberg was not confident of his chances. At the beginning of May, he signalled Wavell: 'Force here can and will fight, but without support from Navy and Air Force cannot hope to repel invasion.'[4] Freyberg also warned his own government that in light of the 'grave situation' the New Zealand Division was in, they should lobby London to reinforce Crete or abandon it. Some 27,000 tons of munitions were duly sent to the island, but little of it was landed; most of the ships were forced to turn back in the face of repeated air attack.

BATTLE COMMENCES OVER CRETE

Student's initial assault force had taken off at 0430 hours on 20 May, consisting of a battalion transported in 53 gliders. The rest, some 5,000 men, were to jump at 400 ft (122 m). At 0705 hours, the Luftwaffe's bombers pounded the village of Maleme, the nearby airfield and Hill 107 that overlooked it. The area was defended by Brigadier James Hargest's 5th New Zealand Brigade. Just ten minutes later, Major Koch, with the staff of the Assault Regiment, landed beside Hill 107.

Many of the glider pilots were blinded by the rising sun. An early morning mist and smoke rising from the bombing did not help visibility either. Although the Germans were widely dispersed, Koch and some of his men secured Hill 107. Shortly after, paratroopers began to come down to the east and west of Maleme. When Major Scherber's battalion dropped at 0720 hours east of Maleme they ended up scattered over the surrounding hills. They suffered heavy casualties and Scherber and almost 400 of his men were killed. This meant that Maleme could only be attacked from the east.

In the meantime, Süssmann and his staff from the 7th Parachute Division were killed in a crash near Athens. His force was tasked with capturing Canea. Once again, the initial glider-borne troops suffered heavy casualties. The New Zealanders beat off all attempts on the city.

In Athens, General Student could only assume that things were going well, as only seven aircraft of the first wave had failed to return. Soon, however, Student learned that Canea, neighbouring Suda Bay and Maleme had not been taken. In response, he delayed the assaults on Heraklion and Rethymnon. The orders did not reach the men in time and they were dropped piecemeal.

By the end of the day, more than 7,000 Germans had been delivered, but they had suffered heavy casualties. 'Fortunately for us,' recalled regimental physician Dr Heinrich Neumann on Hill 107, 'the New Zealanders did not counter-attack. We were so short of ammunition that, had they done so, we should have had to fight them off with stones and sheath-knives.', The airfield, though, remained in British hands.

'The night of May 20th-21st was critical...' recalled Student. 'If the enemy had made an organized counterattack during this night or the morning of May 21st, he would probably have succeeded in routing the much battered and exhausted remnants of the Assault Regiment...', Freyberg, however, more concerned about the prospect of a seaborne assault between Maleme and Canea, kept his men in their coastal defences. He assumed that the air attack was a secondary operation in support of the main invasion.

For Freyberg, time was running out. The Luftwaffe had air superiority over the island and it was difficult for his men to move without being bombed. The following morning, German airborne reinforcements and much-needed supplies arrived. German transports landed at Maleme under British fire, losing a third of their number. In the Maleme area, the 5th New Zealand Brigade fell back towards Canea and Suda. General Ringel, who was now in command after taking Canea, was to outflank the Suda defences.

Suda Bay was cluttered with wrecked ships, including the cruiser *York*, which had been hit by two Italian explosive motorboats in March. She had continued to act as an anti-aircraft platform until damaged beyond repair by German bombers on 18 May. The unloading of supplies at Suda became impossible once the Germans had secured their landing grounds. The bay provided the best anchorage on Crete and once it was in their hands the Germans could take delivery of seaborne supplies and heavy equipment from Melos. This was to include anti-aircraft and anti-tank guns, artillery and a few tanks. They were also going to ship over two battalions of the 5th Mountain Division. The German flotilla, consisting of Greek caiques and Italian motor torpedo boats, was advised that the British Fleet was still at Alexandria.

Admiral Cunningham, alert to the danger of the Germans trying to send reinforcements to Crete, deployed his ships to the north. Just before midnight on 21 May, Rear Admiral Glennie, with the cruisers *Ajax*, *Dido* and *Orion*, intercepted a convoy of about 20 heavily laden little vessels. 'There began then one of the most fantastic actions ever fought in the Mediterranean,' wrote war reporter Alan Moorehead. 'The British ships found themselves in the midst of a fleet of caiques, each carrying about a hundred soldiers ... the Navy turned its pompomps and four-inch guns upon the caiques – often at point blank range.',[7] Three of these were immediately blown out of the water.

The survivors fled, but over the next two-and-a-half hours more were sunk. The night was filled with gun flashes and the screams of drowning men. Estimates of the casualties varied wildly, with the British claiming thousands and the Germans reporting just 300. 'Not a living man landed that night,' said Moorehead. 'Some nine thousand Germans were either drowned or killed.',[8] This seems highly improbable as the caiques' capacity was only about 2,000. Nonetheless, the loss of the Germans' heavy weapons greatly handicapped operations on Crete.

'The Luftwaffe avenged this setback,' said Student, 'by "pulling a lot of hair" out of the British Navy's scalp.',[9] At 0530 hours, German bombers took off to attack the cruisers *Fiji* and *Gloucester* and the destroyers *Greyhound* and *Griffin*. The ships zigzagged madly and although the *Gloucester* and *Fiji* were hit, no real damage was done. Rear Admiral Rawlings, with the battleships *Warspite* and *Valiant* plus eight destroyers, deployed west of Crete looking for the Italian fleet. He was confident that his anti-aircraft guns would keep the Stukas at bay.

About 25 miles (40 km) south of Melos, the Luftwaffe attacked Rear Admiral King's force, which had intercepted another German convoy. For the next three-and-a-half hours, the British weathered the storm. The destroyer *Juno* was sunk. The cruiser *Naiad* was hit, putting out of action two of her gun turrets. She was also holed but the bulkheads held. On HMS *Carlisle*, the captain was killed. King, running low on anti-aircraft ammunition, asked Rawlings to rendezvous with him in the Strait of Antikythera between Greece and Crete.

Just after the two forces came together, Rawlings' flagship *Warspite* was hit, causing some damage. Next, the destroyer *Greyhound* was caught on her own and sunk. When the destroyers *Kandahar* and *Kingston* went to pick up survivors, with the *Fiji* and *Gloucester* providing anti-aircraft cover, they too were attacked. The *Gloucester* was hit, caught fire and sank. The others retreated. At 1745 hours, the *Fiji* was caught by a lone German fighter-bomber. A single 500-lb bomb tore her hull open. About 30 minutes later, a second attack took place, scoring a direct hit and at 2015 hours, the vessel capsized.

The battered Mediterranean Fleet did what it could to help the beleaguered garrison on Crete. Five destroyers were summoned from Malta and two risked shelling Maleme airfield. The following day, *Kashmir* and *Kelly* were caught by the Luftwaffe and sunk. At 0700 hours on 23 May, the fleet headed for Alexandria, shaken by its deadly encounters with the Luftwaffe. HMS *Decoy* took the Greek king to safety.

Between 21 and 23 May, the Royal Navy had lost two cruisers and four destroyers, and two battleships and three other cruisers had been damaged. By 1 June, they had lost another cruiser and two more destroyers. Cunningham felt it fortunate that the carrier *Formidable* was not available for the defence of Crete, otherwise she would have probably been sunk, too.

THE ALLIES WITHDRAW FROM CRETE

By 27 May, it was clear that Freyberg's garrison could not hold out much longer. Wavell signalled Churchill: 'Fear we must recognize Crete is no longer tenable … It has been impossible to withstand weight of enemy air attack…'[10] There was no other option but to abandon the island. It would be up to the Royal Navy to rescue the garrison. It was decided to evacuate around 22,000 men mainly from the beach at Sfakia on the south coast. A rearguard was formed by 750 Commandos, who had only just landed at Suda under Colonel Laycock, and the survivors of the 5th New Zealand Brigade and the 7th and 8th Australian battalions. Stuka dive-bombers mercilessly swooped in to bomb and strafe the Allied troops as they streamed southwards across the White Mountains. The Commandos were tasked to protect Sfakia, but there was nothing they could do against the continual air attacks.

Only now did Mussolini join the battle for Crete by sending General Angelo Carta's Sienna Division. For the past week, the Italian Air Force had taken part in the Luftwaffe attacks on British warships, but its results had been limited. Likewise, the Italian Navy confined itself to the unsuccessful attempts to reinforce the Germans. Carta's troops, sailing from the Dodecanese, finally landed on the north-eastern end of Crete near Sitia on 28 May. Although his men were 'veterans' of the Albanian front, this part of the island was safely out of the firing line.

On the night of 28 May, four British destroyers arrived and took off 700 men at Sfakia. At the same time, Rawlings, with three cruisers and six destroyers, attempted to rescue the Heraklion garrison. They had run the gauntlet of the Kaso Strait between north-eastern Crete and the island of Scarpanto. The latter was host to Stuka bases. These launched five raids that afternoon against Rawlings' warships, damaging the *Ajax*, which was obliged to turn back for Alexandria, and the *Imperial*. The anti-aircraft gunners had expended more than half their ammunition by the time the ships reached Heraklion at 2330 hours. Despite air attack, by 0320 hours some 4,000 men had been embarked. Men at Khoudesion who held the roadblock, and casualties at the Knossos dressing station had to be left behind. Most Greek troops were not told of the evacuation.

Unfortunately, the damaged steering gear of the destroyer *Imperial* failed, so the *Hotspur* was sent to rescue her crew and 400 soldiers before sinking her. This was achieved but it greatly delayed Rawlings' return passage through the Kaso Strait. It also meant that his RAF fighter cover flying from North Africa never found him. At 0600 hours, the air attacks started, involving more than 100 dive-bombers. What followed that morning was carnage. Some 25 minutes later, the *Hereward* was hit and had to be left behind. She was run aground north of Cape Plaka and the men took to the lifeboats. Next, an Italian seaplane appeared and began to circle them like a harbinger of death. Instead of strafing them, however, the gallant Italian pilot protected them from two Stukas that had intended to attack the survivors.

In addition, the cruisers *Dido* and *Orion* were hit, as well as the destroyer *Decoy*. Their decks became splattered in blood and human remains. Tragically, on the first vessel, 103 of its 240 passengers were killed. *Orion* was carrying 1,100 soldiers and a bomb killed 260 and wounded 280 of them. The ship was hit three times in two hours and her captain killed. 'I had always wondered what it must have felt like to take part in the Charge of the Light Brigade,' remarked a naval officer on the *Orion*. 'Now I know.'[11] At midday, just two Fulmars arrived to provide some limited measure of protection. By the time the ships reached Alexandria, one-fifth of the Heraklion garrison was dead or wounded.

Wavell was appalled by these losses and told Cunningham he would not ask the Royal Navy to undertake any more rescue missions. In response, he recalled that Cunningham 'thanked us for our effort to relieve him of responsibility but said that the Navy had never yet failed the Army in such a situation, and was not going to do so now.'[12] Cunningham had little choice but to continue committing his warships to the evacuation from Sfakia. They worked miracles.

By the morning of 29 May, almost 5,000 men had been rescued. That night, 6,000 men were embarked by Admiral King. The following day, another 1,500 men were rescued from Sfakia. Wavell also instructed Freyberg to fly out. At this point, the garrison at Rethymnon surrendered. The Germans found the Australians were holding 500 parachutist prisoners and had buried another 550. Admiral King returned on 31 May and ferried almost 4,000 men to Alexandria. During this operation, the cruiser *Calcutta*, which had been built at the end of the First World War, was sunk in an air attack.

In Cairo, Freyberg reported to Wavell. 'It was a difficult meeting, and we were both overwrought,' he recalled. 'I presented a dishevelled appearance as I had not had my clothes off for several days, and had no clothes except what I stood up in.'[13] According to one of Wavell's staff, Freyberg was 'almost in tears'.[14] Freyberg was understandably worried that he would be made a scapegoat for what had happened. Around 13,000 men had been killed, wounded and taken prisoner during the battle. About 16,500 were evacuated to Egypt, including some 2,000 Greeks. The Royal Navy suffered almost 2,000 casualties.

Wavell sent a personal message to all the commanders of the units that had served on Crete. 'I thank you for the great courage and endurance with which you attempted the defence of the island of Crete,' he said. 'I am well aware of the difficulties under which you carried out your task and that it must have appeared to many of you that you had been asked to do the impossible...' He then shouldered the blame, adding: 'I accept the responsibility for what was done.'[15]

'The capture of Crete by an invasion delivered purely by air was one of the most astonishing and audacious feats of the war,' wrote respected military historian Basil Liddell Hart. 'It was also the most striking airborne operation of the war.'[16] Although Hitler now controlled Crete, his victory had been at enormous cost. Of the 22,000 men Student committed to the assault, more than 6,500 were dead, missing and wounded. Half the transport planes employed had been destroyed.

So incensed was Hitler by these casualties that he ordered his parachute divisions to fight as infantry from that point on. Also, Hitler's distrust of the Italian Navy grew to a point where he would not rely on it. Crucially, this meant that Student was unable to carry out any of his ambitious plans for airborne assaults on Malta, Cyprus, Alexandria and the Suez Canal. The result was that the Commonwealth sacrifice in trying to defend Crete had not been in vain. 'The New Zealanders and other British, Imperial and Greek troops who fought in the confused, disheartening, and vain struggle for Crete,' wrote Churchill, 'may feel that they played a definite part in an event which brought us far-reaching relief at a hingeing moment.'[17]

Wavell was extremely grateful to the Royal Navy, which, at great cost, had saved the garrison. He signalled Cunningham:

> I send to you and all under your command the deepest admiration and gratitude of the Army in the Middle East for the magnificent work of the Royal Navy in bringing back the troops from Crete. The skill and self-sacrifice with which the difficult and dangerous operation was carried out will never be forgotten and will form another strong link between our two services.[18]

The campaign had taken a terrible toll on Cunningham's Mediterranean Fleet. He had lost three cruisers and six destroyers, with another nine cruisers and destroyers undergoing repairs. The battleships *Barham* and *Warspite*, along with the *Formidable*, his only carrier, would have to sail from Alexandria to be repaired elsewhere. All that Cunningham had available were two battleships, three cruisers and 17 destroyers. His losses had largely nullified the Royal Navy's achievements at Taranto, Spartivento and Matapan. Thanks to Hitler's overwhelming air power, the balance had shifted. The big question was: would Mussolini's fleet venture forth and attempt to take advantage of the situation?

'The resistance against the enemy in Crete did not stop when we evacuated the island,' wrote Cunningham after the war with some satisfaction. 'For the next four years the German garrison would not be left idle. The guerrilla groups which immediately were formed would become their continuous headache…'[19]

CHAPTER 10:

Adventures in the Levant

IT WAS not long before Hitler was mischief-making in the Levant and the Middle East. At the beginning of May 1941, Rashid Ali, the pro-German Iraqi leader, orchestrated a rising against the British. His forces attacked the British airbase at Habbaniya, outside Baghdad, and he turned to Hitler for help. This offered an opportunity to stretch the British even further. Admiral Raeder was pressing Hitler to allow Rommel to prepare for a decisive offensive against Egypt and Suez. 'This stroke,' Raeder told Hitler, 'would be more deadly to the British Empire than the capture of London.'[1] He also said that the attack on the Soviet Union must not distract from the chance of victory in the Mediterranean.

Hitler, though, would not be swayed. 'Whether – and if so, by what means – it would be possible to launch an offensive against the Suez Canal,' he said, 'and eventually oust the British finally from their position between the Mediterranean and the Persian Gulf cannot be decided until Operation Barbarossa is completed.'[2] Nonetheless, he agreed to send limited support to the Iraqis. Hitler requested Vichy Syria's co-operation with this. Admiral Darlan, commander of the French Navy and one of Pétain's key supporters, agreed to let 75 per cent of the military equipment gathered in Syria under control of the Italian Armistice Committee be transferred to Iraq to assist the revolt. He also granted the Luftwaffe landing rights.

Darlan signalled General Henri Dentz, Vichy high commissioner and commander-in-chief in Syria, on 6 May stating:

Conversations of a general nature are in progress between the French and German Governments. It is of the greatest importance for their success that if German aeroplanes heading for Iraq land on an airfield in our mandated territories, all facilities should be given to them to continue their route.[3]

Meanwhile, Wavell set about crushing the Duke of Aosta's Italian Army in East Africa. The 1st South African Division and the 11th and 12th African divisions under General Alan Cunningham, invading from Kenya, successfully occupied Italian Somaliland at the end of February 1941. A small force from Aden took Berbera on 16 March and joined Cunningham's forces at Jijiga in northern Ethiopia. Addis Ababa, the Ethiopian capital, was liberated on 6 April 1941 just as Hitler was rolling into Greece and Yugoslavia.

In Eritrea, the Italians, under attack from General William Platt's 4th and 5th Indian divisions striking from Sudan in late January, put up a stiffer fight. The Italian 4th Colonial Division, holding Agordat south-west of Keren, was supported by ten medium tanks and a number of light tanks. Against this force, the 4th Indian Division could muster just four Matilda tanks and a number of carriers to help force the defensive line based on the Laquetat ridge. Having broken through, they successfully engaged Italian armour beyond Mount Cochen on 31 January 1941. The carriers lured the Italian tanks into a trap and the concealed Matildas attacked them from the rear, destroying six M11 medium tanks and five L.3 tankettes.

To attack Keren, the Indians had to manhandle their armoured cars through the Dongolaas Gorge. The Italians held up Platt's advance until a squadron of Matilda tanks from 4RTR turned the tables at the end of March. The Eritrean capital, Asmara, fell on 1 April, followed by the Italian naval base at Massawa seven days later. Aosta, having lost all his armour, withdrew to Amba Alagi in Ethiopia with 7,000 men and 40 guns, but with less than three months of supplies he was forced to surrender on 19 May 1941. Lingering Italian resistance in Ethiopia was overcome by the end of November. 'Thus ended,' said Churchill, 'Mussolini's dream of an African Empire to be built by conquest and colonized in the spirit of ancient Rome.'[4]

Britain was next compelled to act against French Madagascar. Fearing that the pro-Vichy French governor might shelter Japanese submarines, British forces seized the naval base at Antsirane (Antsiranana) in Diego Suarez Bay on 5 May 1941. A squadron of light tanks and a squadron of Valentine tanks took part in the invasion. The French garrison resisted and although Operation *Ironclad* was successful, after two days of fighting, the British had suffered around 400 casualties. In some quarters, it was felt there was little military advantage in invading Madagascar and that the mission was a political move rather than a military one.

The subsequent attack on the battleship *Ramillies* and a tanker while lying in the harbour by Japanese mini-submarines seemed to justify the operation. Beyond Antsirane, the Vichy governor continued to refuse to surrender so *Ironclad* was followed by a second operation in September to occupy the entire island. Despite a series of landings, Vichy resistance was not overcome until 6 November. However, Mers-el-Kébir and Madagascar proved to be a sideshow compared with what was to come and Britain's war with Vichy soon escalated.

SAFEGUARDING SYRIA

The first major bloodletting came in the Levant when General de Gaulle suggested his Free French forces in Palestine invade Vichy-controlled Syria and Lebanon. The problem faced by the Allies was that they did not know how the Vichy administration and the French garrison would react to an invasion. The French colonies tended to be a law unto themselves, while the colonial forces and locally raised troops operated independently of the metropolitan French Army.

Churchill telegraphed Wavell in Alexandria on 9 May:

You will no doubt realise the grievous danger of Syria being captured by a few thousand Germans transported by air. Our information leads us to believe that Admiral Darlan has probably made some bargain to help the Germans to get in there. In face of your evident feeling of lack of resources we can see no other course open than to furnish General Catroux with the necessary transport and let him and his Free French do their best at the moment they deem suitable, the RAF acting against the landings.[5]

The fear was that with the Luftwaffe operating from the Greek Islands, the Germans might be tempted to occupy Syria and from there could threaten Britain's position in Cyprus, Cairo, the Suez Canal and the vital oilfields in Iraq.

General Dentz, in Syria, made no attempt to resist the Germans. A year before, he had been given the dubious role of defending Paris, only to have it declared an open city by General Weygand. When the French Army retreated, Dentz had been left behind to arrange the surrender. Moving against the French in Syria was the last thing Wavell wanted. 'Wavell, I believe, was very much against the venture,' recalled Colonel de Guingand. 'He had no doubt been shaken by the reverses in Cyrenaica and the disaster in Greece, a campaign which had received his backing. He still had active fronts in Eritrea and Abyssinia, in Cyrenaica and Iraq. He was also planning a limited offensive in the Western Desert.'[6]

By late May 1941, large numbers of German and Italian aircraft had landed in Syria. Alarm bells began to ring in London that a German takeover was imminent, especially in the light of German airborne landings in Crete. Wavell responded to Churchill with gloomy news: 'This Syrian business is disquieting, since the German Air Force established itself in Syria and are closer to the Canal and Suez than they would be at Mersa Matruh. The [Vichy] French seem now wholly committed to the Germans. I am moving reinforcements to Palestine…'[7]

Churchill felt compelled to act to safeguard Egypt's eastern flank. It had been hoped that Free French Forces could achieve the task, but after the disastrous attempt to wrest Dakar from Vichy control, it was decided that British forces should assist General Georges Catroux. Besides, the Free French in the region numbered only 4,000 men with just nine tanks and would be easily overwhelmed by Dentz's forces. He commanded more than 50,000 men, including colonial troops of the Syrian Legion, supported by almost 100 tanks, 150 armoured cars and 120 guns.

Wavell's defence of Egypt and Crete had to take priority, which greatly restricted the resources available for the Syrian adventure. His invasion force under General Wilson consisted of the 7th Australian Division, part of the 1st Cavalry Division, the 5th Indian Infantry Brigade and the Free French Forces of General Paul Louis Le Gentilhomme, consisting of six battalions, an artillery battery and a company of tanks.

Operation *Exporter* was launched on 8 June 1941 and met practically no opposition at first. Next, the Free French were held up 10 miles (16 km) from Damascus and the Australians on the coast road made slow progress. British and Free French forces found themselves under attack when Vichy troops launched a counter-attack with two battalions of tanks at Kuneitra. They overwhelmed a British battalion, but British artillery fire then succeeded in destroying a large concentration of Vichy tanks outside Sidon on 13–15 June and the port quickly fell. This success was marred when two British destroyers were damaged in a Vichy air attack off Sidon.

British troops also invaded from Iraq and by 21 June, after three days of heavy fighting, the Australians captured Damascus. Following the fall of Beirut, the Vichy regional headquarters, it was all over and the Free French took control. General Dentz, although he still had 24,000 men under arms, knew continued resistance was pointless. Churchill recalled: 'At 8.30 on 12 July Vichy envoys arrived to sue for an armistice. This was granted, a convention was signed and Syria passed into Allied Occupation.' He added: 'Our casualties in killed and wounded were over 4,600; those of the enemy about 6,500.'[8] Once again, Churchill was cursed in Vichy France.

Lebanon and Syria were placed under the control of Catroux's Free French. Dentz and the bulk of his troops chose repatriation rather than to join Catroux. Out of the 37,736 men offered this choice, just 5,668 chose to support de Gaulle's cause and only 1,046 of them were native Frenchmen. The rest were mainly Germans or Russians from the Foreign Legion, North Africans or Senegalese.

OPERATION *BATTLEAXE*

By 9 June 1941, all the British armoured squadrons in Egypt had received their new tanks, but at General Creagh's request were given another five days' training before the launch of Operation *Battleaxe*. Later, Creagh admitted he was not confident about their chances of victory:

An answer was difficult since it depended on which side could reinforce the quicker – though we could concentrate on undoubted initial superiority, the Germans could reinforce with their second

Armoured Division from Tobruk, only eighty miles distant, while as far as I knew we had no means of reinforcement at all.₉

Lieutenant-General Sir Noel Beresford-Peirse was placed in command, with the 7th Armoured and 4th Indian divisions acting as his strike force, though both lacked a brigade each. The latter was to push along the coast through Halfaya towards Sollum and Capuzzo. The 7th Armoured comprised the 4th and 7th Armoured brigades. The former had two regiments 4RTR and 7RTR equipped with Matildas, while the latter's 2RTR had to make do with inadequate cruiser tanks, which although old designs were recently delivered new builds, and the 6RTR was issued with the Crusaders. Ninety-eight Hurricanes and Tomahawks as well as more than 100 bombers supported the ground forces.

Under *Battleaxe*, Churchill's ill-prepared 'Tiger Cubs' were thrown perhaps recklessly into action on 15 June with the intention of overwhelming Rommel. Lieutenant-Colonel Walter O'Carroll, commander 4RTR, watched the attack on Halfaya Pass go in:

> The sun was rising behind and light forward was excellent. No guns sounded. The tanks crept on. At Halfaya the month before, Major Miles had found the enemy still in bed or shaving when he arrived, but they were Italians. Now it seemed almost too good to be true that the [German] garrison should be so caught again...₁₀

He was right.

At 0600 hours, Rommel's 88-mm guns opened up and the Matilda dubbed the 'Queen of the Battlefield' after soundly thrashing the Italians met its match. All but one of 13 Matildas went up in flames and the attack along the top of the escarpment collapsed. At the bottom of the pass, six tanks of A Squadron 4RTR ran into a minefield; four blew up, blocking in the survivors. The attack on the pass ended in a confused shambles. The 7RTR reached Capuzzo only to lose five Matildas to German counter-attacks, with another four damaged.

The 2RTR attacked, with 6RTR's Crusaders held back for a surprise blow, but both were bested to the west at Hafid Ridge. Two cruisers were lost to German 88-mms. Armed with only solid shot, there was nothing they could do against the dug-in anti-tank guns. To the south, a flanking attack failed and five tanks were lost after they could not be recalled for the lack of radios. The Crusaders were then thrown in and ran straight into a German gun line, losing 11 tanks and another six damaged. Others simply broke down. In the face of more than 30 Panzers and failing light, the rest withdrew.

At Point 206, A Squadron 4RTR swung in from the west, but German gunners claimed eight Matildas. The point changed hands twice until 16 Matildas of B Squadron rumbled up from the east and settled the issue.

North of Sollum, at the port of Bardia, German defences consisted purely of administrative units and a few 88-mm flak guns guarding the harbour. At the approach of about 20 Matildas advancing from Capuzzo, the local senior officer redeployed the guns and by a quirk of fate was able to halt a passing supply column bearing 88-mm anti-tank rounds. Very quickly, 11 tanks were knocked out but only one 88-mm remained; however, this last gun claimed the rest of the attacking tanks, ending the British breakthrough.

By the end of the day, of the 100 Matildas committed to the battle only 37 remained operational, although the mechanics had another 11 battleworthy by the following day. It was discovered that 7th Armoured Brigade had lost half its tanks, while 2RTR had 28 tanks and 6RTR some 50 remaining. Disastrously for Beresford-Peirse, he had lost half his tanks without even bringing Rommel's main Panzer force to battle.

Rommel was feeling the pressure having lost Capuzzo: he had men isolated at Halfaya, suffered casualties along Hafid Ridge and lost Point 206. He must have been very reassured by the reports filtering in that the surrounding landscape was littered with knocked-out and broken-down British tanks. Furthermore, a Panzer battalion from the 5th Light Division had just arrived at Hafid Ridge and the rest of the division was en route. Similarly, the 15th Panzer Division had yet to fully commit itself to the fight, its artillery and anti-tank units having borne the brunt of most of the fighting. Those Panzers involved around Capuzzo had been used solely to lure the 'Tiger Cubs' on to the waiting anti-tank guns.

In the early hours of 16 June, Rommel wrote to his wife: 'There was heavy fighting in our eastern sector all day yesterday, as you will have seen long ago from the Wehrmacht communiqués. To-day – it's 2.30am – will see the decision. It's going to be a hard fight, so you'll understand that I can't sleep.'[11]

At 0500 hours, 80 Panzers counter-attacked at Capuzzo only to run into British 25-lb artillery, 2-lb anti-tank guns and hulled-down Matildas acting as anti-tank posts. The British could not retreat, as this would have meant abandoning their infantry, so held their ground and slogged it out. The battle raged for five hours and 15th Panzer found itself reduced to just 30 operational tanks; the rest were either burned out or awaiting recovery. The fighting also continued at Halfaya and at Hafid Ridge, when the 7th Armoured Brigade tangled with the 5th Light Division.

Lieutenant Heinz Werner Schmidt, who accompanied Rommel to view the battle, recalled:

> It was bonny fighting that we saw. Wavell's tanks broke into a number of infantry positions, despite the intensive fire of our 88mm guns, which they had scarcely expected to meet. The crews manning the 88's sat high up and unprotected at their sights. When one man fell, another of the crew took his place … despite the heavy losses caused by the artillery, the British infantry with rare gallantry pressed forward across the Halfaya wadis.[12]

By the afternoon, the 6RTR had withdrawn to the frontier with just ten operational Crusaders. The Panzers launched another attack at 1900 hours and rolled over 6RTR and 2RTR; only the onset of darkness saved them from compete annihilation. The following day, Rommel, massing his Panzers, struck west of Sidi Suleiman, reaching the town at 0600 hours. The Matildas withdrew from their exposed position at Capuzzo and a six-hour battle followed. *Battleaxe* had been stopped in its tracks and the Germans were left in possession of the battlefield. Rommel remarked: 'Great numbers of destroyed British tanks littered the country through which the two divisions had passed.'[13] Large numbers of Churchill's 'Tiger Cubs' had fallen intact into his hands.

Rommel observed:

> Thus the three-day battle of Sollum was over … It had finished with a complete victory for the defence, although we might have dealt the enemy far greater damage than we actually had done. The British had lost in all, over 200 tanks and their casualties in men had been

tremendous. We, on the other hand, had lost about twenty-five tanks totally destroyed.[14]

In fact, according to British figures, 64 Matildas were lost along with 27 cruiser tanks, though more Crusaders fell into German hands due to mechanical troubles than through battle damage. Although the Crusader was under-gunned, Rommel was quite impressed by it, noting: 'Had this tank been equipped with a heavier gun, it could have made things extremely unpleasant for us.'[15]

Some of the captured Matildas were subsequently reused by the Panzer divisions; likewise the Afrika Korps put a number of Crusader tanks back to work. Lieutenant Schmidt recalled:

I accompanied Rommel on a personal inspection of the battlefield along the frontier from Halfaya to Sidi Omar. We counted 180 knocked-out British tanks, mostly Mark IIs [Matildas]. Some of them were later recovered from the battlefield, repaired, marked with the German cross, and in due course sent into battle against the men who had manned them before.[16]

THE FALL-OUT FROM OPERATION *BATTLEAXE*

Churchill by his own admission was disconsolate at the failure of *Battleaxe* and retreated to his house at Chartwell for a while, noting: 'Although this action may seem small compared with the scale of the Mediterranean in all its various campaigns, its failure was to me a most bitter blow. Success in the Desert would have meant the destruction of Rommel's audacious force.'[17]

Wavell fell on his sword on 21 June and signalled Churchill:

Am very sorry for the failure of *Battleaxe* and the loss of so many Tiger Cubs, especially since I have realised from figures produced by the liaison officer how short we are of requirements at home ... I was over optimistic and should have advised you that 7th Armoured

Division required more training before going into battle ... but ... I was impressed by the apparent need for immediate action.[18]

Churchill chose to ignore the last remark. Wavell was to take the blame and to avoid embarrassment to Churchill was made to swap places with General Claude Auchinleck in India. Churchill cabled back: 'I have come to the conclusion that public interest will best be served by appointment of General Auchinleck to relieve you in command of [the] Armies of [the] Middle East.'[19] Wavell stoically took it on the chin and replied: 'I think it wise to make change and get new ideas and action on the many problems in the Middle East and am sure Auchinleck will be successful choice.' He was not even allowed to return to London on leave.

Rommel was far more complimentary of Wavell's efforts than Churchill, remarking:

Wavell's strategic planning of the offensive had been excellent ... He knew very well the necessity of avoiding any operation which would enable his opponent to fight on interior lines and destroy his formations one by one with locally superior concentrations. But he was put at great disadvantage by the slow speed of his infantry tanks, which prevented him from reacting quickly enough to the moves of our faster vehicles.[20]

Despite Churchill's efforts, the 'Tiger Cubs' had been a failure.

The 'Tiger' convoy stretched Britain's resources to the limit. Churchill by early July 1941 could muster 1,141 infantry and cruiser tanks for the defence of Britain, but just 391 of these were operational. Still smarting about the very public failure of his 'Tiger Cubs', he wrote to the minister of supply and the chief of the imperial general staff in a state of irritation in late August bemoaning:

The Germans turned up in Libya with 6-pounder guns in their tanks, yet I suppose it would have been reasonable for us to have imagined they would do something to break up the ordinary 'I' tank ... The Germans had specimens of it in their possession taken at Dunkirk, also some cruiser tanks, so it was not difficult for them to prepare weapons which would defeat our tanks.'[21]

After the success of the 'Tiger' Convoy, the Royal Navy, feeling its luck could not hold in the Mediterranean, escorted another 50 cruiser and 50 infantry tanks round the Cape but they did not reach Suez until mid-July. When Rommel's Panzergruppe Afrika was established, consisting of the 15th and 21st Panzer divisions, it had about 170 Panzers, as well as a dozen British Matildas and 17 British Valentines. Had Churchill known, he would have been publicly outraged at the misuse of his 'Tiger Cubs' while privately probably full of admiration for German ingenuity. Rommel's 'Tiger Cubs' went into action with 21st Panzer on 14 September 1941, when three armoured columns pushed into Egypt.

OPERATION *CRUSADER*

By November, the British 8th Army had come into being, and a newer generation of British infantry and cruiser tanks along with the American light Stuart tank had reached North Africa. The production runs for Britain's early 'A' series cruiser tanks was fairly limited and all were withdrawn from service in late 1941, having been replaced by the Crusader and Stuart. They enjoyed mixed success during Operation *Crusader*, launched on 20 November and employing two whole Corps instead of just two divisions.

Auchinleck massed 756 tanks, mostly Matildas and Valentines, for Operation *Crusader*. Once more, the British tanks were lured into a trap sprung by concealed armour and anti-tank guns and the attack quickly came unstuck. Nonetheless, the British held on and Rommel lost by a narrow margin, as his two Panzer and single Italian armoured division were overextended and forced to retreat. During these engagements, Rommel's 'Tiger Cubs' caused confusion on both sides.

Lieutenant Schmidt, with the 15th Panzer, was involved in an action near Sidi Azeiz in November 1941. Heading southwards towards Maddalena, he was alarmed to be informed that there were 12 Matilda tanks behind him. His three anti-tank guns were set up to block them. Two of the latter were destroyed and the rest fanned out. Schmidt and his gunners were in danger of being surrounded and were considering retreating when two more Matildas came up behind them. Schmidt takes up the story: 'I glanced back with a vague idea of withdrawal if that were possible amid this fire … Then to my gasping relief I recognised swastika markings on them: they were two of the British tanks that had been captured at Halfaya during "Battleaxe" months before.'[22] The British, assuming that Schmidt and his men had been captured, broke off their attack long enough for him to flee with Rommel's Matildas covering his retreat.

It was now that Rommel got a new boss. Field Marshal Albert Kesselring was appointed German armed forces commander-in-chief in the south. Although a Luftwaffe officer, he was sent to Rome to take charge of German air, ground and naval units operating across the Mediterranean. His task was to focus on the bigger picture and not just Egypt. Keeping Rommel resupplied would prove a major challenge for him.

PART 3:
The Sicilian Narrows

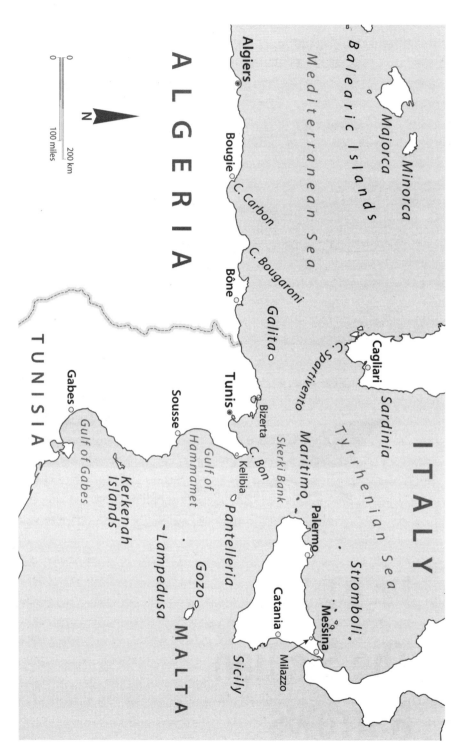

Map C

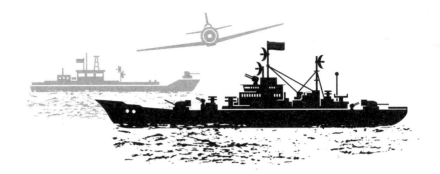

CHAPTER 11:
Maltese Sickness

IN THE central Mediterranean, the population of British-held Malta found itself in the midst of a gathering Axis storm. 'The eyes of all Britain, and indeed of the whole British Empire,' wrote Churchill, 'are watching Malta in her struggle day by day...', Its proximity to Sicily and the Italian islands of Lampedusa and Pantelleria meant that it was fenced in on three sides. As a result, it was easy to attack and a long way from help. 'I have twice made the flight between Malta and Sicily,' wrote war correspondent Alan Moorehead. 'Each time it took less than half an hour.', Mussolini and Hitler decided to crush the troublesome defenders under a hail of bombs. Not only did they want to beat the island into submission, but they also needed to distract the RAF and Royal Navy while Rommel's divisions were shipped to Tripoli.

Early in the afternoon of 16 January 1941, the Luftwaffe threw its Ju 88 and Ju 87 Stuka dive-bombers at the damaged carrier *Illustrious* moored at Parlatorio Wharf. The *Illustrious* had been hit six days earlier getting to the island and the defenders had devised a 'box barrage' to protect her while under repair. The bombers were greeted by the anti-aircraft guns of the Royal Artillery, Royal Malta Artillery and in particular the Dockyard Defence Battery. Field Marshal Kesselring recalled that they 'put up a barrier of fire to be penetrated only by stout hearts and at the loss of many aircraft'., Bombs fell indiscriminately on the neighbouring cities of Senglea, Vittoriosa and Cospicua, but miraculously the carrier only received a single hit on the quarterdeck.

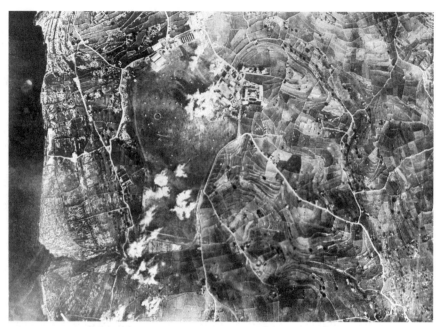

Malta under air attack by the Italians in 1940. The island provided Winston Churchill with a strategic choke point in the central Mediterranean.

Two days later, the Luftwaffe was back and struck the *Illustrious* again, causing damage beneath the waterline. Local civilians were caught in the crossfire. 'The noise and commotion was fantastic,' said Joseph Caruana, 'and my memories are a kaleidoscope of terror.' Once again, the anti-aircraft batteries and the *Illustrious*' own guns threw a hail of hot metal up into the sky. Caruana noted: 'The whining warcry of the diving Stukas (so different from the normal steady drone of the Italian high level bombers)...'[4] The harbour became engulfed in a choking white dust thrown up by collapsing houses and damage to the ancient fortifications. Once more, the carrier survived the bombardment and on 23 January headed for Alexandria. She was then sent to America for repair and returned two years later to take part in operations against Sicily.

Churchill was very impressed and signalled General Sir William Dobbie, Malta's governor: 'I send you, on behalf of the War Cabinet, our heartfelt congratulations upon the magnificent and ever-memorable defence which your heroic garrison and citizens, aided by the Navy and above all the Royal Air Force, are making...'[5] Dobbie, who was a very religious man, had done all he could to prepare, and replied: 'By God's help Malta will not weaken.'[6] It was as if he were invoking the heroic Knights of Saint John.

Malta desperately needed more fighter aircraft to ward off the raiders. In early March 1941, Air Chief Marshal Sir Arthur Longmore, commander-in-chief of the RAF in the Middle East, sent a dozen Hurricanes with long-range drop tanks from Egypt. The only way to get larger numbers to the island was by flying them off carriers, which either transported them from Britain or picked them up at Gibraltar. This type of operation was conducted on 3 April, when the carriers *Ark Royal* and *Argus* launched a dozen Hurricanes from 400 miles (640 km) west of Malta. They repeated this exercise on 27 April, but this time sent 23 aircraft. By June 1941, some 224 fighters had been delivered in this way, with 109 for Malta and the rest sent on to Egypt.

George Fabri, a Maltese war correspondent, was appalled by the Luftwaffe's unrelentingly destructive attacks on Valletta in the spring of 1941. 'In the sunny, cloudless afternoon the bombers made a deliberate, devastating, devilish attack,' he wrote. 'All those monuments, which took tens and even hundreds of years to build, were destroyed by the Luftwaffe in a few minutes.', In defiance, the angry Maltese scrawled on the ruins: 'Bomb Rome'.

Axis bombs falling on Malta. Its defiance became seen as a decisive turning point in the battle for the Mediterranean.

Air Vice-Marshal Hugh Lloyd was appointed air officer commanding RAF Malta. His job was to co-ordinate the island's air defences and undertake attacks on Axis shipping supporting Rommel. Lloyd was just the man for the job. A violent maelstrom was coming and it needed someone who could weather it. He faced a challenge as his Hurricanes were increasingly outclassed by the newer German Messerschmitts. Squadron Leader Laddie Lucas considered Lloyd a 'quite exceptional' commander, who was 'ruthless' and took 'calculated risks'.(8) This was not to say that he did not care about his men. He was experienced enough to know that indecision cost lives and squandered opportunity. Fighter pilot Tom Neil recalled that the air vice-marshal 'cultivated a rather Cromwellian sternness and brevity of speech'.[9]

In the meantime, what was clear to Mussolini, Hitler and Kesselring was that Malta had to be crushed or Rommel and his Axis forces would be lost. Before the war, Malta was not a defence priority for Britain. France was Britain's ally and its navy safeguarded the western Mediterranean. All the time Italy was neutral, it left the Royal Navy dominating the eastern half. Although the navy continued to view Malta as an important base, the nearest help was at Gibraltar or Alexandria. Indeed, when it looked certain that Mussolini would enter the war on Hitler's side, Admiral Cunningham prudently withdrew his ships to the safety of Alexandria.

The Italian Navy attempted to penetrate the defences of Malta's Grand Harbour and Marsamxett Harbour on 26 July 1941. Their intention was to attack the submarine base and destroy a convoy that had arrived two days earlier. The assault by Italian motor torpedo boats started at 0444 hours and was supported by a simultaneous air attack. The coastal batteries swiftly foiled the Italian boats, while in the air the RAF beat off the air raid. Those craft not sunk were destroyed by the island's Hurricanes. 'From the sea Malta is practically invulnerable,' said Luftwaffe General Erich Quade, '... the Italian MTBs tried to penetrate the Malta defences and enter the harbour of Valletta. Not one of these courageous naval units returned.'[10]

That autumn, Secretary of State for Air Sir Archibald Sinclair was moved to write to Lloyd, in praise of him and his brave squadrons:

The brilliant defence of the Island by the Hurricanes, the audacious attacks by Beaufighters on enemy air bases, the steady and deadly slogging of the Wellingtons at the enemy airports, the daring and dextrous reconnaissance of the Marylands, culminating in the tremendous onslaughts of the Blenheims and Fleet Air Arm Swordfish on the Axis shipping in the Mediterranean are watched with immense admiration by your comrades in the RAF and by your fellow men at home.[11]

THE FOCUS OF SUSTAINED ATTACK

The previous 12 months had been tough for Malta's garrison. After Mussolini declared war at midnight on 10 June 1940, the following morning at 0655 hours, ten Italian bombers and their escort fighters struck Malta for the first time. They divided into two groups with one formation attacking Grand Harbour and Marsamxett, while the other hit the Delimara area and Hal Far. Some of the first bombs hit Fort Saint Elmo, killing six men of the Malta Royal Artillery. Several civilians were also killed and a number wounded.

At that stage, the defenders had few anti-aircraft guns and the old naval monitor *Terror*, along with *Aphis* and *Ladybird* moored in Marsamxett, did what it could to bolster the flak. The raid was followed by six others that day, as well as a reconnaissance sortie by the Italians to assess the damage. In response, the Maltese began to burrow deep into their island to create more effective air raid shelters. At Valletta and Floriana, for instance, the old railway tunnels were used as public shelters, while almost every village and town dug their own communal protection.

Two weeks later, France surrendered and the balance of power in the Mediterranean shifted very dramatically. The western Mediterranean was left undefended and a Royal Navy squadron, later known as Force H, was deployed to Gibraltar in a bid to maintain communications with Malta and Alexandria. However, the complete lack of air cover over Malta meant that the Royal Navy could not operate safely from the island. As far as Mussolini was concerned, Malta was immediately neutralized as a threat to his operations in Libya.

Fortunately for Churchill, the Maltese have a streak of stubbornness running through their psyche. In 1565, the plucky little island had faced off the military might of the Ottoman Empire and won. No matter what the Turks had thrown at them, the islanders and the Knights of Saint John never gave up. Surrender was simply not an option. In the summer of 1940, therefore, the Maltese looked upon the neighbouring Italians and then the following year the Germans simply as part of a long line of invaders who threatened to despoil and then take their island. As far as the Maltese were concerned, they were not going to roll over. George Fabri noted that the islanders were imbued with 'bulldog tenacity'.[12]

Although the British were occupiers, they were far better than the alternative. If the British departed, the island would be unable to hold out. Together, there was a glimmer of hope that Mussolini's air force could be held at bay. The RAF and the Maltese needed each other. However, not all Maltese were keen on continued British sovereignty and there were Italian agitators among the population. This had been a problem ever since Mussolini took power. 'The Italians have been stirring up the Maltese for a long time,' noted Captain Henry Hawkins a decade before the war, 'and getting them all excited about kicking out the British and becoming part of Italy.'[13] There had even been fanciful talk of a 'coup'. To be on the safe side, in 1940 those with known Italian connections were interned and a few were deported to Africa for safekeeping. Mussolini's subsequent attempt to get an agent on to the island was a complete farce.

Where the RAF and British Army were concerned, Malta was considered wholly indefensible in the face of Axis attack. In theory, there were supposed to have been four squadrons of Hurricanes on the island, but in early 1940 there were none. The island had just four very exposed airfields: Hal Far near the south coast, which was used by the navy's Fleet Air Arm; Kalafrana on the south-east coast, which was a flying boat base; and Ta'Qali inland near Mdina and Luqa, which were the only two airfields available for the RAF. The garrison comprised five infantry battalions, a mix of British and Maltese troops. This force and the island's ancient fortifications were hardly capable of repelling a full-scale invasion.

Churchill gave some consideration to abandoning the eastern Mediterranean and Malta, with the navy taking refuge in Alexandria. To have done so, though, would have made it almost impossible to push supply convoys through the western half to British forces in Egypt. In addition, such a move would have opened the road to the Suez Canal to the enemy. Churchill therefore instructed that Malta must be held no matter what was thrown at it.

REINFORCEMENTS ARRIVE IN MALTA

Two fleet carriers, *Illustrious* and *Eagle*, were tasked with protecting convoys passing in and out of Malta. Admiral Cunningham assessed that to keep the island supplied would require two convoys a month each bearing 40,000 tons of supplies. This, though, did not immediately help the air defence of Malta. By good fortune, however, the navy indirectly came to the island's aid with this problem.

At Kalafrana, the naval air station in Marsaxlokk bay, eight long-forgotten crated fighters were discovered in a hangar. These were Gloster Gladiator biplanes that had belonged to the carrier *Glorious*, before she had headed for the Norwegian campaign. They were initially to be handed over to the *Eagle* but instead four were passed to the RAF, who put them together and had them up in the air fighting the Italian Air Force. One was to be lost and the others became known as *Faith*, *Hope* and *Charity*. On 21 June 1940, these Gladiators were reinforced by the welcome arrival of a few Hurricanes.

The aptly named Operation *Hurry* saw the old carrier *Argus*, protected by Force H, steam from Gibraltar to fly 12 Hurricanes from south of Sardinia to Malta in August 1940. This was followed by Operation *White* in November when *Argus* tried to deliver another dozen Hurricanes. Due to navigational error, only four reached the island. The following year, another attempt was made to get more aircraft to Malta. In March 1941, the cargo steamer *Paracombe*, with RAF ground crew, plus 21 Hurricanes and other stores, sailed from Gibraltar, then tragically vanished. The American consul in Tunis reported on 2 May that the ship had been sunk by a mine and that 18 survivors who had been rescued were in Bizerta.

Hitler, determined to stop the British from reinforcing Malta, deployed his U-boats to the Mediterranean. During the second half of 1941, the *Ark Royal* had continually managed to fly off large numbers of Hurricanes bound for the island. She was returning from one such mission when, on 12 November 1941, a U-boat torpedoed her and she sank 30 miles (48 km) east of Gibraltar while under tow. This was a disaster as two carriers were under repair and a third was being docked after grounding. This left Force H without a carrier and it could therefore no longer escort convoys to the island. It also meant that the supply of aircraft to Malta ceased. To make matters worse, shortly after, Admiral Cunningham lost the battleship *Barham* to U-boat attack.

Concentrated Axis air attacks continued throughout 1941 and reached their height in early 1942. 'Right through the spring they turned such a blitz upon Malta,' observed Alan Moorehead, 'as no other island or city has seen in this war. It was a siege of annihilation.'[14] Luftwaffe General Quade cautioned on 3 April 1942: 'To fight Malta we have to attack from the air and cut off her sea communications. But you cannot expect the Luftwaffe to sink the island with bombs.'[15] To the islanders and the garrison it felt as if they were giving it a good try. Seven days later, Kesselring noted: 'The aerial attack on Malta has I feel, eliminated Malta as a naval base … I intend to carry on with the attack until 20 April.'[16] Air Vice-Marshal Lloyd had but one solution: 'Malta's need is for Spitfires, Spitfires, and yet more Spitfires.'[17]

Churchill first tried to get Spitfires to Lloyd at the end of February 1942, but this attempt failed. By the end of March, 31 had been successfully delivered after being flown off the *Eagle*, which had prudently remained out of range of Italian and German Sicilian-based bombers. The problem by April was that Churchill did not have any carriers seaworthy that could transport and then fly off aircraft. In answer to his prayers, President Roosevelt stepped into the breach and agreed to 'loan' Churchill the carrier USS *Wasp*. She arrived in Britain in early April and took on 47 Spitfires. The *Wasp* and escorts then set sail mid-month and by 19 April was southeast of Mallorca. The next day, the Spitfires took to the air to start their 700-mile (1,125-km) journey to Malta. This would take a gruelling four hours and ten minutes.

Air Vice-Marshal Lloyd was overjoyed and gathered his officers together. 'The arrival of these new aircraft today means that the climax of the battle is upon us,' he told them. 'On its outcome will depend Malta's future as an attacking base against the Axis.'[18] Then disaster struck. German radar based on Sicily detected the Spitfires and the Luftwaffe jumped them once they were on the ground. Forty-eight hours later, just seven remained serviceable.

By this stage, there were some 300 German and 200 Italian fighters and bombers operating from airfields around Catania and Palermo in Sicily. Once the Luftwaffe's powerful 2nd Air Corps deployed there, life became much more difficult for Malta's garrison. This highly experienced formation had redeployed from the Eastern Front and refitted for subtropical warfare, comprising five Gruppen of Ju 88, one of Ju 87 and one of

Bf 110. Fighter protection was provided by Jagdgeschwader 53 with four Gruppen of Bf 109Fs. This totalled 325 aircraft, though only 229 were operational.

Malta, in contrast, could muster just 20 or 30 serviceable fighters. 'The enemy [air]fields were so close that it was possible,' said Moorehead, 'for the British in Malta to detect the noise of the Nazi machines warming up at Catania, and so our fighters, always outnumbered, were repeatedly in the air to accept battle.'[19] The raids, though, were relentless. The Luftwaffe conducted 5,807 sorties, dropping 6,557 tons of bombs between 20 March and 28 April 1942.

It was agreed that the *Wasp* would make a second run with another batch of Spitfires. She was to be joined by the *Eagle*, which would carry a further 16 Spitfires. On 9 May, 61 aircraft successfully reached the island. Malta's six remaining Spitfires were scrambled to help protect their arrival. 'Soon the air was filled with a great mass of Spitfires coming in. What a wonderful sight!' said Squadron Leader David Douglas-Hamilton. 'To say we welcomed them put one's feelings mildly.'[20] This time, each was turned around in six minutes and put back in the air to meet the oncoming Luftwaffe. By nightfall, the RAF had destroyed eight enemy aircraft and claimed another eight 'probables'. Churchill was elated by the success of this operation and signalled Roosevelt: 'Who says a wasp can't sting twice?'[21]

The following day, the second part of the operation was completed. The fast minelayer, HMS *Welshman*, arrived from Gibraltar with vital spare parts for the Spitfires and much-needed anti-aircraft ammunition. At 1100 hours, Kesselring launched an attack aimed at sinking her. Lloyd was able to put up 37 Spitfires and 13 Hurricanes to meet the Luftwaffe. In Grand Harbour, *Welshman* was deliberately shrouded by a thick smokescreen. 'Then the harbour barrage went up. It was a stupendous sight,' observed Douglas-Hamilton from his Spitfire, 'and put to shame all other efforts at "flak" which anyone had seen over Malta or France.'[22] The Germans dropped 40 tons of bombs, with one just missing the minelayer.

During the series of engagements fought over Malta on 10 May, 63 enemy aircraft were destroyed or damaged by the fighters and anti-aircraft fire. That night, Rome radio admitted that 37 Axis planes had been lost and claimed 47 Spitfires had been shot down. In reality it was just three Spitfires. Under the cover of darkness, the *Welshman* departed for Gibraltar.

'In the last few days we and the Germans have lost many feathers over Malta,'[23] confessed Count Ciano, the Italian foreign minister. A further 16 Spitfires were delivered on 18 May. From this point on, the air battle was decisively turned.

Thanks to American assistance, 126 planes were safely delivered to the garrison, which led to an end in Axis daylight raiding. This, though, was not before many of the new Spitfires had been destroyed and the island's airfields and ports put out of action. Such was the ferocity of the Axis attacks that by the spring of 1942 the islanders had built 6,000 air raid shelters with another 1,500 under construction. Subsequently, between June and October, *Eagle* and *Furious* delivered another 226 Spitfires, with the bulk of them landing safely. In the meantime, Malta was running out of food and fuel.

The island's heroic resistance did not go unnoticed. On 15 April 1942, the fortress of Malta was awarded the George Cross by King George VI, in recognition of the inhabitants' outstanding bravery. By this point, the tiny island had endured more than 2,000 air raids and alerts. It was not until 13 September that the medal was formally presented to Sir George Borg, the chief justice, by the new governor, Viscount Gort. The tide of war now began to turn in Malta's favour.

THE GERMANS CHANGE TACK

Rommel desperately needed the island occupied, but it never happened, as Tobruk was always his priority. Although Operation *Hercules* was formulated, which envisaged Malta being assaulted by three airborne divisions supported by 1,100 aircraft, it never came to fruition. Hitler was not keen on the scheme after the heavy losses incurred taking Crete. Ultimately, Rommel argued convincingly that the men and resources allocated to Hercules would be better deployed supporting his drive on Suez.

When Rommel captured the port of Tobruk in late June 1942, this victory seemed to negate the need to occupy Malta. General Student, who had spent months planning an airborne landing, was bitterly disappointed. He had learned from the mistakes made in Crete and had first-class intelligence. 'We knew much more about the enemy's dispositions,' said Student. 'Excellent aerial photographs had revealed every detail of his fortifications, coastal and flak batteries, and field positions.'[24] Regarding the proposed assault force, he recalled that it was: 'five times as strong as we had against Crete'.[25]

Nevertheless, the fierce air war over the island continued unabated. Eight Spitfires took off from Ta' Qali airfield (known as RAF Ta Kali) on 8 July 1942 to intercept enemy bombers and their escorts. During the dogfight, the Spitfires succeeded in damaging three Bf 109 fighters and three Ju 88 bombers. This engagement, though, cost two aircraft. Flight Lieutenant L.V. Sanders found himself under attack by two 109s and was forced to ditch in Marsalforn Bay in Gozo, from where he was rescued by locals Frank and George Debono.

Journalist George Fabri wrote:

By day the Luftwaffe attacks in raiding force, varying from three to five planes. The average is five Ju 88s with say, twice that number of yellow-nosed Me. 109 fighter escorts ... Flying at great height, they keep crossing the island at half-hourly intervals, searching for gaps in the clouds through which to drop their bombs.[26]

Fabri also observed that many of these hit-and-run attacks caused negligible damage. On cloudless days, the Luftwaffe tended to keep away for fear of tangling with the RAF, although limited dive-bombing was carried out on clear days.

The 'Cromwellian' Air Vice-Marshal Lloyd now moved on. He was posted on 14 July 1942 and replaced by Sir Keith Park, a veteran of the Battle of Britain. Before he left, Lloyd was presented with a cigarette case bearing the abbreviation MTAP – 'Malta thanks air protection.' Park was of the view that it was time to take the war to the enemy even more. It was not enough to intercept Axis aircraft over the island: they must be shot down before they ever reached it. Rommel's convoys were keeping well out of range of Malta's Swordfish, so Park employed the Fleet Air Arm pilots flying Hurricanes as bombers over Sicily.

OPERATION *PEDESTAL*

The gallant attempts to resupply battered Malta culminated with Operation *Pedestal*, when a large convoy entered the Mediterranean via Gibraltar on

10 August 1942. This force included the carriers *Eagle*, *Indomitable* and *Victorious*. There was no way to hide them from spies along the Spanish coast monitoring Allied shipping movements. Once the convoy was south of the Balearic Islands, the Axis was thus fully alerted and ready.

Kesselring closely co-ordinated operations to stop *Pedestal* with Admiral Eberhard Weichold, the German naval liaison officer in Rome, Admiral Arturo Riccardi commanding the Italian Navy and General Rino Corso Fougier, commander of the Italian Air Force. Between them, they mustered more than 700 aircraft, 21 submarines (only three of which were German) and 18 motor torpedo boats. The German U-boats were given the special task of penetrating the destroyer screens and attacking the carriers. The Italian and German motor torpedo boats lay in wait north of Cap Bon. Once the British convoy had been severely mauled, six Italian cruisers and 11 destroyers were standing by to finish it off with supporting air attacks.

The *Eagle* disappeared beneath the sea north off Algiers on 11 August. This happened just after a batch of Spitfires had taken off, when a German U-boat stuck four torpedoes in her with the loss of 260 lives. 'I remember seeing the planes that were on the flight decks slipping off,' said Leading Seaman Donald Auffret aboard the *Warspite*. 'She went down in eight and a half minutes.'[27]

'About five hours later came the first enemy air attack', wrote reporter Captain Norman Macmillan. 'Bombers, torpedo-bombers and Stukas swarmed out from their bases in Sardinia and Sicily, but one attack after another was smashed either by our carrier fighters … or by the tremendous barrage of shells from the naval and merchant ships.'[28] This was just a taste of things to come. What followed was carnage. A five-day running battle resulted in nine merchantmen, one aircraft carrier, two cruisers and a destroyer being lost. It seemed that *Pedestal* would inevitably fail in the face of such a brutal onslaught. However, quite remarkably, three days later, four supply ships reached Malta.

It was Mussolini who inadvertently saved *Pedestal* from complete destruction. There was not sufficient fighter cover to protect both the Axis bombers and the Italian naval task force. Kesselring and Fougier favoured finishing off the convoy employing bombs, whereas Riccardi and Weichold wanted to commit the surface vessels. Mussolini sided with the air commanders. The final air attacks only claimed a single merchant ship. If the Italian warships had been let loose, the damage could have been far greater, though they would have run into half a dozen British submarines. Instead, north of Sicily, as the redundant Italian warships were returning to port, a British submarine damaged the cruisers *Bolzano* and *Muzio Attendolo*, putting them out of action.

The American oil tanker *Ohio*, which was torpedoed by an Italian submarine and had a dive-bomber crash on its deck, was nursed into Grand Harbour on 15 August. The crippled vessel had lost her engines 60 miles (97 km) out and was slowly sinking. It took three destroyers and two minesweepers to get the tanker to safety. 'At 1800 two motor launches and a minesweeper, *Rye*, came out from Malta to assist us,' said her captain Dudley Mason. 'I called for a small number of volunteers to return to the *Ohio* to make the two ropes fast, but the whole crew voluntarily returned.'[29] The tanker had only just made it. 'The fuel was all drawn off, and none too soon,' recalled Squadron Leader Douglas-Hamilton, 'for the damage had been altogether too great; and before long her back broke and she sank in the harbour.'[31] The arrival of these five vessels with desperately needed provisions partially lifted the siege.

On the Axis side, Lieutenant-Commander Renato Ferrini, captain of the Italian submarine *Axum*, was the hero of the hour. Firing a single salvo of four torpedoes on 12 August, he damaged the cruiser *Nigeria*, sank the anti-aircraft cruiser *Cairo* and almost sank the *Ohio*.

MEDALS FOR GALLANTRY

Captain Mason was the first Merchant Navy officer to win the George Cross. He also later received the Lloyd's War Medal for Bravery at Sea. His chief engineer, James Wyld, became the first merchant seaman to gain the Distinguished Service Order, which was a military decoration. Ten other members of the crew were awarded gallantry medals for their efforts in saving the *Ohio*.

Sources in Rome told the reporter for the *Geneva Tribune*:

No further attempts to neutralise Malta will be made for the present – the Axis Command considers that the supplies which got through with the last great convoy have assured an effective resistance by the island for some time to come. The German and Italian Air Forces in the Mediterranean are now being diverted to the defending of convoys from Italy and Sicily to Libya and Egypt, against increasing Allied attacks.'[31]

Deep rifts were growing among the Axis commanders over how best to deal with Malta's continued defiance. The Italians were losing faith in the Luftwaffe's abilities. Marshal Ugo Cavallero wrote in his diary on 5 September 1942: 'Fresh efforts must be made to subdue Malta. If the Island is neutralised, we will win all the battles in Africa. If not, we will lose them all.' Two days later, he added: 'On the importance of subduing Malta, Kesselring tells me that he cannot do it with the two fighter groups at his disposal; the German airmen are tired ... they have developed a state of tension defined as "Maltese sickness".'[32]

Kesselring firmly held the Italians to blame for the situation:

Italy's missing the chance to occupy the island at the start of hostilities will go down to history as a fundamental blunder.

The Oberkommando der Wehrmacht [German Armed Forces High Command] very soon recognised the crucial importance of the island but, in spite of my reiterated argument for its occupation, afterwards supported by the [Italian] Commando Supremo and Rommel, they were satisfied with trying to neutralise it by air bombardment. This deliberate refusal to repair the first mistake was the second fundamental strategic error which placed the Mediterranean Command at a decisive disadvantage.[33]

COUNTING THE COST

The Axis had lost their initial chance and were now to pay the price. After weathering the brutal Axis storm of 1942, Malta began acting as a key base for the Allies' offensive missions across the Mediterranean. Captain Macmillan noted:

Meanwhile, Malta, supplied by convoys, increased its value as an air base. December 1942 saw Malta's heaviest air offensive, bombing

Tunis port with 4,000lb bombs (Wellingtons), sinking two ships in a convoy of four off Sicily with "tin-fish" (Albacores), and bombing Sicilian aerodromes.[34]

The RAF and newly arrived United States Army Air Force were also flying from North Africa. These attacks were coupled with warship and submarine operations. Those pilots operating from Malta had an enormous operational area. Air Vice-Marshal Lloyd observed:

> We patrol the seas to the east and to the west every day and all day. To the east it is over 350 miles to Greece. When we arrive there we have to cover something like 500 miles of Greek coast and open sea from Italy to Africa. To the west we have 200 miles to the Tunisian coast, and in the south 200 to Tripolitania [Libya].[35]

The losses in aircraft between 1940 and 1943 are testament to just how fierce the air battle for Malta had been. The RAF claimed 1,252 Axis planes, while anti-aircraft gunners accounted for another 241. The British lost 547 aircraft in the air and another 160 destroyed on the ground. One of the unsung heroes of the air battle was the RAF's rescue launch. Between mid-1940 and the close of 1942, it fished 123 RAF, 34 German and 21 Italian pilots out of the sea.

Some 26,000 Axis sorties were logged against Malta. In 1940, there were 211 air raid alerts, which escalated alarmingly to 2,031 in 1942. The following year, there was a very dramatic decline with 127. This was in part thanks to the Allied victories in North Africa. The focus shifted on to Sicily and then Calabria. In 1944, there were just eight air raid alerts, with the final all clear being given on 28 August 1944. The battle for Malta was finally over. The Maltese people suffered 1,190 men, women and children killed and another 296 who died of their injuries. It was a terrible price to pay for such a small island, but the Axis had been kept at bay.

CHAPTER 12:
Back to Tripoli

ROMMEL STRUCK in North Africa in May 1942, defeating the
British at Gazala. Then, on 21 June, he seized his prize – Tobruk. By
the time he had captured the port his forces had taken 45,000 prisoners,
along with 1,000 armoured fighting vehicles and almost 400 guns. His
reward from Hitler was elevation to field marshal. Rommel pushed on
until he reached a place called El Alamein, just 60 miles (97 km) west of
Alexandria. At the front, the rumours were not encouraging. 'The talk
was all of evacuating Egypt, perhaps going to Palestine, or even to India,'
said Private A. Lewis who was retreating back towards El Alamein with
the Royal Army Service Corps 'and the German victory was considered
inevitable.'[1] To the south-east, a 100-mile (160-km)-long British military
convoy was rolling towards the Egyptian capital. The atmosphere in
both cities was very tense.

If Rommel broke through he could avoid Alexandria's defences and
then loop south to cut it off from Cairo. However, German propagandists
were so confident that the Axis would shortly be in the port, they broadcast
an invitation suggesting: 'The ladies of Alexandria should get out their
party dresses.'[2] When he heard Tobruk had fallen, Sir Miles Lampson, the
British Ambassador to Egypt, who was holidaying in Alexandria, quickly
cut short his visit. Lieutenant Newby, while on leave in the city, attended
a luncheon that included the king and queen of Albania. He noted Queen
Géraldine 'was extremely good-looking, if not down-right saucy-looking'.

By contrast, King Zog 'looked a tough customer'.₃ Newby did not get to talk to them; instead, a British general gave him a good dressing down for not being in uniform. His excuse was that it was in tatters. The last thing Zog and Géraldine wanted to do was to fall into the hands of Rommel, for fear of ending up in Rome.

Naval and merchant ships left Alexandria's harbour, most of the shops closed and the place became subdued at the news of the advancing enemy forces. A military curfew was imposed to keep order. Admiral Sir Henry Harwood, who had succeeded Cunningham, sent the fleet to Beirut, Haifa and Port Said. The departure of the Mediterranean Fleet triggered 'the Flap'₄ as a general sense of panic engulfed the city and people fled. Sir Gerard Wells, the retired vice-admiral in control of the Egyptian ports and lighthouses administration, had a senior moment and abandoned his office. He had to be rounded up before his absence became an issue with the local Egyptian authorities.

The city was full of tempting targets for the Luftwaffe. Captain Burt-Smith, an advisor on air raid precautions, grumbled: 'the situation in Alexandria could hardly be worse ... innumerable tanks of crude oil and benzene clustered together in a small area...',₅ It was not long before the Luftwaffe came calling.

The British, fearing the worst, commenced evacuating non-essential personnel from Cairo. At the embassy and military headquarters, staff began frantically burning classified documents. General Auchinleck, commander-in-chief in the Middle East, put his headquarters on standby to destroy his correspondence with Churchill. Elements of the American military headquarters headed for Khartoum and Asmara in former Italian Somaliland.

Convoys of packed cars headed for Palestine and the eastbound trains were crammed with civilians trying to get to safety. The families of some British servicemen were put on ships at Suez or sent to Palestine. Many were given just 24 hours to leave. Alan Moorehead and his wife Lucy did not know what to do for the best. She was Auchinleck's private secretary, but the couple had a baby to think of. This was a slightly unusual job in light of Alan Moorehead being a journalist. In the end, it was agreed that she, the baby and Eve Smith, another secretary, would get on the train to Palestine. Sisters Jane and Margaret Coonan, the daughters of a British Army officer, were put on lorries bound for South

Africa. 'I remember we were told we couldn't take anything with us,'[6] said Margaret. Both were upset and the duty officer relented, allowing them to take one toy each.

Auchinleck's chief of staff, Lieutenant-General Thomas Corbett, found himself in command of Cairo after his boss headed for the front. He ordered a night-time curfew. Luckily for him, the Egyptian government continued about its business and there was no panic or riots on the streets. Most Egyptians decided that the Germans and Italians would be much worse colonial masters than the British ever were. Auchinleck and Corbett felt relaxed enough to leave the Egyptian Army responsible for internal security.

In contrast, a few Egyptian nationalists led Rommel to believe there would be a rising once he had broken through the British defences at El Alamein. 'It was known from Egyptian officers,' noted Manfred, Rommel's son, 'who were in touch with the Germans that such a revolt was contemplated.'[7] Rommel planned to take the Nile bridges in Alexandria and Cairo using an airborne *coup-de-main*. At that point, it was anticipated the Egyptians would side with the Axis forces. 'Now that he's got this far,' remarked Prince Abbas Halim, raising a toast to Rommel, 'let's hope he doesn't fall at the last fence.'[8] Halim, who had fought for the Germans in the First World War and made no secret of his pro-Nazi sympathies, was arrested shortly after.

The Egyptians were prepared to wait things out. They had seen it all before with foreign invaders. Napoleon had captured Alexandria in 1798 and defeated the Egyptians at the Battle of the Pyramids. Admiral Nelson's subsequent decisive naval victory over the French fleet at the Battle of the Nile put an end to Napoleon's aspirations for conquering Egypt. Later, it had been the turn of the British, who shelled Alexandria and set about defeating a nationalist uprising in 1882. From that point on, Britain assumed control of Egypt in defiance of the authority of the Ottoman Empire.

HITLER'S GRAND PLAN FAILS

Since mid-1941, Hitler had considered a grandiose scheme that would see Rommel's troops and those fighting in the Caucasus linking up in the Middle East. Hitler believed that if he captured Grozny then his forces in the Caucasus could reach the Gulf. In reality, Plan *Orient* was wishful thinking as he simply did not have the resources to conduct such a giant pincer movement. However, it was a strategic threat that the Allies could not ignore. By the summer of 1942, the Germans were bearing down on Grozny and it was not clear if the Red Army could hold them. Now that Rommel was advancing on Alexandria, all this added to Churchill's unease over the fate of Egypt and indeed the whole Middle East.

Churchill certainly had no intention of abandoning Egypt. Even if Alexandria were lost, a defence could be conducted in the Nile delta and in the deserts between the Nile and Suez. If Rommel got across Sinai, he would still have to fight his way through Palestine and Iraq. There was no strategic reason for him to head south into the desert wastes. For the Europeans in Cairo, it was hard to imagine the Egyptian capital falling, but Hitler had conquered most of Europe's major cities. British Ambassador Sir Miles Lampson stoically refused to leave Cairo. To show that it was business as usual, he even decided the embassy railings could do with a new coat of paint.

Mussolini, convinced that nothing could stop Rommel, flew to Libya on 29 June. He took with him his Sword of Islam ready to brandish it at the anticipated triumphal parade through Cairo's streets. Mussolini accepted that the victory would be Rommel's, but the majority of his troops were Italian. He would therefore turn it into an Italian propaganda coup.

However, as always happened in the fighting in North Africa, the attackers reached the end of their lines of communication. Rommel's advance ran out of steam. Supplies became low, his forces were exhausted and he desperately needed reinforcements.

The British, along with their Australian, Indian, New Zealander and South African allies, readied themselves and lay in wait. Rommel was halted at the First Battle of El Alamein. Auchinleck had chosen a good defensive position. Rommel's only way to get to Alexandria, Cairo and Suez was through a 40-mile (64-km)-wide gap between the Mediterranean and the Qattara Depression. The latter was more than 328 ft (100 m) below sea level and was wholly unsuitable for tanks. Auchinleck's forces dug in on the ridges that dominated the gap, in particular Alam el Halfa and Ruweisat Ridge. Rommel's tanks failed to bludgeon their way through.

It was at this point that Hitler lost his key source of intelligence in Cairo. Auchinleck had an unwitting spy in his headquarters, who furnished the Axis with information on reinforcements for Malta and advanced warning of commando raids on Italian airbases. Rommel also gained a detailed order of battle for the British 8th Army. American military attaché Colonel Bonner Fellers attended Auchinleck's daily morning briefings then reported back to Washington. Unbeknown to him, the Italians had cracked the US diplomatic codes. It was not until Rommel was poised to strike Alexandria that these were changed and could not be broken.

Mussolini stayed at Derna for three weeks, 460 miles (740 km) from the front line, and then on 20 July flew home via Athens. There, he was dismayed by the starvation he saw on the streets. Next, Mussolini himself fell ill and began to lose weight. 'The wheel of fortune ... turned on 28 June 1942, when we halted before El Alamein...' Mussolini later observed. 'The Germans have never grasped the importance of the Mediterranean, never...', The following month, Churchill sacked Auchinleck and replaced him with General Harold Alexander. Corbett was also replaced.

THE SECOND BATTLE OF EL ALAMEIN

Rommel flew to Rome on 23 September to warn the Italians that unless massive logistical support was provided it would be impossible for the Axis to remain in Egypt. The following day, he saw Mussolini. 'I left him in no doubt that unless supplies were sent to us at least on the scale I had demanded,' wrote Rommel, 'we should have to get out of North Africa ... he still did not realise the full gravity of the situation.'[10] Rommel then flew to see Hitler, who was full of platitudes. To Rommel's despair, very little was done to help.

The turning point for Rommel finally came in October/November 1942 at the Second Battle of El Alamein, by which time his forces were completely outnumbered. General Bernard Montgomery's 8th Army had about 200,000 men. Rommel, by contrast, had about half that number. Crucially, the 8th Army had amassed 1,029 tanks against 491 Axis tanks. The ratio of aircraft was very similar. After much heavy fighting, Rommel was thrown back with the loss of more than 400 irreplaceable tanks. Montgomery lost half his tank force but many were repairable. Axis casualties amounted to 20,000 killed or wounded and 30,000 captured. Montgomery's casualties numbered 13,500. Rommel had no choice but to conduct a slow fighting retreat back towards Tripoli. His fate was sealed with the Allied landings in his rear at the end of the year.

German prisoners taken during the Second Battle of El Alamein, which was the turning point in North Africa.

OPERATION *TORCH*

Allied plans to trap Rommel required the co-operation of French North Africa. Churchill had tried to get General Weygand, the commander in the region, to break with Vichy, but to no avail. Even if he had been sympathetic, he was forced out in November 1941 following Hitler's threat to occupy the whole of France. The following April, pro-German Pierre Laval replaced Darlan as the political power behind the throne in Vichy. To complicate matters further, Algeria was administered as a province of France ruled directly by Vichy, whereas Morocco was a protectorate and the French resident-general, General Auguste Noguès, could only 'advise' the Sultan.

By 1942, the Allies hoped that General Henri Giraud, who had escaped imprisonment by the Germans, supported by General Charles Emmanuel Mast in Algeria and General Antoine Béthouart in Morocco, would rise up against Vichy. In September, General Dwight D. Eisenhower warned his military planners about the risk of the French Army resisting the proposed landings in North Africa. He cautioned:

> In the region now are some fourteen French divisions rather poorly equipped but presumably with a fair degree of training and with the benefit of professional leadership. If this Army should act as a unit in contesting the invasion, it could, in view of the slowness with which Allies forces can be accumulated at the two main ports, so delay and hamper operations that the real object of the expedition could not be achieved, namely seizing control of the north shore of Africa before it can be substantially reinforced by the Axis.'[11]

Eisenhower hoped the French would not resist but noted: 'There was nothing in the political history of the years 1940–42 to indicate that this would occur; it was a hope rather than an expectation. Consequently, we had to be prepared to fight against forces which in all, numbered 200,000.'[12] There were actually some 50,000 ground troops in Algeria, 55,000 in Morocco and 15,000 in Tunisia, equipped with 250 tanks and up to 500 aircraft.

At a secret conference with Deputy Allied Supreme Commander General Mark Clark, held on the Algerian coast in late October, Mast guaranteed there would be little resistance from the French military and air force in the event of an invasion. It was perhaps understandably felt that the French Navy would resist the landings. To try to avoid antagonizing the French, it was decided that Operation *Torch* would largely be an American-led affair. However, there were insufficient American forces for the attack on Algiers so they were to be supported by British troops.

Early on 8 November 1942, Pétain was informed that Britain and America had just invaded French North Africa. He faced a difficult choice: resist and defend that which he had sought to preserve or acquiesce to Allied military demands. Pétain made his decision and broke off diplomatic relations with America, warning the US chargé d'affaires that his forces would resist the Anglo-American invasion.

The Moroccan ports of Casablanca and Safi on the Atlantic coast and Algerian ports of Oran and Algiers on the Mediterranean had to be secured as quickly as possible in order for the Americans to land their tanks over the quayside. In particular, the landings at Safi would have to prevent the strong French garrison at Marrakech from intervening at Casablanca – key to deterring Spanish Morocco to the north, potentially sealing the Straits of Gibraltar. At Casablanca, the French fleet attempted to interfere with the American transport ships and the US Navy was forced to put out of action seven warships.

At Oran, as well as a direct assault, three task forces landed either side of the city. To the west, a tank landing ship had to be grounded 120 yards (110 m) from the beach and a pontoon bridge built before its Sherman tanks could be unloaded. First contact came at 0800 hours when American anti-tank gunners knocked out three armoured cars at point-blank range. To the east, the French lost another five armoured cars at Renan, but further down the road, even using self-propelled guns, the Americans were unable to budge French troops who eventually had to be bypassed. Despite stiff resistance, American armoured units had penetrated Oran by 1000 hours and at noon the French garrison surrendered.

Completely unknown to the Allies, Darlan was in Algiers visiting his ill son. This compromised the city's military commander, General Alphonse Juin, who had planned to act for the Allies. The eastern advance on Algiers itself was brought to a temporary halt by the threat of attack by just three French tanks. Similarly, with the landings at Casablanca, French tank and infantry columns approaching from Rabat had to be driven off by aircraft from the American battleship *Texas*.

The French also resisted landings at the Moroccan port of Safi. The garrison was only 450 strong under Major Pierre Deuve, but several batteries of powerful fixed coastal guns and mobile artillery units supported them. The major was roused from bed at 0335 hours local time with news of the Allied invasions at Oran and Algiers. Just over 30 minutes later, his guns began to engage the American warships offshore. By daybreak, American troops had secured the harbour, railroad station, post office and roads entering Safi, but they were still coming under small arms fire.

General Ernest Harmon, leading the American landings, found he was without armour. Those light tanks that had been landed were inoperable due to faulty batteries or drowned engines. To make matters worse, the two ships carrying additional tanks that had come into the harbour suffered critical delays unloading their cargo thanks to frustrating winch and crane problems. In the meantime, the French organized a counter-attack with

1,000 French troops from Marrakech. Carrier-borne dive-bombers soon located the convoy, which they bombed for half an hour.

In Safi, French troops held out in the old walled barracks near the waterfront and launched a counter-attack using three Renault tanks, but the Americans knocked out two using rifle grenades and the third crashed into a wall. Still lacking tanks of their own, the Americans redirected the Renaults' guns on to the barracks. The defenders finally surrendered at 1530 hours. When the Shermans of Task Force Blackstone finally landed near Safi, they arrived too late to see any combat.

The Americans encountered a similar reception at Port Lyautey. The coastal guns opened up on the transports and warships, while French aircraft strafed the beach and bombed some of the landing craft. Those forces landing on Green Beach opposite the town, lacking tank and artillery support, found themselves under attack by Renault tanks and Moroccan colonial infantry. Lieutenant Charles Dushane and Corporal Frank L. Czar manned an abandoned French anti-tank gun and succeeded in knocking out one of the tanks before the lieutenant was killed. Task Force Goalpost, assigned to capture the airport at Lyautey and Sale, included M5 light tanks of the 66th Armoured Regiment, US 2nd Armored Division. They anticipated encountering up to 45 French tanks.

General Lucian K. Truscott was warned that a French armoured column was on its way from Rabat and he became worried about a dawn attack on his exposed southern flank. Fortunately for Truscott, seven M5 light tanks under Lieutenant-Colonel Harry H. Semmes from 2nd Armored arrived just in time to block the Rabat-Port Lyautey road. On 9 November, Semmes came under attack from two battalions of French infantry and up to 18 Renault tanks. The latter were completely outclassed with their inadequate 37-mm guns and attacked in groups of two or three in a vain effort to overwhelm the Americans. Within ten minutes, Semmes' tanks knocked out four Renaults and their machine guns mowed down the French infantry.

The French tanks, whose armour-piercing rounds largely bounced off the M5s, also found themselves under naval gunfire when the destroyer *Savannah* came to Semmes' assistance. The bloodied French withdrew back down the Rabat road. When Semmes inspected the battlefield, he discovered two armour-piercing shells embedded in his tank's armour. Reinforcements from the 70th Tank Battalion helped drive off an attack by 32 French tanks attempting to break through to the beachhead, and an American counter-attack then forced the French to abandon 24 of them.

Near the vital Tafraoui airfield, south of Oran, another tank battle erupted between French and American armour on 9 November. The day before, elements of the US 1st Armored Division – consisting of M3 light tanks of the 13th Armoured Reconnaissance Company spearheading Red Task Force, under Colonel John Waters (General George S. Patton's son-in-law) – had pushed inland to help the US 509th Parachute Infantry Battalion secure Tafraoui airport. After taking 300 prisoners at Tafraoui, Waters was heading for La Senia airport when he received a message to turn back – a French armoured column was just 7 miles (11 km) east of Tafraoui.

A reconnaissance platoon of tanks led by Lieutenant William Beckett was despatched to hold up the French attack. Joined by Captain William R. Tuck, they knocked out 14 French tanks for the loss of one tank and a halftrack. Green Task Force, including M3s of the 1st Battalion plus elements of the 701st Tank Destroyer Battalion, moved to secure La Senia airfield. En route, French armoured cars fitted with 37-mm guns were encountered at Bou Tlelis and 75-mm guns at Bredeah.

It was only when medium tanks were finally put ashore at Safi and Oran that the Allies were able to field any substantial quantity of armour and by then the French had called for a ceasefire. Darlan ordered this on 10 November, only to have it overruled by Pétain. Continued resistance was futile and Darlan reached a settlement with the Allies, in which the French colonies would be treated as friendly rather than occupied territory.

American forces suffered 1,404 casualties, including 556 killed, 837 wounded and 41 missing in the needless four-day war in French North Africa. The British sustained 300 casualties and the French 700 dead, 1,400 wounded and 400 missing. Privately, the Americans were partly pleased that the French chose to fight, as it gave them the opportunity to blood their inexperienced army before it had to contend with the battle-hardened Axis forces. The invasion also provided a vital testing ground for the subsequent amphibious assaults on Sicily and Normandy.

THE AFTERMATH OF OPERATION *TORCH*

The Allies' inability to extend the landings eastward into Tunisia was to prove a major failing of Operation *Torch*. In the port of Tunis, Admiral

American troops at a roadside cafe in Algeria following Operation Torch.

Jean-Pierre Esteva, resident general in Tunisia, though loyal to Darlan and Vichy, was privately sympathetic to the Allies. Nevertheless, he simply did not have the resources with which to obstruct the Germans who began to arrive in force by air on 9 November. They were quick to react to the Allied landings and arrested Esteva. A quarter of the French garrison remained loyal to Vichy and did nothing to impede the German build-up. At Bizerte, some Vichy French units even joined the Germans who were moving to reinforce Tunisia.

If the French had co-operated, the Allies could have pushed into Tunisia within two days of the landings in Algeria. Instead, the Germans struck eastwards from Tunis, successfully safeguarding Rommel's passage from Libya into Tunisia. Under the Franco-Italian Armistice, Mussolini had imposed a 50-mile (80-km) demilitarized zone between Libya and Tunisia but this now counted for nothing as German and Italian tanks would soon be crossing to secure their exposed western flank.

The majority of the French garrison in Tunisia chose to observe the ceasefire and join the Allies when elements of the 1st Army, after landing in eastern Algeria, moved into western Tunisia. General George Barre, the French ground forces commander in Tunisia, withdrew with about five battalions into the mountains west of Tunis and towards the Allies in Algiers, while other French troops moved into the Grande Dorsale. General Juin's force was some 30,000 strong. Consisting of Barre's weak division, a division raised in the Constantine area and some Saharan units, it was assigned the two Dorsale ranges. Its job was to prevent the Germans penetrating the Tebessa area of Algeria and to cover the right flank of the British for the forthcoming Tunisian campaign. In France, *Torch* sealed the fate of Pétain and the Vichy regime, as Hitler's response was to occupy the rest of the mainland.

ROMMEL ATTEMPTS TO REASON WITH HITLER

Rommel met with Field Marshal Kesselring and Italian Marshal Ugo Cavallero on 24 November on the frontier between Cyrenaica and Tripolitania to discuss the deteriorating situation in North Africa. Rommel was of the view that it was futile for the Axis to remain in the region and he urged the immediate evacuation of Tripolitania. He saw reinforcing Tunisia as a pointless exercise as they would be trapped. His superiors refused and informed him that Mussolini wanted to counter-attack.

Rommel tried taking matters into his own hands and four days later flew to see Hitler at Rastenburg. He put his case forcefully, arguing that:'the abandonment of the African theatre of war should be accepted as a long term policy ... If the army remained in North Africa, it would be destroyed.'(13) Rommel then explained that most of his weapons and equipment had been blasted to pieces by the British. In response, Hitler flew into a rage and said there was to be no retreat.

On his way back to Libya, Rommel stopped off in Rome and tried to persuade Kesselring to permit him to withdraw to Gabès in southern Tunisia. Kesselring refused on the grounds that it would increase the threat to the Luftwaffe's Tunisian airbases. Mussolini was more sympathetic and called Rommel's withdrawal at El Alamein a 'masterpiece'. He also gave permission for Italian units to withdraw in the face of a British attack. Rommel appreciated that it was only a matter of time.

THE ASSASSINATION OF ADMIRAL DARLAN

To the horror of many, following the ceasefire in French North Africa, Darlan was made high commissioner. Churchill and de Gaulle were furious that a collaborator should be given this office. A violent solution to this shaming arrangement soon presented itself. Darlan and his staff officer, Captain Hourcade, were shot and wounded in Algiers, just after 1500 hours on 24 December 1942. Their assailant, 20-year-old Fernand Bonnier de La Chapelle, hit Darlan in the face and the abdomen. The admiral, still conscious but unable to speak, was rushed to hospital. He was quickly pronounced dead on the operating table. Hourcade was also shot twice, with one bullet grazing his cheek and the second hitting his thigh, but survived. Bonnier was caught at the scene and executed two days later.

Eisenhower and Giraud were immediately recalled from the Tunisian front for fear of unrest or even a coup. They faced a bleak 30-hour drive through winter weather to get back to Algiers. Eisenhower sent a note of condolence to Madame Darlan: 'You have the consolation of knowing that he died in the service of his country and that we view his passing with regret.'[14] Nobody who hated collaborationist Vichy, Bonnier included, shared this rather generous sentiment. Churchill could never forgive Darlan for forcing him to attack Mers-el-Kébir. 'If I could meet Darlan, much as I hate him,' Churchill once told Eisenhower, 'I would cheerfully crawl on my hands and knees for a mile if doing so I could get him to bring that fleet of his into the circle of Allied forces.'[15]

Darlan's funeral was held on 26 December and was attended by among others Generals Clark, Eisenhower and Giraud, and Admiral Cunningham. 'Darlan's murder, however criminal,' Churchill later wrote, 'relieved the Allies of the embarrassment of working with him, and at the same time left them with all the advantages he had been able to bestow during the vital hours of the Allied landings.'[16]

That Bonnier was part of a conspiracy is beyond dispute, although he initially claimed he had acted alone. On being apprehended, he had cried: 'Don't kill me. Don't kill me.'[17] Although sentenced to death, Bonnier told the police: 'I am calm, London has been advised.'[18] He spoke of a mock execution before being spirited away to Tangiers. 'Powerful personages,' Bonnier said, 'will get me out if I continue to say nothing.'[19] No reprieve came and General Giraud ordered Bonnier before a firing squad. Just before he died, Bonnier implicated Abbé Cordier, who worked with the French Secret Service, and Henri d'Astier de la Vigerie, secretary general of the police.

Vichy media sources reported that Darlan's last words in the car were:

'Nothing more can be done for me ... England has attained her goal.'[20]
This was nonsense as his wounds were such that he could not communicate.
Intriguingly, just before Darlan's death, Sir Alexander Cadogan, head of the
Foreign Office with responsibility for MI6, Britain's overseas intelligence
service, wrote: 'we shall do no good till we've killed Darlan.'[21]

It has since been claimed that Sir Stewart Menzies, MI6's boss, made
a clandestine visit to Algiers in late 1942.[22] The evidence regarding his
movements does not support this, but is it conceivable that on the orders
of Churchill, he travelled to North Africa to co-ordinate the assassination
of Darlan with French contacts. Eisenhower ordered an investigation,
with the proviso that if there was the slightest hint of American or British
complicity, he be relieved of command. He kept his job and Giraud
replaced Darlan.

Charles de Gaulle sensed blood in the water. He realized this leadership
crisis in French North Africa presented an opportunity for him to
manoeuvre himself in to a position of greater power. He messaged Giraud,
stating: 'I propose, mon general, that you should meet me as soon as possible
on French soil, either in Algeria or in Chad, in order to study the means
of grouping under a provisional central authority all French forces inside
and outside the country...'[23] Algeria was considered part of metropolitan
France and de Gaulle knew if he headed the provisional authority there he
would be on his way to assuming power on the mainland.

THE AXIS RETREAT

At the end of December 1942, a desperate Mussolini sent Hitler a message,
once again pleading for help: 'Stop all offensive operations in Russia. Hold
the line with fewer men and assign troops to North Africa.'[24] In response
to the Allied landings, Hitler occupied southern France and seized eastern
Tunisia to protect Rommel's rear. It was a futile gesture that consigned
North Africa to another six months of bitter fighting. It also left the Italian
and German armies trapped, between the Anglo-American 1st Army and
the British 8th Army, conducting a two-front war. Tripoli fell on 23 January
1943 and Italian Libya ceased to exist. So did Mussolini's dream of creating
a new Roman Empire. Rommel evacuated the city without a fight, but not
before his engineers comprehensively wrecked the harbour; blockships were
sunk in the entrance and the quays and other installations were blown up.

At the gates of Tripoli, civic dignitaries greeted Montgomery to offer their formal surrender. British tanks clattered along the city's tree-lined streets and into the main square by the harbour. A British photographer was on hand to capture the moment as they fanned out and took up defensive positions just to be on the safe side. The tanks were followed by lorries and tracked carriers bearing infantry. The men dismounted and looked up at the pockmarked buildings. Shortly after, the Union Jack was hoisted over the Libyan capital.

Montgomery took a tour and stopped by the harbour to eat his sandwiches. When he was offered the governor's palace as his headquarters, he replied: 'Certainly not.'[25] Instead, a location was chosen several miles to the south of the city. 'The defeat of the enemy in the Battle of Alamein, the pursuit of his beaten army and the final capture of Tripoli,' Montgomery later told his men, 'a distance of some fourteen hundred miles from Alamein, has been accomplished in three months. This achievement is probably without parallel in history...'[26]

Germans in Tunisia scanning the border with Algeria. After the Axis surrender in North Africa, the Allies invaded Sicily, Italy and southern France.

Rommel, retreating to Tunisia, made use of the French-built Mareth Line to delay Montgomery's advance. At the end of the first week of March 1943, he handed command to General von Arnim and flew to Rome. 'I told Mussolini briefly and plainly what I thought of the situation...' Rommel wrote, 'but he ... seemed to lack any sense of reality in adversity and spent the whole time searching for arguments to justify his views.'[27] Time was running out for the Axis forces in North Africa.

General Alexander reported: 'On 6 May First Army delivered the final successful blow. Next day the unfailing and ever-unflagging 7th Armoured Division led the advance into Tunis. Almost simultaneously, on the same day American and French forces of the United States II Corps entered Bizerta.'[28] The British 1st Army entered Tunis in the late afternoon, to be greeted by machine-gun and sniper fire from pockets of last-ditch resistance. Axis troops were located in a block of half-built flats and there were snipers in a brewery building. Tanks were brought forwards to deal with them. Despite the sporadic gunfire, French and Tunisian civilians were soon welcoming the Allied vehicles as they moved down the streets.

'Tunis was the first major city to be liberated by the Allies during the war,' recalled Lieutenant Alan Whicker, with a British Army film unit, 'the streets full of deliriously happy people when men proffered hoarded champagne and pretty girls their all...'[29] They impeded progress into the city as the Allies edged forwards to take control. 'The crowd around us in the Avenue Jules Ferry was so jammed and ecstatic we could not move,' added the young lieutenant.

The swiftness of the Allied breakthrough caught many Axis troops in Tunis by surprise. In the city centre, British troops discovered Germans sitting at pavement cafes enjoying an aperitif, while others were promenading the streets with their girlfriends. All they could do was stop and stare as British armoured cars rolled by. The surviving Italian and German troops were herded north-east into the Cap Bon Peninsula. However, 8th Army encountered continued resistance in the mountains between Enfidaville and Zaghouan. Despite this, they were in Hammamet by 9 May.

The defeated Axis forces surrendered in Tunis on 12 May 1943 with the loss of more than 240,000 prisoners. They consisted of around 125,000 Germans and 115,000 Italians. Among them was the German commander. 'The fact that von Arnim himself had not been able to get away was proof of the speed and completeness of our victory,' wrote war reporter Alan

Moorehead. 'All the Axis generals, with only one notable exception, had now been taken.'[30] On the airfield at Korba on the road to Cap Bon, the British found around 5,000 Axis soldiers forlornly waiting in vain to be evacuated.

Lieutenant Heinz Schmidt, who had been with Rommel from the start, by good fortune had flown home two weeks earlier to get married. He was on his honeymoon in the spa town of Baden-Baden when he heard the terrible news on the radio. The broadcast was blunt and to the point: 'After an heroic fight the German-Italian Panzer Army in Tunisia has suspended the struggle against terrific odds. With this, the battle in Africa has ended.'[31]

The following day, General Alexander signalled Churchill in London: 'Sir, it is my duty to report that the campaign in Tunisia is over. All enemy resistance has ceased. We are masters of the North African shores.'[32] The prime minister could hardly hide his glee when he responded to this news: 'All the way from Alamein to Tunis in ceaseless fighting and marching of the last six months you and your brilliant lieutenant Montgomery have added a glorious chapter to the annals of British Commonwealth.'[33]

Churchill also sent his gratitude to Eisenhower, saying: 'Let me add my heartfelt congratulations … on the brilliant result of the North African campaign…'[34] He then hopped on to a plane to join the celebrations. Lieutenant Whicker's next job was to film Churchill, who flew in to address 3,000 troops from the British 1st Army gathered in the Roman amphitheatre at Carthage. The symbolism of this could hardly be missed. Apart from Spanish Morocco, the Allies controlled the entire coastline. The battle for the Mediterranean would now enter a new phase.

'Great Britain, the classical Mediterranean power, had been able,' wrote Field Marshal Kesselring, 'with the aid of the Americans, to establish a jumping-off base for an assault on Europe from the south.'[35] Certainly, Italy was wide open to attack. The remains of Mussolini's army were tied up in southern France, the Balkans and the Aegean. The navy was short of fuel and the air force was struggling to defend Italian airspace from Allied bombers. After his shattering defeat at Stalingrad, Hitler had little interest in helping Mussolini in the Mediterranean. His preoccupation was trying to retrieve the Eastern Front from complete disaster. Mussolini had become expendable and his days were numbered.

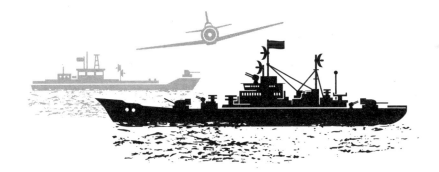

CHAPTER 13:
Where Next?

FOLLOWING THE Axis defeat in North Africa, Mussolini and his generals were in a state of panic. They did not know what to do, as the initiative had very firmly passed over to the enemy. The Allies could attack anywhere in the Mediterranean at their leisure. The question was: where would they go next? They might hope to open the liberation of France by landing on the Riviera; they might opt for the Balkans and land in weakly defended Greece; or they might strike the Italian mainland. If the Allies were looking to capture Rome, then operations against Corsica and Sardinia seemed most likely. Possession of the latter could also support an Allied assault on southern France.

Mussolini was tired of his entanglement with Hitler. His African adventure had gone horribly wrong, even with the intervention of Rommel. Now, the Allies were poised to attack Italian soil. Mussolini was in a very bad position to defend his homeland. He had lost around 300,000 men killed or captured from the 1st, 5th and 10th armies in North Africa. In Russia, his 8th Army had collapsed in December 1942, with the loss of 150,000 men, contributing to the Germans' defeat at Stalingrad. The ill-equipped 2nd and 9th armies were bogged down in the Balkans fighting Albanian and Yugoslav partisans. The 11th Army was tied up on occupation duties in Greece. All he had left was his weak 6th Army to protect Sicily and southern Italy.

Now that the Allies controlled Tunisia they posed a direct threat to Sicily and Sardinia. 'At the time of the capitulation of Tunis the outlook in Sicily,' wrote Kesselring, 'as everywhere, was very black.', Hitler's commanders were warning him that the beating heart of the Italian armed forces had been torn out in Africa. Mussolini would not be able to defend Italian soil without German help. To Hitler, this must have felt like Libya and Greece all over again. However, he was not unduly concerned about the threat to Sicily, because he did not anticipate that the Allies would attack it next.

The situation in the Mediterranean was not helped by disunity in the Italian high command. General Mario Roatta, Army chief of staff, accepted that neither Italy nor Sicily could be defended without major German assistance. In contrast, General Vittorio Ambrosio, who had replaced Cavallero as the senior Italian commander, actively disliked the Germans. Whereas Cavallero had happily co-operated with their allies, Ambrosio wanted to end his country's reliance on them. This resulted in Roatta asking for more German help, with Ambrosio continually declining it.

Field Marshal Kesselring and Admiral Doenitz tried to resurrect the idea of attacking Gibraltar. This, they pointed out to Hitler, would help them regain the initiative in the Mediterranean and threaten the Allied flank. It would also distract the Allies from Italy. Hitler knew he could not move into neutral Spain without Franco's permission and that was unlikely to be given. German resources were already stretched and the ongoing partisan wars in the Balkans and on the Eastern Front showed what might happen if he invaded Spain.

Hitler appreciated that once the Axis forces had been defeated in North Africa, the Allies would next attempt a major seaborne operation against Italy or the Balkans. In early 1943, Hitler therefore decided he would defend the entire region and a skeleton army headquarters was established in Munich to co-ordinate the planning for the defence of Italy. However, the growing drain on resources on the Eastern Front and the question over the reliability of the Italian Army made the prospect of occupying and defending the whole of metropolitan Italy fairly slim.

Mussolini did not want additional German troops in his homeland, but rather, German supplies with which to replenish his exhausted and demoralized army. When Kesselring told Mussolini he was forming three new German divisions to help defend Italy, Mussolini stated they would make no difference and what he really needed was tanks and aircraft. His requests included enough armoured vehicles to equip 50 tank and self-propelled artillery battalions.

Mussolini, increasingly ill under the strain, went to see Hitler, who reassured him that once he had smashed the Red Army at Kursk he would send all the help the Italians needed. Allied deception plans, not least Operation *Mincemeat*, were such that Hitler was convinced that the Allies' next objective would be Greece. Churchill, who was in Washington, received a telegram on 14 May 1943, confirming: 'Mincemeat swallowed rod, line and sinker by right people and they look like acting on it.', Hitler chose to reinforce the Luftwaffe in the Aegean, Ionian and Tyrrhenian seas.

STRIFE IN THE STRAIT OF SICILY

The following month, the Allies took the Italian islands of Lampedusa and Pantelleria located between Sicily and Tunisia. Mussolini had hoped that heavily fortified and garrisoned Pantelleria would act like an Italian Malta. Instead, it rapidly became an American airbase. The tiny island was first treated as a guinea pig. The only place to land was the harbour, so the Allies decided to beat the 12,000-strong garrison, under the command of Admiral Gino Pavesi and General Achille Maffei, into submission.

Pantelleria received 4,656 tons of bombs during May and early June. On top of this, it was bombarded relentlessly by British warships. The island became shrouded in a cloud of dust and smoke. The garrison and the civilian population were forced to cower in subterranean caves. On the night of 10 June, Maffei radioed Mussolini: 'The situation is unendurable. If this happens again we cannot carry on. Everything is destroyed. We cannot even resist invasion now.', Mussolini told him not to let down the honour of the country. It was little wonder that Pavesi capitulated on 11 June when the Allied invasion fleet came into view. Neither Pavesi nor his men wanted to fight. He signalled Rome beforehand for permission to give up, but decided to do so before Mussolini sent authorization. His last message read: 'I cannot oppose landing, now I must surrender.',

Lampedusa had a similar experience and yielded another 4,600 prisoners. The latter surrendered to Sergeant Pilot Sydney Cohen, who force-landed on the island after his Swordfish developed engine trouble. 'I was taken to the Commandant's villa and presented to a high ranking officer,' recalled Cohen. Despite the harbour being under attack by Allied fighter-bombers, Cohen and his crew took off with a surrender note, which they flew to

Tunis. 'Now they call me "The King of Lampedusa",'[5] joked Cohen after safely reaching Tunisia. To the north-east of Lampedusa, a small British force landed on Linosa, where they had to kick the island commandant out of bed in order to accept his surrender.

ISLANDS OF EXILE

Aside from their garrisons and civilian population, who mainly eked out a living as fishermen, these islands harboured a dark secret. They were part of Mussolini's gulag and were places of exile for those who displeased his Fascist government. A British writer noted that on Pantelleria: 'The citadel needless to say contained an Italian penal colony.'[6] Similarly to the north of Sicily, one-third of the population of the island of Ustica were political prisoners. Lipari, also to the north, served a similar purpose.

Kesselring and Mussolini's senior generals felt the loss of these islands without a fight was reprehensible. It proved to the Allies that even when defending their own territory the Italians were poorly motivated. This did not bode well for the defence of Sicily. General Alfredo Guzzoni and his Italian 6th Army, which had responsibility for Sicily, were directly in the front line. By early July 1943, there were 200,000 Italian and 32,000 German troops, as well as 30,000 Luftwaffe ground personnel, on the island. These numbers meant little, as most of the Italians were reservists in coastal units and there were just four regular army divisions. Only one of these, General Domenico Chirieleison's 4th Livorno Division, was truly mobile. Most of the static forces were tied up defending Sicily's main ports: Catania, Messina, Palermo and Syracuse.

Initially, Roatta had been placed in charge of the 6th Army, when he was sent to take command in February 1943. He did not like what he found: the garrison was poorly trained and ill-equipped and morale was low. He did not stay long and returned to Rome. Guzzoni was recalled out of retirement following the loss of Tunis, and replaced Roatta on 20 May. He was an experienced commander, having been involved in Albania and Greece, but had not seen active service since 1941. Guzzoni and Kesselring could not agree on the best defensive strategy for Sicily.

Kesselring was able to deploy two Panzer divisions to support Guzzoni. These were actually units that had been lost in Tunisia and were in the process of being reconstituted as the 15th Panzergrenadier Division and 1st Fallschirm-Panzer Division Hermann Göring. The former simply consisted of units in Sicily that had been waiting to ship to Tunisia, while the latter was made up of Luftwaffe personnel who had no combat experience. Nonetheless, they had tanks. He also had a division in Sardinia and a weak brigade in Corsica. All these forces were backed by Luftwaffe anti-aircraft and fighter units. In Kesselring's view, the defences on Corsica were the best, then the ones in Sardinia and Sicily, while those on the Calabrian coast: 'left much to be desired'.

The Germans operated an independent ferry service across the Straits of Messina directed by Admiral William Meendsen-Bohlken. Thanks to this, Kesselring was able to get reinforcements across to Sicily swiftly and largely unhindered. When the Hermann Göring division arrived in late June and early July, some 3,600 men, 610 vehicles and 750 tons of supplies were ferried over in a single day. About 9,500 men, 1,300 vehicles, 50 guns and 40 tanks arrived during the first week of July. It was only once the Herman Göring was in Sicily that it started training.

OPERATION *HUSKY*

The target of Eisenhower's next seaborne assault, dubbed Operation *Husky*, was indeed Sicily. Eisenhower and his senior officers knew that it would not be easy. This would be of a much different magnitude to the landings in Algeria and Morocco, where the resistance had been sporadic and half-hearted. The island had a garrison of comparable strength to the invasion force and was well fortified. A major concern was the Axis air forces. Although the Allies had command of the sea, General Alexander noted they had 'a somewhat doubtful degree of superiority in the air...',[7] The Axis air forces based in Sardinia and on the mainland would easily be able to intervene.

Alexander observed:

Messina was heavily guarded by fixed defences and beyond the range of our fighters. Catania was only just within fighter cover, and was also heavily defended and under the fighter umbrella of the Luftwaffe based on the Catania group of airfields … Syracuse and Palermo were both within our fighter cover and not so heavily defended.[8]

Initially, it was suggested that the British would land in the Syracuse region to the east and the Americans near Palermo in the north-west. The flaw with this was that it would leave the British 8th and US 7th armies unable to support each other. Instead, the Allies decided to assault south-eastern Sicily. Air Chief Marshal Tedder wanted to secure the Italian airfields in this area as soon as possible. Admiral Cunningham was in agreement, otherwise the enemy's air forces could pose a threat to his fleet.

THE AMERICANS MAKE USE OF THE MAFIA

There was another player on the island involved in the Allied invasion – organized crime. America did the Mediterranean a great disservice in this respect. Although Mussolini had attempted to stamp out the Sicilian mafia in the 1920s, it managed to endure his brutal methods. The Americans decided to get the US mafia to help facilitate the landings through its connections on the island. They turned to crime boss Charles 'Lucky' Luciano, who was serving time in New York, to reach out. Vito Genovese, another New York thug, would turn up in Sicily as a US military liaison officer. Worst of all, Don Calogero Vizzini, the unofficial head of the Sicilian mafia, was waiting in the wings to take over the administration of the island with the Americans' blessing.

Cunningham and the other naval commanders anticipated that the Italian fleet would not interfere. Nonetheless, regular reconnaissance flights were conducted over Genoa, to keep an eye on the Italian cruisers, La Spezia, which was hosting the Littorio battleships, and Taranto, home to the Cavour class battleships. Allied torpedo-bombers were placed on standby just in case. They need not have worried. 'I had lost all faith that the Italian Navy would carry out any of the plans prepared for different eventualities,'[9] said Kesselring with resignation. The Italian naval commander in Sicily was Rear Admiral Pietro Barone, but he had little in the way of resources and his main role was fortress commandant of the Messina-Reggio area.

For *Husky*, the Allies gathered 150,000 troops, 1,000 guns, 600 tanks and more than 2,500 vessels. Just before the invasion, Cunningham, commander-in-chief of the vast armada, signalled to all his ships' captains: 'We are about to embark on the most momentous enterprise of the war – striking for the first time at the enemy in his own land.'[10] The airborne and seaborne assault on Sicily commenced on 9/10 July 1943. The airborne drops by the US 82nd and British 1st Airborne divisions did not go well. These were larger and much more ambitious than the modest operations conducted against French North Africa, involving 400 transports and 137 gliders. This aerial armada was fired on by Allied warships and many of the gliders crashed into the sea.

The defenders knew exactly what to expect after the terrible treatment of Pantelleria. Allied warships and fighter-bombers pounded Italian coastal defences, both in the invasion area and elsewhere. The British and American landings swiftly succeeded in creating bridgeheads. Inland, Italian resistance just seemed to vanish. Lieutenant Alan Whicker observed: 'The Italian defences in our sector seemed admirably sited. Their pillboxes commanded excellent fields of fire, were strongly constructed and most had underground chambers full of ammunition ... All sites were deserted: their crews had melted away.'[11] Elsewhere, the Italian coastal and regular army divisions began to surrender. Where the Italians did conduct counter-attacks, they were lacklustre and beaten back with the help of naval gunfire.

Guzzoni launched an unco-ordinated counter-attack against the American landings on 11 July involving the Livorno and Hermann Göring divisions. The Italian attacks towards Gela were repelled, with a battalion from the Livorno being decimated, in part thanks to poor training. Although Italian light tanks got into the town, the Americans hunted them down using bazookas, grenades and even TNT, which they dropped from the rooftops. The Germans, with armour support, penetrated the Gela plain before they were also stopped. Their tanks struggled to manoeuvre in the terraced olive groves and were forced to withdraw in the face of the Allies' firepower. The powerful German Tiger tank, first encountered in Tunisia, once again proved it was no wonder weapon.

There was some talk about Mussolini flying to the island to inspire the defenders. 'It would be grave if for a move of this kind the Duce should lose his life or be captured,' King Victor Emmanuel said to General Paolo Puntoni, 'though the thing would facilitate the solution of many important questions.'[12] Mussolini, not one to lead from the front, decided against the idea.

When Hitler heard of the assault on Sicily he halted his ill-advised Kursk offensive. This was because he wanted to immediately send reinforcements to Italy, but also it enabled him to save face, as he knew that he simply could not win at Kursk. He also ordered Rommel to prepare secret plans for a military takeover in Italy.

Two days after the landings, Kesselring authorized Lieutenant-General Richard Heidrich's 1st Parachute Division to be flown in as reinforcements. He then personally flew to Sicily to assess the situation. His view was that there was little point in trying to hold the western part of the island. They would be better off anchoring the defence around the towering heights of Mount Etna. Arriving in northern Sicily by flying boat, Kesselring told General Hans-Valentin Hube, commander of the XIV Panzer Corps, to hold at all costs. Although Kesselring paid lip service to this being an Italian-run defence, he knew it fell to him and Hube to safeguard their men.

At 1815 hours on 12 July, Heidrich's advance guard, in the shape of 1,400 men of the 3rd Parachute Regiment, parachuted into Sicily. The following day, Kesselring got Mussolini and Hitler's approval for his plans, plus permission to deploy the 29th Panzergrenadier Division. On 14 and 16 July, Allied bombers tried to destroy the Messina ferry service. They sank three steamers, but this did not stop the Italian and German troop movements. Kesselring was also grateful that Eisenhower did not launch a simultaneous attack on Calabria on the Italian mainland. He knew that his reinforcements would be sufficient to cover the German withdrawal when the time came.

IL DUCE'S DOWNFALL

Mussolini's fate was sealed by the fighting in Sicily, which triggered a political crisis in Rome. The writing was already on the wall for him after the surrender of the Axis forces in Tunisia. His generals and opposition leaders rapidly began to plot his downfall. On 5 July, Ambrosio held a meeting with, among others, Badoglio and King Victor Emmanuel. They agreed Mussolini had to go, but they did not know when to move against him for fear of how the Fascists and the Germans might react. Ambrosio saw the king again four days after the Allied landings commenced in Sicily. Time was running out for the Duce.

Mussolini held a meeting with Hitler at Feltre, not far from the Italian border with Austria, on 19 July. Hitler vented his anger, blaming Axis failures in North Africa and the Mediterranean on Italian ineptitude. During the meeting, Mussolini was informed that Allied bombers had hit Rome for the first time. At midday, Ambrosio informed Mussolini he must tell Hitler that Italy needed to make peace. The general warned Mussolini that if he did not do so then Ambrosio would order the Italian armed forces to cease fire within 15 days. Instead, Hitler promised that the defence of Italy was a priority and Mussolini missed his chance. Ambrosio knew he must act.

Within a week of the landings, General Patton's US 7th Army had overrun western Sicily. The Americans captured some 45,000 Italian soldiers and Palermo fell on 22 July. The scar-faced General Giuseppe Molinaro simply surrendered the city without a fight at 1900 hours that night. Montgomery's 8th Army faced a tougher slog in the east, pushing north towards Catania and Mount Etna. British troops took until 5 August to enter Catania. Kesselring was highly critical of the Allies' failure to encircle his troops on the island or seal the Straits of Messina to cut off his inevitable retreat.

In Rome, Mussolini was summoned by the king on 25 July. 'My dear Duce, it's no longer any good,' said Victor Emmanuel solemnly, 'Italy has gone to bits … The soldiers don't want to fight any more … At this moment you are the most hated man in Italy…'[13] The night before, Mussolini had been deposed by a specially convened meeting of the Fascist Grand Council. He had taken no notice. In a fury, he turned to his Fascist colleagues and said: 'The session is over. Gentlemen, you have provoked the crisis of the regime.'[14] He could not accept that the crisis was of his own making.

Now, Mussolini was sacked by Italy's monarch and arrested. He was dumbfounded, as he naively thought he could ride out this latest political storm. Instead, he was driven under armed guard to a police station in an ambulance. Italy's modern-day Roman Caesar had ignominiously fallen from power without a shot being fired. Mussolini claimed that his monarch tried to be conciliatory, saying: 'You will always be deemed Italy's greatest son, and I shall always call you cousin!'[15] His parting words to the king were a warning: 'You are making an extremely grave decision.'[16] He was right: the war would go on in the Mediterranean, with or without him.

Twenty-one years of Fascist dictatorship vanished overnight. The new government, under Badoglio, did not include a single member of Mussolini's Fascist Party. It was not long before they were secretly negotiating with the Allies in an effort to get out of the war.

THE AXIS WITHDRAWAL

When Hitler was informed of Mussolini's incarceration he was furious. He did not trust Badoglio's claims that Italy would remain loyal to the German cause. General Jodl, Hitler's chief of operations, urged caution, but the Führer knew the situation called for decisive action before Germany's southern flank in the Mediterranean became completely unhinged. Rommel, who had just arrived in Greece to inspect the four German divisions, was immediately summoned to Rastenburg.

The Axis evacuation of Sicily officially commenced on 11 August. In reality, both Kesselring and Guzzoni had started the process much sooner. Kesselring was determined to avoid a repeat of the disastrous losses suffered in Tunisia. 'The fact that I was for a long time *persona ingrata* because I took the decision to evacuate Sicily on my own initiative,' said Kesselring, 'did not trouble me unduly in view of the successful military withdrawal from the island.'[17] The job of overseeing the German escape fell to Colonel Ernst-Günther Baade, who had been appointed commandant of the Messina Strait. Some 235 anti-aircraft guns were deployed either side to protect the vulnerable ferries, a number of which were converted into floating flak ships. Batteries of heavy German and Italian guns were also deployed on the coast.

Just after the Allies landed, the Germans had begun withdrawing non-essential staff to Calabria. Then, when Patton began to push on Palermo, equipment and stores were removed, though in the case of Palermo just 100 tons were saved. When the German ferries returned to the harbour, four were sunk by Allied fighter-bombers. Most of western Sicily was overrun so quickly that very little could be saved and 10,000 tons of fuel were lost.

Guzzoni first ordered Admiral Barone to commence evacuating Italian personnel on 3 August. He gathered the only remaining train ferry, the *Villa*, and two steamers, which got across 7,000 men before Rome gave the green light eight days later. When the *Villa* broke down, the Italian Navy deployed ten motor rafts and another steamer to keep everything moving. As the German and Italian troops withdrew, so their front contracted, allowing men to be released to head for Messina and other ports. The anti-aircraft guns and coastal batteries on either side of the straits successfully helped to keep Allied aircraft and warships at bay. Three British motor torpedo boats tried to interfere on the first night of the authorized evacuation. They attacked six small craft with machine guns and torpedoes, chasing them into Messina. This, though, was a risky exercise and four days later, the British lost a motor torpedo boat after it was caught by the shore batteries.

Patton's forces captured the flattened city of Randazzo on 13 August, but they were still 50 miles (80 km) from Messina. Montgomery was held up at Gerbina long enough for Patton to beat him to Messina three days later. Barone had rescued 62,000 men by midday on 16 August thanks to the Italian Navy, which lost six minesweepers, 15 landing barges and many other small craft in the process. General Guzzoni escaped to the mainland and was later charged with treason, but was spared the firing squad after German commanders argued he had done all he could to hold the island. The Germans completed the process at dawn the following day, having ferried over 40,000 men plus almost 15,000 casualties. Remarkably, they also retrieved 18,665 tons of supplies, almost 10,000 vehicles, 163 guns and 51 tanks.

Kesselring left behind about 5,000 dead and 6,600 captured. Despite the evacuation, Guzzoni essentially lost the bulk of his army, with 137,000 men captured. Italian casualties amounted to 2,000 killed and 5,000 wounded. Among the prisoners was General Giulio Porcinari, commander of the Italian Napoli Division, which had been decimated by mass defections. The battle for Sicily cost Patton 3,000 dead or missing and 6,000 wounded. Montgomery lost 5,000 killed or missing and 7,000 wounded. The Royal Navy suffered 314 killed and 411 wounded. The US Navy lost 546 dead and 484 wounded.

Among the Allies, there were immediately recriminations over who was responsible for letting so many Axis troops escape. On the whole, the Allied chain of command had not helped. General Spaatz, in charge of the Northwest African Strategic Air Force, was preoccupied with bombing Rome and other mainland targets. Air Vice-Marshal Coningham, commanding the Northwest Tactical Air Force, did what he could in the face of intense flak, but the naval forces failed to put in place a maritime barrier. Admiral Cunningham, with good reason, was loath to risk exposing his warships to the enemy's artillery, mines and torpedoes. Despite this, yet another Axis stronghold in the Mediterranean had been overcome. 'Our last pictures of the Sicilian campaign showed Generals Eisenhower and Montgomery,' recalled Lieutenant Whicker, 'staring symbolically through field glasses out across the Straits of Messina towards the toe of Italy, and the enemy.'[18]

CHAPTER 14:
Il Duce Resurrected

AFTER THE fall of Mussolini, his country's fate hung in the balance. Had Badoglio acted swiftly and decisively he could have sealed the border and cut off the German units in Italy. Italian engineers prepared the Brenner Pass for demolition and if they had blown the vital rail link it could have been severed for at least six months. However, defecting took time and Badoglio first had to establish contact with the Allies and agree terms for an armistice before he could act against his new foe. Six vital weeks were to be wasted – leaving Italy vulnerable to German occupation.

Hitler knew the Italians were wavering in their commitment to the Axis and that he needed to secure Rome and the Balkans against the Allies. Kesselring, with very few forces, was to pressure the Italians into disarming without even firing a shot. Just two days after Mussolini's fall, Hitler held an emergency meeting to discuss four options, which got progressively more ambitious. The first simply envisaged an airborne or maritime mission to rescue Mussolini; the second called for the seizure of Rome in order to reinstate Mussolini; the third proposed the complete occupation of Italy and the fourth planned for the capture or destruction of the Italian fleet. The latter was particularly important, because if Italy's warships sided with the Allies they would pose a threat to the German position in the Aegean and the Balkans. It was eventually decided that the last two military options would to be combined under the ironic code name *Axis*. Ultimately, it would need a combination of all these options to get the Italians back in line.

Initially, Hitler, far from reassured by Italian platitudes, ranted:

We'll play the same game while preparing everything to take over the whole crew with one stroke, to capture all that riffraff. Tomorrow I'll send a man down there with orders for the commander of the 3rd Panzergrenadier Division to the effect that he must drive into Rome with a special detail and arrest the whole government, the king and the whole bunch right away. First of all, arrest the Crown Prince and take over the whole gang, especially Badoglio, and that entire crew. Then watch them cave in, and in two or three days there'll be another coup.[1]

Fearing the worst, Hitler began to draft a directive outlining the occupation of Italy and all her overseas possessions. This was never issued, but on 31 July a series of orders were sent out instructing commanders what to do if the Italians dropped out of the war. Although Hitler was dissuaded from putting troops on to the streets of Rome, he swiftly secured the Alpine passes between Germany and Italy and between Italy and France. To rescue those German forces in Italy and Sicily, eight divisions were assembled from France and southern Germany under Field Marshal Rommel.

Rommel, rather than occupy all of Italy, drew up plans for a defensive line in the Apennines well north of Rome. Hitler was determined to hold the Italian capital and Kesselring was confident that he could do so. On 1 August 1943, Hitler's forces rolled over the border prepared for possible resistance. In the event, the only casualties were two Tiger tanks, which did not like the concrete roads; one overturned and another caught fire. The Italians could not miss what was going on and part of an Italian Alpine division was deployed to Milan, but with only ten rounds per man. According to the German intelligence, the Italian Army was suffering acute ammunition shortages. Rommel was not surprised; he already had a low opinion of Italian weapons' factories after his experience with the ill-resourced Italian Army in North Africa.

'General Feuerstein reports that a critical situation developed on the Brenner about midday yesterday,' recorded Rommel in his diary, adding, 'when the Italians tried to hold up the advance of 44th Infantry Division. General Gloria had given orders for fire to be opened if 44th Division attempted to continue their march.'[2] Fortunately, the Italian troops on the ground chose not to obey and instead withdrew. The Italians concentrated some 60,000 men in the Verona-Bolzano area, but in the face of elements of the 1st SS Panzer Division, which crossed the Brenner Pass on 3 August, chose not to commit them. Belatedly, the Italians moved elements of three divisions – the Alpine, Julia and Trentina – towards the Brenner. The road to the Italian Naval base at La Spezia was also blocked.

On 9 August, Rommel wrote to his wife: 'The situation with these unreliable Italians is extremely unpleasant. To our faces they protest their truest loyalty to the common cause, and yet they create all kinds of difficulties for us and at the back of it all seem to be negotiating.'₃ The rest of the 1st SS Panzer together with 25th Panzer and the 65th Infantry divisions passed through the Brenner Pass on 14 August and deployed to the Verona area. Kesselring also became alarmed by the news that the Italians were withdrawing their occupation forces from southern France and moving two divisions from southern Italy to the north.

Rommel on 15 August travelled to Bologna to discuss the situation with General Roatta, chief of staff of the Italian Army. To his consternation, intelligence indicated that the Italians planned to either poison him or have him arrested. In response, he ordered his men to secure the conference building beforehand. Roatta claimed the withdrawal of Italian troops from southern France was to help fight the British and that the Alpine division had moved north to resume garrison duties. He confirmed a second division had moved north to secure the railways from sabotage. Roatta dismissed any ideas that these refitting formations were in any way a threat to German interests.

Roatta reiterated that the defence of Italy must be left to the Italian Army, though the Germans could assume responsibility for air defence. He tried to get rid of the 1st SS Panzer by suggesting it be sent to Sardinia in case of invasion. He also suggested that other German units should be moved into southern Italy and thereby away from Rome. The meeting ended without agreement and the following day an Italian delegation approached the British Ambassador in Madrid – offering Italy's unconditional surrender.

THE GERMANS MOVE IN

That month, a total of seven German divisions crossed the frontier. In central Italy, the German 10th Army was activated, able to call on five divisions and another two deployed near Rome. Up until the end of the Sicilian campaign and the successful escape of four German divisions, Hitler only had two divisions covering the whole of southern Italy. The Badoglio regime were not pleased about the presence of these German troops and General Siegfried Westphal, Kesselring's chief of staff, spent a great deal of time trying to smooth things over. Badoglio, though, had missed his chance.

By September, the Italian Army had 21 divisions on the mainland, although half of these were of poor quality and not fit for combat, four in Sardinia and another 36 overseas. To fend off a German occupation of northern and central Italy, the Italians had eight infantry and two motorized/armoured divisions, supported by another eight weak infantry divisions. Against these forces, Kesselring could field about 16 battle-hardened divisions.

After securing Sicily, the Allies attacked mainland Italy at Reggio, Salerno and Taranto. Had the Allied invasion fleet, gathered off Naples on 8 September, sailed north and landed troops near Rome, the Italian Army would probably have used its remaining tanks against the Germans and Hitler would have abandoned Kesselring's seven divisions. Instead, fate took a cruel hand and the US 5th Army landed not near the Italian capital but at Salerno, south of Naples.

Following the Italian armistice on 9 September, Hitler issued the code word 'Axis'. He had intended to capture the Italian fleet, but most of the major surface vessels were already on their way south from Genoa, La Spezia, Taranto and the other Italian naval bases to Malta. Churchill instructed Cunningham that they should be: 'received in [a] kindly and generous manner'.[4] The Germans did what they could to intercept them. Thus the unfortunate Admiral Carlo Bergamini and his flagship *Roma*, along with 1,400 crew, were immediately lost to the Luftwaffe employing glider-bombs. A cruiser and three destroyers rescued the survivors and rather than risk the wrath of the Luftwaffe again, headed west for the Balearic Islands. Upon reaching port Mahón, the crews of two of the destroyers decided to scuttle their warships, rather than have them interned by the Spanish.

In the meantime, the battleship *Italia* suffered damage after being torpedoed, but managed to escape towards Malta. The elderly destroyer *Audace* departed Trieste, but developed engine troubles and was seized by the Germans in Venice harbour. The battleship *Giulio Cesare* and her destroyer escort escaped from Venice to reach Malta. The cruiser *Gorizia*, which had been undergoing major repairs, was taken by the Germans along with the damaged *Bolzano* at La Spezia. The *Taranto*, another non-operational cruiser at La Spezia, was scuttled by her crew.

Now under Admiral Alberto Da Zara, the operational backbone of the Italian Navy – comprising two battleships, five cruisers and four destroyers – pressed on for Malta. They were greeted by their old adversaries, including *Warspite*, *Valiant* and *Illustrious*, on 10 September and escorted to the island. It was a historic moment for *Warspite*, as the old warhorse had been at Scapa Flow in 1918 when the German fleet surrendered. Admiral Cunningham and General Eisenhower sailed from Bizerta aboard the destroyer *Hambledon* and took great joy in touring the combined fleets. The Italian battleships and cruisers were gathered outside Grand Harbour. Da Zara came ashore to be greeted by a full naval guard of honour and was then taken to see Cunningham.

By the end of the day, other flotillas arrived, bringing the total up to 27 Italian vessels, which included four battleships, seven cruisers, ten destroyers, four submarines and other smaller craft. The following morning, Cunningham signalled the Admiralty: 'The Italian battle fleet now lies at anchor under the guns of the fortress of Malta.'₅ It seemed a fitting tribute to the island's defiance. Among the cruisers was the *Raimondo Montecuccoli*, which Eric Newby had sensibly declined to attack with a manned torpedo back in 1941. Subsequently, two battleships, two cruisers and a destroyer arrived from Taranto. Some of the Italian warships were thereafter sent to Alexandria to join the Allied war effort. By the end of the month, 21 submarines had also surrendered at the island.

Meanwhile, General Westphal, trying to reach Roatta at Monte Rotondo, found himself obstructed by Italian troops. Fearing something was wrong, he insisted on seeing Roatta, who upon arrival informed him that Italy had signed an armistice with the Allies. Westphal, returning to Frascati, acted quickly and with more aggression than Kesselring would have liked. He called a meeting with the officers of General Carboni's Corps, which was responsible for the defence of Rome. Westphal told them, having served alongside them in North Africa, that he was very sorry that they were no longer comrades in arms. He then got to the point: either they lay down their weapons or they would be subjected to dive-bomber attack. To support his threat, Field Marshal von Richthofen had 80 aircraft at his disposal in Italy. The next day, an Italian officer signed the surrender order for the Carboni Corps. Kesselring and Westphal had achieved a bloodless coup.

Rommel, writing to his wife on 10 September 1943, said with genuine regret:

The events in Italy have, of course, long been expected and the very situation has now arisen which we have done all we could to avoid. In the south, Italian troops are already fighting alongside the British against us. Up north, Italian troops are being disarmed for the present and sent as prisoners to Germany. What a shameful end for an army![6]

German units moved to occupy key points and installations throughout Italy, as well as Italian positions in southern France, the Balkans and the Aegean. Hitler took possession of two-thirds of Italy, including the industrial north, where factories were soon put to work producing arms for the German war effort. Everywhere, demoralized Italian troops were disarmed almost without firing a shot and their weapons confiscated. The Italian Army handed over all its equipment, except in Albania, where a whole division joined the partisans rather than surrender to the Germans. Hitler only managed to retain about half of Yugoslavia and the partisans seized considerable quantities of weapons. 'Our units had disarmed two Italian armies and liberated practically the entire coast,' recalled Milovan Djilas, one of Tito's key partisan commanders, with satisfaction. 'The booty in weapons, food, and motorized vehicles exceeded all imagination, if not all hope.'[7]

These unfolding events immediately put Allied prisoners being held in Italy in an unpleasant position. 'I absconded in order to avoid being sent to Germany,' said Eric Newby, 'as did thousands of other prisoners-of-war in camps all over Italy.'[8] He had been held for a year after being caught in Sicily in August 1942, where he was involved in a raid on a Luftwaffe airfield. Thanks to the kindness of local people, he remained on the run in the Apennines until he was caught by the Fascist militia in early 1944. Just as he had feared all along, he was shipped to a camp in Germany.

Hitler's occupation of Italy was swift and efficient, as Churchill records:

The Germans clamped down their military occupation upon the regions lying north of Rome; a skeleton Administration of uncertain allegiance sat in Rome, now open to the movements of the German Army; at Brindisi the King and Badoglio set up a rump Government under the eyes of an Allied Commission and with no effective authority beyond the boundaries of the administrative building of the town. As our armies advanced from the toe of the peninsula Allied military government took over the task of controlling the liberated regions.

Italy was now to pass through the most tragic time in her history and to become the battle-ground of some of the fiercest fighting in the war.[9]

THE BATTLE FOR THE AEGEAN

In light of Hitler's defeat at El Alamein, the subsequent *Torch* landings and expulsion from North Africa and Sicily, he must have been highly relieved that he had stabilized such a disastrous situation. In the Aegean, things went particularly badly for the Allies, where an ineffectual campaign was fought to try to prevent the German takeover.

Hitler appreciated that he needed to occupy Crete and Rhodes as this would maintain his dominance of the Aegean, as well as giving him a foothold in the eastern Mediterranean. In addition, taking Rhodes would reassure Turkey, which although neutral was pro-Nazi, that it was business as usual despite the defection of Italy. He was certain that with the British and Americans committed to attacking Italy, they would not have the resources to launch a major operation elsewhere in the Mediterranean.

Churchill had wanted to secure Rhodes in mid-September, but there was not the shipping available to transport the earmarked forces. These were to have consisted of an infantry division, supported by an armoured brigade and a parachute drop at Marizza airfield. Instead, penny-packets of troops and aircraft were deployed to various other islands in a futile attempt to pre-empt Hitler. Churchill and General Wilson overplayed their weak hand and paid the consequences.

Governor Campioni had a garrison of 35,000 men in Rhodes, facing General Ulrich Kleemann's 8,000 German troops, which were supported by armoured cars, self-propelled guns, tanks and the Luftwaffe. They were mainly located around the town of Rhodes, with artillery dominating the two main approach roads and the port. This left Campioni effectively a prisoner in his own headquarters. The scattered Italian units lacked transport, so were unable to concentrate. Kleemann's forces acted quickly to take the three main airfields and other key positions on 9 September 1943. Only at Marizza were they met by Italian artillery fire.

Lacking guidance from Rome, Campioni dithered, uncertain what to do. He did not want his men massacred by their former allies. The following day, Campioni learned that the Italian forces in Crete and Greece had surrendered to the Germans. This meant he could expect no help from them and was therefore on his own. At this point, a small British delegation, under Major Jellico, arrived by parachute to ask Campioni to side with the Allies. Campioni enquired what forces were available to assist him. When advised that Allied help would be very limited, Campioni argued his men were unable to fend off Kleemann's superior firepower. The British then withdrew to a neighbouring island. Kleemann duly seized full control of Rhodes on 11 September and Campioni's men laid down their arms. Tragically, 6,000 Italian prisoners were subsequently drowned while being transported to Greece.

Kleemann also attacked the scattered British outposts. He invaded Cos, overrunning the RAF base there, taking 600 British prisoners and 2,500 Italians. Leros and Samos suffered similar fates, both of which had British and Italian garrisons. In the case of Leros, this comprised three British infantry battalions and 5,000 Italians. 'Once again our forces were fighting without adequate air cover, as in Norway, Greece and Crete,' wrote L. Marsland Gander, a British correspondent, who witnessed the assault on Leros involving German paratroops. 'This time, however, it was not a shortage of aircraft pilots which brought about such a disastrous situation,' he added, 'but merely the geography and the distance of our nearest fighter bases from the scene of the action.'[10] Vice-Admiral Sir Algernon Willis, commander-in-chief in the Levant, agreed: 'We failed because we were unable to establish air fields in the areas of operations.'[11]

During these operations, the Royal Navy, trying to support the isolated garrisons, needlessly endured considerable losses at the hands of the Luftwaffe. 'They achieved considerable success against the enemy and held off the attack on Leros for some time,' said Vice-Admiral Willis, 'but not without heavy casualties to our own forces.'[12] Before the fall of Cos, two destroyers were sunk, and by the end of October, three more were lost and four cruisers and two destroyers damaged. It seemed as if nothing had been learned from the battle for Crete. One of the cruiser captains later remarked bitterly that it was: 'the most pointless campaign of the war'.[13]

AN ATTEMPT AT A FASCIST REVIVAL

Back in Italy, Hitler's next move was to locate and 'rescue' Mussolini. For this job, he called on his tough fixer SS-Sturmbannführer Otto Skorzeny. After his arrest, Mussolini had been sent to an island off Ponza. He was then moved to La Maddalen off the coast of Sardinia. Fearing the Germans might try to free the fallen Duce, Badoglio decided to hold him somewhere inaccessible. At the end of August, Mussolini therefore found himself at a mountain resort up in the Abruzzi in central Italy.

To rescue Mussolini, a force consisting of German paratroops and SS was put together, which would be transported in a dozen gliders. They were successful. Dramatically, on 12 September, Mussolini was snatched from the Hotel Campo Imperatore, 100 miles (106 km) from Rome. Skorzeny's glider landed right in the hotel grounds, disgorging his Waffen-SS commandos and an Italian general. The Carabinieri guarding Mussolini were unsure what to do, so some simply fled, while others faced the quandary of whether or not to open fire on an Italian general or indeed their former leader. At the behest of Skorzeny and Mussolini, they decided to surrender. Mussolini was in a sorry state according to Skorzeny: 'He looked very ill, an impression intensified by the fact that he was unshaven and his usually smooth, powerful head was covered with short, stubbly hair.'[14]

Skorzeny escorted the former dictator to a small plane and he was flown to Rome and then on to Munich. 'I never realized that the Italian royal house was, and would remain, my enemy,'[15] lamented Mussolini during the flight. A few days later, he arrived at Rastenburg to meet his saviour. While he was full of gratitude, Hitler was displeased to find his one-time ally less than enthusiastic about his plans to revive Fascism in northern Italy. It seemed the fall of Il Duce could not be reversed. Mussolini had no desire to return to politics and felt Fascism was beyond help. 'Northern Italy will be forced to envy the fate of Poland,' Hitler threatened, 'if you do not accept to give renewed vigour to the alliance between Germany and Italy, by becoming head of state and of the new government.'[16]

The disillusioned Mussolini thus found himself the quisling ruler of his occupied homeland, the so-called Socialist Republic of Italy or Repubblica Sociale Italiana. In reality, all he wanted to do was spend time with his mistress while his country went to ruin. When Mussolini flew home on 23 September, Hitler would not permit him to set up his new government in Rome. Instead, he became effectively a prisoner at Gargnano on the banks of Lake Garda. There he was 'advised' by the German ambassador Rudolf von Rahn and SS-General Karl Wolff, who was in control of internal security. Conspicuously, Mussolini's guard comprised not Italians but an SS battalion.

Marshal Badoglio sailed from Taranto, on the cruiser *Scipio Africano*, and arrived at Malta on 29 September for a face-to-face meeting with the Allies. Aboard the battleship *Nelson*, he was welcomed by Eisenhower, Cunningham, Alexander, Tedder and Lord Gort, the island's governor. Together, they discussed the future of Allied-Italian co-operation in the Mediterranean. For the Allies, it must have felt like poetic justice. In the meantime, the Allied landings at Salerno on the Italian mainland had met determined German resistance. It was evident that Italy would not be wrestled from Hitler's grasp as swiftly as some had hoped.

The armistice did not have a happy outcome for the Italian people and resulted in a bloody civil war. Churchill noted:

> Mussolini's bid for a Fascist revival plunged Italy into the horrors of civil war. In the weeks following the September armistice officers and men of the Italian Army stationed in German-occupied Northern Italy and Patriots from the towns and countryside began to form Partisan units and to operate against the Germans and their compatriots who still adhered to the Duce.[17]

Kesselring had a very easy solution to this problem. The 150,000-strong Guardia Nazionale Repubblicana (GNR) was established by the Germans in early December 1943 to maintain order behind the front line. Kesselring was not foolish enough to allow Mussolini's new armed forces to have significant numbers of tanks. Instead, the GNR Combattente had a single armoured battalion; similarly, only two armoured groups equipped with some Italian medium tanks supported the four new divisions of Mussolini's revived army. This totalled 400,000 and with the GNR was restricted to fighting Italian resistance groups. Along with the SS, they would wage a brutal and horrific campaign.

Churchill became fixated on following up the Allied victories in the Mediterranean by attacking the Germans in Italy and the Balkans. He felt this strategy should be given priority over opening a second front in France. However, by early October, Hitler had reinforced his forces in Italy with 27,000 troops withdrawn from Corsica and Sardinia. Kesselring had managed to keep the Allies at bay and disarm the Italian Army at the same time. He then brought the invaders to a halt 100 miles (160 km) from Rome. Eight months were to pass before the Allies reached the Italian capital and it would take another eight months before they managed to break out into the plains of northern Italy. Any aspirations Churchill harboured about attacking Germany from the Mediterranean floundered in the face of Hitler's tough Italian defences.

CHAPTER 15:
Air, Sea and Land

BY 1944, the Allies still had unfinished business in the Mediterranean as the Germans remained entrenched in northern Italy, southern France and the Balkans. Hitler had 55 divisions tied down in the Mediterranean, with almost half of them in Italy. General Alexander was very pleased by this state of affairs, noting: 'There can be no doubt at all that the indirect effect of our menacing position in Italy resulted in this diversion of Germany's limited strength to guard her Balkan flank.'₁

Allied success against the Axis forces had gathered momentum following victory in North Africa, the capture of Sicily and the subsequent invasion of southern Italy. That year, the proposed invasion of southern France, initially dubbed Operation *Anvil* (then *Dragoon*), emerged to support Operation *Hammer* (which later became *Overlord*) – the attack on northern France. The idea was to prevent German forces moving north to oppose the cross-Channel invasion.

Stalin also pressed for an attack on southern France, as he wanted the Allies distracted from the Balkans so that the Red Army would have a free hand to crush Hitler's east European Axis allies and secure Yugoslavia. It was he who gained both Churchill and Roosevelt's undertaking for *Anvil* at their Tehran Conference in 1943. Churchill and the British chiefs of staff really wanted all military resources directed to opening the Second Front in Normandy and continuing the fight in Italy. In late February 1944, Eisenhower got agreement for continued planning on *Anvil* by the Combined Chiefs of Staff and approval by Roosevelt and Churchill.

However, Churchill saw this as a waste of effort, needlessly drawing troops and equipment from Italy. There was also some concern that German troops in Italy might strike west at the *Anvil* forces' eastern flank. The British argued that resources would be better committed to Italy, which would enable a decisive thrust up the Italian peninsula, through Austria and into southern Germany – an action that would render both *Anvil* and even *Overlord* unnecessary. The Americans argued that geography and logistics were against such a plan; crossing the English Channel meant shorter lines of communication and a line of advance that was not obstructed by the troublesome Alps.

To General Wilson, British theatre commander in the Mediterranean, the American preoccupation with France's southern ports seemed to imply a strategy aimed at defeating Germany during the first half of 1945 at the cost of an opportunity of defeating her before the end of 1944. Wilson warned the British chiefs of staff that a diversion of forces for *Anvil* would cause a pause of offensive operations in the Mediterranean of six months and allow the Germans to establish themselves strongly in Italy along their Pisa-Rimini Gothic Line.

Likewise, Hitler saw the Italian front as the key. Holding on there helped reduce Allied air attacks on his factories in central Europe and protected the vital raw materials of the Balkans. In contrast, southern France was of no strategic value to him as the Mediterranean was already lost. A withdrawal from there would surrender nothing of strategic or economic value and would give the Allies airbases no nearer to his war industries than they already possessed. His U-boat bases on the Bay of Biscay were no longer of any utility and the disruption of the French railways had already curtailed what raw materials he got from France and Spain.

Field Marshal Gerd von Rundstedt, commander-in-chief in the west, expected an Allied invasion of northern France soon after three Panzer divisions rolled into neutral Vichy France. Rundstedt's forces were divided into two Army Groups, the strongest of which was in the north under Rommel holding Belgium and northern France. To the south, General Johannes Blaskowitz's Army Group G, with his headquarters in Toulouse, consisted of General Kurt von der Chevallerie's 1st and General Friedrich Wiese's 19th armies. These totalled 17 divisions stationed on the Biscay and Riviera coasts respectively. Wiese was based at Avignon north-west of Marseilles.

The key armoured formations were the 11th Panzer and the 17th SS Panzergrenadier divisions under Chevallerie, and the 2nd SS Das Reich and 9th Panzer divisions under Weise. The latter desperately needed a refit and had been sent to southern France in March, where it was strengthened by a reserve Panzer division. There were in fact only four infantry divisions of any note in the whole of southern France; the rest were refitting or forming.

The Allies ran a series of deception operations in the Mediterranean designed to mislead Hitler as to the true strength of Allied forces in the region, and to convince him that they would attack Crete or western Greece, or Romania via the Black Sea. Churchill was in favour of thrusting into the Balkans, partly to forestall Stalin's plans; years later, Eisenhower was to concede that this should have been their course of action. In the meantime, the Allies won a pyrrhic victory in Italy.

ALLIED 'VICTORY' IN ITALY

General Clark's 5th Army liberated Rome on 4 June 1944 and in doing so allowed Kesselring's 10th and 14th armies to escape. 'If he had succeeded in carrying out my plan the disaster to the enemy would have been much greater,' observed General Alexander diplomatically. 'Indeed, most of the German forces south of Rome would have been destroyed.'[2] Others were much less generous. 'Clark's vainglorious blunder, the worst of the entire War in my experience,' said Lieutenant Whicker, who was in Rome to photograph the event, 'lost us a stunning victory, lengthened the war by many months, cost numberless lives and earned Mark Clark the amazed contempt of other American and British Generals.'[3] Alexander concluded: 'I can only assume that the immediate lure of Rome for its publicity value persuaded him to switch the direction of his advance.'[4]

Alexander's aim, perhaps naively optimistic, was to deliver a decisive blow against Kesselring in the Mediterranean before the opening of the long-awaited Second Front in France. He instructed Clark to strike northeast from the Anzio bridgehead towards Valmontone and the retreating Germans, rather than directly north towards the Italian capital. This it was hoped would sever the Via Casilina and trap the German 10th Army between the rest of Clark's 5th Army pushing up from the south. It could also have enabled Clark to encircle Rome with a right hook and potentially cut off the 14th Army. In light of the mountainous terrain and Kesselring's tough defence, Clark was sceptical this could be achieved. Furthermore, the Via Casilina was just one of five main routes the Germans were using to escape.

Controversially, Clark opted to attack in both directions from Anzio, hoping to destroy the 14th Army on the road to Rome. The result was that the Allies mauled both Kesselring's armies, but failed to destroy the 10th as Alexander had intended. Although Clark's actions did not help matters, the British 8th Army's slow progress up the Liri Valley permitted the 10th to withdraw to the north-east. Kesselring was thus able to conduct a fighting retreat to the defences of the Gothic Line, which stretched from Viareggio on the west coast to Rimini on the east.

Although Rome had been declared an open city the previous year, Mussolini wanted it defended to the last. Kesselring, however, had no intention of holding it and on 3 June received permission to evacuate. Even Hitler agreed that Rome was a 'place of culture' and should not become the 'scene of combat operations'.₅ Clark, thanks to work at Bletchley Park, was well aware of this decision. For Mussolini, the loss of Rome was yet another humiliation, especially as he was not consulted over its fate. When he heard the news, by way of mourning, he demanded that all bars, cinemas, restaurants and theatres shut for three days. Few Italians took much notice.

Despite the acrimony among the Allies, Kesselring's defence south of Rome was successfully overcome. He suffered 50,000 killed, wounded and captured, which were irreplaceable. The Allies lost almost 44,000 men. Clark, in justifying his actions, stated that Roosevelt had personally ordered him to liberate the Italian capital before D-Day. Ultimately, his headline-grabbing antics were a waste of time, because two days later they were completely overshadowed by the opening of the Second Front.

OPERATION *DRAGOON*

The invasion in Normandy on 6 June 1944 quickly impacted on Blaskowitz's command and many of his units were ordered north. The day after D-Day, the 17th SS Panzergrenadier Division received instructions to head for Normandy. General Heinz Lammerding, commanding the 2nd SS Panzer Division, was also ordered to Normandy, but his forces were already bogged down fighting the French resistance. On 27 July, 9th Panzer was put on notice to be ready to march north from the Avignon area. By 1 August, 9th Panzer and six infantry divisions of varying quality were heading for the Normandy battlefield, as it was clear that the American Operation *Cobra* represented a very real threat.

At the end of June, in the meantime, General Wilson withdrew the bulk of the American units assigned to *Anvil* in Italy, as well as four French divisions, but all were exhausted and in need of rest and refit. Churchill was conscious that Allied forces in Italy had already lost seven divisions sent back to Britain for the cross-Channel assault, and the loss of a further seven for *Anvil* seemed the final straw. He feared that by weakening the Allied forces in Italy further, they would be unable to destroy the occupying German armies or reach Vienna to counter Stalin's influence in central Europe.

Churchill therefore stepped up his campaign to derail *Anvil* and cabled Roosevelt pleading: 'Let us resolve not to wreck one great campaign for the sake of another. Both can be won.'[6] Roosevelt would not give in and on 29 June he cabled back: 'In view of the Soviet-British-American agreement, reached at Tehran, I cannot agree without Stalin's approval to the use of force or equipment elsewhere.' This of course was not strictly true and Churchill refused to accept it to the last.

Throughout July, Churchill bombarded Eisenhower with cables, driving the Allied supreme commander to the point of despair. Even the week before the landings, Churchill sought to bully Eisenhower into getting his own way. Relations became particularly acrimonious when he arrived at Eisenhower's Normandy headquarters, near the village of Tournières, on 7 August. Churchill wanted Eisenhower to shift *Anvil* to Brittany or the Channel ports, which would have piled the pressure on the Germans in northern France, though in reality there was a lack of available ports as the Germans resolutely clung on to them.

Eisenhower, although pushed to the brink by his recalcitrant ally, would not budge; he was committed to making the Germans fight on as many fronts as possible. He pointed out that America had acceded to Britain's desire to invade North Africa first, thereby pushing the opening of the Second Front back from the spring of 1943 to June 1944. The fall of Rome and the success of Operation *Cobra* in Normandy in July 1944 had finally convinced Eisenhower to green-light the secondary invasion.

Eisenhower was clearly shaken by his encounters with Churchill and wrote to him:

> To say that I was disturbed by our conference on Wednesday does not nearly express the depth of my distress over your interpretation of the recent decision affecting the Mediterranean theatre. I do not, for one moment, believe that there is any desire on the part of any responsible person in the American war machine to disregard British views...[7]

Despite Churchill's behaviour, Eisenhower held the British leader in high regard, describing him as 'a cantankerous yet adorable father'.[8] Churchill, the highly experienced politician, knew that despite his brinkmanship this was the high-water mark of Britain's dominance of the alliance. Previously, British and American chiefs of staff rarely disagreed on major issues; from now on, they would rarely agree and with Britain now the junior partner, they would rarely prevail.

The Americans won the day and *Anvil* became *Dragoon* using the forces of General Alexander Patch's US 7th Army from Italy and General Jean de Lattre de Tassigny's French II Corps – his units having been built up in North Africa following the invasion. The Riviera landings were scheduled for ten weeks after D-Day on 15 August. Blaskowitz had no way of stopping the fleet of 2,000 Allied warships and landing craft bearing 151,000 American, British, Canadian and French troops. The Riviera, once a playground for the wealthy, was now dotted with German pillboxes, gun emplacements, mines and booby traps, though 19th Army was hardly in a fit state to effectively defend it.

As the deadline for *Dragoon* loomed, Blaskowitz had very few Panzers remaining in southern France. Most of his armoured divisions, along with elements of the four infantry divisions, had already been drawn north to the bitter fighting in Normandy. Only 11th Panzer remained in the south, which was refitting north-east of Bordeaux after being mauled on the Eastern Front.

During the Allied naval build-up in the Mediterranean, the Luftwaffe kept General Weise appraised of developments, though he and Blaskowitz did not know exactly where the blow would fall and had insufficient forces to defend the entire coastline. The heavy bombing of Toulon and other targets in the days before the landings alerted Blaskowitz that something was likely to happen. By 14 August, suspecting attack in the Marseilles-Toulon region, Blaskowitz moved 11th Panzer and two infantry divisions east of the Rhône.

By the evening of 14 August, transport aircraft and gliders had been gathered to ferry the airborne assault force. Le Muy, to the north-west of Saint-Raphaël, screened the invasion area and provided access to the Argens valley corridor. For this reason, it was to be secured by Allied airborne troops. The parachute assault on the Le Muy-Le Luc area was carried out by the Anglo-American 1st Airborne Task Force. While these airborne landings suffered heavy losses – only 60 per cent of the paratroops landed on their drop zones and about 50 gliders were lost – the seaborne landings themselves were largely unopposed.

The main assault commenced at 0800 hours on 15 August 1944. The US 3rd Infantry Division stormed ashore on the left at Cavalaire-sur-Mer, the US 45th in the centre at Saint-Tropez and the US 36th on the right at Saint-Raphaël. The 3rd struck the boundary of the German LXII Corps' 242nd and 148th Infantry divisions. French commando units landed between Cannes and Hyères, flanking the assault beaches. There was no firing on the Allied fleet and many of the prisoners taken were Russians who had volunteered to fight Stalin but had found themselves in the south of France on the receiving end of the Allies. Those who did offer token resistance were swiftly dealt with.

Churchill joined the invasion fleet aboard a British destroyer, but slept through the initial landings. Later, while standing on deck, passing American troops yelled 'Winnie, Winnie!' i.e. Winston at him. They were pleased to see him, little knowing he had threated to resign over *Dragoon* He later noted rather sourly: 'One of my reasons for making public my visit was to associate myself with this well-conducted but irrelevant and unrelated operation.'[9] Eisenhower's recollection of the situation was far more generous: 'As usual the Prime Minister pursued the argument up to the very moment of execution. As usual, also, the second that he saw he could not gain his own way, he threw everything he had into support of the operation.'[10]

That first day, more than 94,000 men and 11,000 vehicles came across the beaches. The US 3rd and 45th Infantry divisions were soon pressing towards Marseilles and the Rhône, while the 36th made towards the Route

Napoléon and Grenoble. Follow-up forces – including the US 7th Army headquarters, US VI Corps headquarters and the French II Corps (1st French Armoured, 1st, 3rd Algerian and 9th Colonial divisions) – came ashore the following day and passed through VI Corps on the Marseilles road. Due to the rapidity of the advance, lack of fuel became a greater impediment than German resistance. What followed was dubbed 'the champagne campaign'.

The failure of Hitler's Mortain counter-attack in Normandy and the developing Falaise pocket meant that by 16 August it was imperative to save Army Group G before a wider collapse occurred in France. General Weise tried to establish a defence line using the 242nd Infantry Division in the Toulon area, the 244th guarding Marseilles, and elements of the 189th and 198th as they came across the Rhône. Blaskowitz was ordered to move his forces north-east, except for the 148th Division in the Cannes-Nice area and a reserve mountain division at Grenoble, which were instructed to move into Italy. Marseilles and Toulon were to remain German fortresses. Blaskowitz duly abandoned Toulouse and started withdrawing north. General Ferdinand Neuling's LXII Corps at Draguignan, a few miles north-west of Le Muy, was not so lucky and was surrounded by American paratroopers. His two infantry divisions were trapped at Marseilles and Toulon. Weise sent the 189th Infantry Division to clear Le Muy and relieve LXII Corps, but the Americans easily fended off their feeble counter-attacks.

It was not long before the US 7th Army and the French forces were pushing up the Rhône Valley towards Avignon, Montélimar and, ultimately, Lyon. Between 21–23 August, French troops forced their way to Toulon, suffering 2,700 casualties and capturing 17,000 Germans. At Marseilles, they lost 1,800 men, taking another 11,000 prisoners. Once the Americans were at Montélimar, 11th Panzer was despatched to try to hold open the German escape route. For nine days, the Germans fought the Americans before retreating on Lyon. In particular, on 25 August, 11th Panzer and supporting units launched five attacks. Two days later, the bulk of the division and most of the retreating infantry had crossed the Rhône north of Drôme, having lost 2,500 prisoners. They left the Montélimar region in the hands of General Baptist Kniess's newly arrived LXXXV Corps.

General Otto Richter's 198th Infantry Division, plus a rearguard engineer detachment to the south, remained at Montélimar. On the night of 27/28 August, he led his remaining two regiments and other survivors in a bid to escape. Richter's group ran straight into the US 36th Division's push on the town and the general and some 700 of his men were captured, but not before the Americans suffered around 100 casualties. To add to German woes in the south of France, Toulon on 26 August, followed by Marseilles two days later, was liberated. The Allies secured the region between Nice and Avignon as far north as Briançon via Grenoble to Montélimar, effectively destroying General Wiese's 19th Army.

The Allied forces in southern and northern France linked up at Châtillon-sur-Seine on 12 September 1944, when the French II Corps made contact with the French 2nd Armoured Division, which formed part of General Patton's US 3rd Army. The French II Corps then expanded to become the French 1st Army, and along with the US 7th Army, formed the US 6th Army Group under Lieutenant-General Jacob Devers. It has been estimated the Germans lost up to 7,000 dead in southern France and about 21,000 wounded. In total, Blaskowitz lost perhaps half of his 250,000 troops. The Americans suffered about 4,500 casualties and the French slightly higher.

In strategic terms, *Dragoon* was largely a waste of time. It was not conducted at the same time as *Overlord*, due to shortages of amphibious transport, and the success of D-Day meant Army Group G would have been forced to withdraw from southern France to avoid being cut off regardless of the attack on the Riviera. The timing of *Dragoon* also meant it did not take any pressure off the Allies fighting in Normandy because Blaskowitz's better units, especially his Panzer divisions, had already been drawn north. Nonetheless, the Riviera landings served to drive the Germans away from the shores of the western Mediterranean.

THE GERMANS LOSE THEIR GRIP

Hitler's foothold in the eastern Mediterranean soon collapsed like a house of cards. The German position in the Balkans was rapidly compromised by the defection of Bulgaria and Romania. Hitler, with his resources stretched beyond breaking point, abandoned mainland Greece in October 1944. British troops arrived in Athens and the Russians liberated Belgrade. Forlorn German garrisons were left trapped in Crete and the Dodecanese to await the end of the war.

The following month, the Germans were driven from Albania by Enver Hoxha's partisans. His communist forces based in the south of the country had emerged as the dominant guerrilla group. It took them three weeks to finally liberate Tirana, which thanks to Mussolini had been in enemy hands since 1939. Although occupation forces remained in Yugoslavia, they came under increasing pressure from Josip Broz Tito's men and the Russians. Slowly but surely they were pushed northwards and away from the Adriatic. Croatia, which sat astride the German lines of communication into Austria and Italy, became an epicentre for the fighting. 'Constantly surrounded in a small hilly area, amid snow and frost,' wrote Milovan Djilas, 'the Slavonians fought battles which were amongst the fiercest ever fought by the Yugoslav Partisans.'[11] Everything that Hitler had achieved in 1941 and in 1943 was lost.

In northern Italy, Kesselring became sick and tired of the constant partisan attacks. He took a dim view of his new-found enemies, remarking: 'Altogether the Partisan groups presented the picture of a motley collection of Allied, Italian and Balkan soldiers, German deserters and native civilians of both sexes ... with the result that patriotism was often merely a cloak for the release of baser instincts.'[12] According to his conservative estimates, during a three-month period in mid-1944, the partisan war cost him 5,000 dead and 8,000 wounded or kidnapped. Kesselring's response was to order brutal reprisals that resulted in mass shootings, hangings and the destruction of countless villages. In the name of protecting his lines of communication, he unleashed a wave of senseless massacres. They did little good and simply inflamed the situation even further.

CHAPTER 16:
Deadly Sideshow

ANY SHRED of enthusiasm that Mussolini may have had for his rump socialist republic had evaporated by the summer of 1944. The Allied landings in the Riviera posed a direct threat to him. Although well protected by the Alps, it seemed as if it would only be a matter of time before the Americans were pushing through the mountain passes towards Turin and Milan. Luckily for Mussolini and Kesselring, the Allied forces in the Rhône Valley were more intent on chasing the Germans north towards the Belfort Gap and the Rhine.

'I'm doing my best to help the Axis to win the war,'[1] Mussolini told a visiting Otto Skorzeny with little conviction. Skorzeny observed that: 'The Duce was no longer the active head of state … I had seen him for the last time.'[2] By early 1945, Mussolini was a completely tragic figure, little more than a powerless figurehead, barely legitimizing Hitler's continued occupation of northern Italy. The dogged resistance to the Allied advance remained very firmly in German hands. He understood that with the German armies reeling everywhere, victory was impossible.

The situation was so dire on the Eastern and Western fronts that throughout late 1944 and early 1945 German divisions were regularly withdrawn from Italy. German forces on the Italian front amounted to 23 battered divisions, and two others partly formed, supported by just four Italian divisions. The latter had been trained in Germany and although they were commanded by Italian generals, each had German 'liaison' staff. They were lumped together behind the front lines to create the 'Liguria' Army. Kesselring, mindful of their combat effectiveness and loyalty, would only employ them against their fellow countrymen. Aside from Mussolini's Republican Army, there were also the dubious Fascist National Guard and various militias; similarly. they were all confined to internal security roles.

Kesselring, in late 1944, was badly injured in a car accident and was unable to return until February 1945. The following month, he was appointed commander-in-chief in the west and was replaced by General von Vietinghoff. Kesselring objected to this posting: 'I pointed out that I was needed in the Italian theatre and that not being fully recuperated I had not the necessary mobility for this decisive mission.'[3] It did him no good; instead, he had to preside over Germany's final defeat on the Western Front.

DEATH OF THE MEDITERRANEAN STRONGMAN

By the spring of 1945, the exhausted German troops in Italy continued to fight tenaciously as they were steadily driven north by the Allies. They were finally defeated trying to retreat over the River Po in late April. Mussolini hoped to flee to Switzerland, but was caught on the open road by Italian communist partisans and arrested. They subsequently shot him and his mistress without trial, on 28 April, and drove the bodies to Milan. Mussolini, so accustomed to being in command, even directed his own execution. 'Shoot me here,' he instructed his killers, 'in the chest.'[4] Along with 16 other dead Fascists, his and his mistress's bodies were dumped in the street. They were kicked, spat at and even urinated upon.

Mussolini had gone from addressing adoring crowds at the Palazzo Venezia to a lifeless, mutilated cadaver hung by its ankles above a petrol station in Piazzale Loreto. Before the baying masses strung him up, they smashed his face to a pulp. 'Bloodlust unsated and in a vicious and merciless mood,' wrote Alan Whicker, who witnessed the barbarism, 'an hysterical mob had subjected the corpses to sickening indignities.'[5] It was Mussolini's Mediterranean lust for power that had brought him to this. According to Whicker: 'One woman fired five shots into the corpse, to avenge five dead sons.'[6] The partisans then embarked on an orgy of revenge across northern Italy. Anyone with links to the Fascist Party was

This was how Mussolini's dream of empire ended, strung up with his mistress in Milan.

executed. In Tripoli, the remaining Italians knew the end was in sight for their mother country.

Two days later, Hitler took his own life. By this stage, with the Red Army at the very gates of Berlin, continuing the war in Italy was pointless. Some 230,000 German troops in northern Italy and southern Austria laid down their arms on 2 May 1945, following their unconditional surrender. There were more than 100,000 German prisoners in neighbouring Yugoslavia. 'So ended the Italian campaign,' remarked Field Marshal Alexander, 'exactly twenty months to the day from the date when our forces landed on the peninsula.'[7] The butcher's bill for Italy was considerable: from September 1943 to May 1945, the Allies suffered 312,000 killed, wounded and missing; the Germans lost 434,646 casualties.

The American commander, General Mark Clark, wrote: 'The Eighth and Fifth Armies have reached the end of the long roads from El Alamein and Salerno … I hail and congratulate you in this hour of complete victory…'[8] By this stage, the Allies were in Genoa, Milan, Venice and Trieste. A few days later, they reached the Brenner Pass and linked up with the US 7th Army in Austria. The conflict in the Mediterranean was now officially over. It would be another week before the fighting stopped in Europe.

A SERIES OF STRATEGIC BLUNDERS

When Churchill saw the photographs of Mussolini's demise he was horrified. He was especially dismayed by the brutal treatment of Clara Petacci, the dictator's young mistress. His knee-jerk reaction was that the assassin should be punished. 'Was she on the list of war criminals?' he asked Alexander. 'Had he any authority from anybody to shoot this woman? It seems to me the cleansing hand of British military power should make inquiries on these points.'[9] Nothing, though, could be done.

The hapless Mussolini, for all his bluff and bluster, was completely unable to recreate the Roman Empire. Despite his talk of the Mediterranean being an Italian sea, this proved to be far from the case. At the start of the war, he had 80 admirals, many of whom acted as if they commanded a coastal navy, rather than a seagoing one. After the fiascos of Taranto and Matapan, Mussolini had little faith in them. Even the Germans scornfully dubbed the Italian Navy the 'Fine-weather Fleet'. His admirals had never contemplated taking on the Royal Navy – regardless of their new warships they never believed they could defeat the British Mediterranean Fleet. This was not defeatism, but simple pragmatism. The Italian Navy's inability to operate in the dark and its fuel shortages hobbled it from the start.

One of Mussolini's greatest blunders was deciding that aircraft carriers were unnecessary. Instead, he thought of Italy and her islands as one big aircraft carrier. While his land-based aircraft could dominate the central Mediterranean and Malta, they were too far away from Alexandria or Gibraltar to be of any real value as naval strike aircraft. Co-ordination between the navy and the air force was often poor. Italian warships regularly found themselves bereft of air cover. By the time Mussolini had changed his mind and ordered the construction of two carriers it was too late. They were not ready before the end of the war. On 4 October 1942, he acknowledged that aircraft carriers should have been: 'the umbrellas of our naval forces'.[10] The lack of radar and sonar on Italian warships was also a serious omission. Naval engagements covered vast areas and relying on seaplanes for reconnaissance was a time-consuming and hit-and-miss way of gathering intelligence.

Mussolini's army never really had a chance to prove itself; poorly motivated, badly led and inadequately equipped, it was outclassed from the very start, which led to a crippling inferiority complex. Nor was this something the Germans helped to dispel. In 1939, there were 600 Italian generals, most of whom were promoted on seniority rather than aptitude, and they spent much of their time arguing among themselves. In Libya, British officers were bemused to discover that their Italian counterparts lived in luxury while their men went without even the most basic necessities.

Most of the senior Italian military commanders lacked initiative and tended to be overcautious, just like their naval counterparts. When it came to large-scale war, their tactical and strategic thinking was still influenced by the First World War. They looked to Italy's northern borders and anticipated trench warfare in the Alps conducted by static armies. Their more recent experiences had been against lightly armed tribesmen in Ethiopia and Libya. This was no preparation for modern mechanized warfare.

There is a saying, that a bad craftsman always blames his tools. Had Italo Balbo lived, he might have made a go of the attack on Egypt. Instead, Graziani spent all his time delaying his offensive and grumbling about military shortages. The British, in contrast, made do with what they had and raised hell. Once Graziani stopped his advance, the initiative inevitably passed back to the British, with decisive consequences.

Mussolini's generals never envisaged waging a widespread war across the Mediterranean and as a result had not drawn up detailed operational plans for attacks on Malta and Egypt, or Greece and Tunisia. His botched attack on Greece showed that the Italian armed forces were hardly on the road to becoming the masters of the Mediterranean. The loss of ten divisions and 130,000 men in Libya between 1940 and 1941 caused such damage to the Italian Army that it never really recovered. This left Mussolini's forces in North Africa subservient to the ambitions of Hitler and Rommel.

The trouble Mussolini had, despite all his rabble rousing, was that he failed to inspire his troops to the same level as Hitler did. Sergeant Emilio Ponti, captured in North Africa, shrugged after being questioned and replied: 'When asked why the Italians can't fight, my answer is that this was not our war.'[11] However, while the average Italian soldier did not think much of their own generals, they did look up to a certain German commander: 'Rommel became as much of a mythical figure to the Italians as the British,' recalled Lieutenant Paolo Colacicchi. 'One regiment of Bersaglieri at Tobruk called themselves *Rommeletti* [little Rommels].'[12] There could be no greater compliment.

Crucially, Mussolini failed to concentrate all his military strength in the Mediterranean. Instead, he allowed himself to be distracted by campaigns in the Balkans, East Africa and Russia. If he had ever been serious about defeating the British in the Mediterranean, he should have thrown everything he had at Malta and Egypt. A seaborne assault on Malta in 1940 or 1941 could have unhinged the British defence. Instead, Italian incompetence resulted in temporarily diverting Hitler from his goal – the Soviet Union. Thanks to Mussolini, he found himself obliged to conduct operations in the Balkans, North Africa and finally even in Italy.

Hitler's conduct of the war in the Mediterranean was little better. He committed a series of strategic blunders. The first of these, and probably the most serious, was his failure at Hendaye and Montoire-sur-le-Loire to persuade Franco and Pétain to side with the Axis. If this had happened, the Straits of Gibraltar could have been firmly sealed, cutting off the British Mediterranean Fleet at Alexandria and the British Army in Egypt. The Malta garrison would have been completely reliant on reinforcements coming via the Cape of Good Hope, round the Horn of Africa and up through the Red Sea to Suez. If Hitler had also conducted a concerted aerial campaign to mine the Suez Canal, this would have been a disaster for the British. Rommel, adequately reinforced, could then have stormed eastwards to Cairo. All this would have pre-empted the American-led landings in French North Africa.

Franco, very wisely stayed on the sidelines. From his point of view, there was much to lose and little to gain by helping Hitler and Mussolini in the Mediterranean. His country had been impoverished and torn apart by the civil war. By 1940, the wounds were still very raw. He was grateful for German and Italian military assistance against the Republicans, but there was a limit to that gratitude. Both countries had entered the fray with wider agendas than just fighting Bolshevism. Spain had been cynically used as a military testing ground. Furthermore, the war had served to draw Italy ever closer to Germany.

Franco knew that his countrymen would have been appalled by the idea of the Germans liberating Gibraltar. For the duration of the war, Hitler would have demanded basing rights. Franco would have been trading one foreign power for another. Nor did Franco like the idea of allowing the Italians back on the Balearic Islands, as he had only just got rid of them. On Spain's northern coast, it is conceivable that Hitler would have asked for sanctuaries for his U-boats operating in the Bay of Biscay. More importantly, the weak Spanish fleet, even with French assistance, was incapable of taking on the Royal Navy. Once America entered the war, defending Spain from naval and air attack would have been impossible.

The deployment of the remains of the French fleet from Toulon, Algiers and Oran by Pétain in support of the Axis could have been of immense help, denying the western Mediterranean to the British. Hitler hoped that Churchill's controversial decision to attack Mers-el-Kébir and later the Levant might be a tipping point. He was wrong. Hitler was deluded to think that, with half of France under German occupation, the French would want to rally to the Axis cause.

Vichy's main concern was maintaining the integrity of the French Empire in the face of German, Italian and Spanish territorial claims. Pétain tried to stay neutral, but that did not prevent the Allies from invading the French Levant and French North Africa, nor Hitler occupying Tunisia. If Franco had joined Hitler, he would have almost certainly lost Spanish Morocco to the Allies.

Hitler's other major blunder was to consider North Africa as little more than a sideshow until it was much too late. His preoccupation was always the conquest of the Soviet Union and the seizure of its raw materials. Hitler was dragged into the Mediterranean conflict thanks to Mussolini's failure in Greece and Libya. He knew he could not abandon his troublesome ally, but his plans had never encompassed the Mediterranean. However, Mussolini was a good way of keeping the British preoccupied in North Africa.

Both Mussolini and Hitler must take full responsibility for not capturing Malta. This would have very firmly cut the Mediterranean in half. At the start of the war, Churchill anticipated that Mussolini would first attack Malta or Egypt. Instead, he struck France for little gain and then Greece with the same outcome. Logically, Malta, sat astride the Sicilian Channel between Sicily and Tunisia, was a much better prize and much easier to take. Churchill was surprised that Mussolini did not invade Malta in June 1940 when it was at its most defenceless. By 1942, when General Cavallero, the Italian chief of general staff, urged that it was vital to take the island in order to safeguard the Axis supply lines to North Africa, it was almost too late.

The proposed German invasion, dubbed Operation *Hercules*, was continually postponed. Fortunately for Churchill, Rommel on taking Tobruk persuaded Hitler that seizing Malta was unnecessary. At the same time, Mussolini urged Hitler that it was more necessary than ever. Hitler did not seem to consider what would happen if Rommel was driven back to Tripoli. Rommel, determined to get to Cairo, did not want any delay or resources being diverted elsewhere. The conquest of Egypt seemed within their grasp. Hitler supported Rommel, seeing Malta as an irrelevance to the bigger strategic picture. *Hercules* was postponed permanently.

General Student did Hitler and Rommel a great disservice when he persuaded Hitler that he could take Crete from the air. The subsequent heavy losses convinced Hitler not to carry out any further large-scale operations in the region. This meant that the resources committed to Rommel's campaigns were limited. Hitler should have left it to the Italian Navy and air force to protect the Aegean and given Rommel greater forces from the start. If Rommel had arrived in Tripoli with an army, rather than just a corps, who knows what he could have achieved. After being promoted to field marshal, Rommel said rather sourly to his wife: 'I would rather he had given me one more division.'[13] It aptly summed up his predicament.

Kesselring wrote astutely:

> *Germany*, as the leading Axis partner, had accepted the inevitable extension of the war to important parts of the Mediterranean with a certain lethargy and had missed the chance of exploiting her one opportunity to deal a mortal blow at England in a part of the world vital to her.[14]

Hitler's decision to occupy Tunisia once the Allies were in Algeria and Libya was foolhardy. It left his generals fighting a desperate two-front war and trapped. Ultimately, it was a waste of precious manpower. This rearguard did nothing to save Sicily or Mussolini. 'As a result of the senseless sacrifice of so many German and Italian troops in Tunisia,' said Rommel, 'it became impossible to beat off the landings in southern Italy.'[15] Who knows what would have happened if the quarter of a million men in Tunisia had been withdrawn to defend Sicily and southern Italy?

'The loss of Tunisia, following that of Tripolitania,' observed Kesselring, 'was a particularly severe shock to the Italian Command and people.'[16]

Hitler was able to fight on after the Axis defeat in the Mediterranean, Mussolini was not. 'The moment the first Allied soldier set foot on Italian soil,' noted Rommel, 'Mussolini was finished and the dream of the rebirth of the Roman Empire was probably over for good.'[17] Watching all this unfold from Madrid, Franco must have felt thoroughly vindicated. As far are Kesselring was concerned, Tunisia, not Malta, was the decisive turning point. 'The Allies won a total victory,' he said.[18]

THE ROAD TO VICTORY

In North Africa, Britain scored a series of decisive victories that proved to be landmarks in the battle for the Mediterranean and indeed the Second World War. Notably, first against the Italians at Beda Fomm, then against the German-Italian forces at El Alamein. Rommel was simply unable to overcome Montgomery's growing superiority in men and equipment. This was in part because British forces operating from Malta throttled his supply routes. There is no denying that Rommel was a highly skilled tactician, but he lacked strategic foresight. His decision not to invade Malta was ultimately his undoing. 'The outstanding feature of Rommel's successes is that they were achieved with an inferiority of force,' wrote Basil Liddell Hart, 'and without any command of the air.'[19]

At sea, Matapan stands out as a series of firsts. It was a historic moment, as the first British naval action in the Mediterranean since the Battle of the Nile in 1798. It was also the Royal Navy's first major engagement since the Battle of Jutland in 1916. Matapan was the first time carrier aircraft played a crucial role in a fleet action. It was also the first large engagement where radar-equipped ships tracked down an enemy at night. Some of the Italian fleet were also spotted by eye! Matapan showed what a valuable role Bletchley Park was playing with Ultra-derived intelligence.

The battle for the Mediterranean was caused by the very long shadow of the Roman Empire and the much later European scramble for empire. Mussolini had hoped to recapture ancient imperial glories and become a first among equals. Britain and France's superior attitude towards Italy irked him greatly. At the same time, he wanted to keep Hitler out of the Balkans and the Mediterranean. All this backfired spectacularly and led to the series of campaigns fought across the Mediterranean.

At the crucial moment in 1940, Britain did not blink as it had done five years earlier. Churchill refused to be intimidated or to back down in the face of opportunist Italian aggression. His defiant resolution was backed by the tenacity of the Mediterranean Fleet, the 8th Army and the Desert Air Force. It was this bloody-mindedness that put the Allies on the road to victory, not only in the Mediterranean but also in Europe.

The remaining Germans held out to the very last in the Aegean. After Hitler's evacuation of Greece, the garrison in Crete under General Benthag withdrew into the western half of the island. A British and Greek force arrived to take control in the east, but as 11,000 German and Italian troops remained in Crete, there followed a tense stand-off. Finally, on 8 May 1945, the German high command signed the unconditional surrender and the garrisons on both Crete and Rhodes laid down their arms.

A TUMULTUOUS AFTERMATH

Marshal Pétain, who caused the Allies so much grief in the Mediterranean, was arrested by de Gaulle and charged with collaboration. He refused to recognise the authority of the court and even claimed disengenuously that his actions had helped the Allies 'by ensuring a free Mediterranean and the integrity of the empire'.[20] Found guilty of treason, he was sentenced to death, which was reduced to life imprisonment until his death in 1951.

After the Second World War, the Mediterranean was not to know peace. Greece almost immediately fell into a state of civil war between communist and royalist supporters. British forces helped save Greece from communism, but Albania and Yugoslavia were lost when communist partisans took power there. Palestine, abandoned by the British, was torn by the First Arab–Israeli War. Britain withdrew from Suez in the early 1950s, only to return very briefly with the French in a final futile flexing of imperial power.

France's withdrawal from North Africa was protracted and painful, especially from Algeria. This process was not completed until 1962. Although France and Spain relinquished their Moroccan protectorates in 1956, Spain kept the ports of Ceuta and Melilla. Libya was administered by Britain and France until 1951, when the country was finally granted independence. Britain installed a king who lasted until 1969, when he was deposed by Colonel Gaddafi. Lebanon and Syria were next to be blighted by conflict. As for General Franco, the only surviving hard man of the Mediterranean, he remained in power until his death in 1975.

References

INTRODUCTION: THE CRADLE OF CIVILIZATION

1. Halifax, *Speeches on Foreign Policy*, p.218
2. Farrell, *Mussolini: A New Life*, p.332

CHAPTER 1: RUMBLINGS IN THE MED

1. Viotti, *Garibaldi: The Revolutionary and His Men*, p.40
2. Farrell, *Mussolini: A New Life*, p.260
3. Churchill, *The Second World War*, Vol I, *The Gathering Storm*, p.133
4. Ibid., p.134
5. Ibid., p.135
6. Clark, *Mussolini*, pp.192–3
7. Churchill, op. cit., p.138
8. Farrell, op. cit., p.267
9. Churchill, op. cit., p.138
10. Brendon, *The Dark Valley: A Panorama of the 1930s*, p.281
11. Halifax, *Speeches on Foreign Policy*, pp.144–5
12. Churchill, op. cit., p.138

CHAPTER 2: HEMMED IN

1. Farrell, *Mussolini: A New Life*, p.281
2. Bormann, *Hitler's Table-Talk*, p.320
3. Liddell Hart, *The Other Side of the Hill*, p.41
4. Thomas, *The Spanish Civil War*, p.153
5. Beevor, *The Spanish Civil War*, p.63

6. Mitchell, *The Spanish Civil War*, p.36

7. Thomas, op. cit., p.234

8. Halifax, *Speeches on Foreign Policy*, p.106

9. Bullock, *Hitler: A Study in Tyranny*, p.350

10. Carr, *Images of the Spanish Civil War*, p.100

11. Bullock, op. cit., p.351

12. Brendon, *The Dark Valley: A Panorama of the 1930s*, p.475

13. Tolland, *Adolf Hitler*, p.419

14. Halifax, op. cit., p.146

15. Overy & Wheatcroft, *The Road to War*, p.165

16. Clark, *Mussolini*, p.235

17. Thomas, op. cit., p.542

18. Beevor, op. cit., p.227

19. Mitchell, op. cit., p.181

20. Farrell, op. cit., p.312

21. Brendon, op. cit., p.537

22. Halifax, op. cit., p.252

23. Ibid., p.253

24. Brendon, op. cit., p.537

25. Ibid., p.489–90

26. Weitz, *Hitler's Diplomat: The Life and Times of Joachim von Ribbentrop*, p.233

CHAPTER 3: DESERT FRONTLINE

1. Farrell, *Mussolini: A New Life*, p.300

2. Ibid.

3. Shirer, *The Rise and Fall of the Third Reich*, p.740

4. Brendon, *The Dark Valley: A Panorama of the 1930s*, p.476

5. Perret, *Wavell's Offensive*, p.19

6. Pitt, *The Crucible of War: Western Desert 1941*, p.38

7. Ibid., p.27

8. Ibid.

9. Ibid., p.21

10. Perrett, *Wavell's Offensive*, p.8

11. Macksey, *Beda Fomm*, p.35

12. Pitt, op. cit., p.54

13. Barnett, *The Desert Generals*, p.29

CHAPTER 4: FALLEN ALLIES

1. Thompson, *Pledge to Destiny: Charles de Gaulle and the Rise of the Free French*, p.101
2. Tute, *The Deadly Stroke*, p.124
3. Ibid.
4. Ibid., p.125
5. Ibid., p.128
6. Vader, *The Fleet Without a Friend*, p.74
7. Ibid., p.76
8. Ibid., p.75
9. Arthur, *Forgotten Voices of the Second World War*, p.99
10. Ibid.
11. Vader, op. cit., p.81
12. Griffiths, *Marshal Pétain*, p.271
13. Toland, *Adolf Hitler*, p.631
14. Ibid., p.638
15. Bormann, *Hitler's Table-Talk*, p.515
16. Bullock, *Hitler: A Study in Tyranny*, p.606
17. Liddell Hart, *The Other Side of the Hill*, p.237
18. Shirer, *The Rise and Fall of the Third Reich*, p.816
19. Bekker, *The Luftwaffe War Diaries*, p.236
20. Clark, *Mussolini*, 267

CHAPTER 5: SECOND BLOOD

1. Moorehead, *Mediterranean Front*, p.85
2. Ball, *The Bitter Sea: The Struggle for Mastery in the Mediterranean, 1935-1949*, p.5
3. Moorehead, op. cit., p.90
4. Clark, *Mussolini*, p.148
5. Moorehead, op. cit., p.92
6. Ibid., p.92
7. Roskill, *Churchill and the Admirals*, p.169
8. Ibid.
9. Moorehead, op. cit., p.93
10. Grehan & Mace, *The War at Sea in the Mediterranean 1940-1944*, p.14
11. Moorehead, op. cit., p.93

12. Grehan & Mace, op. cit., p.vii

13. Shirer, *The Rise and Fall of the Third Reich*, p.818

14. Ibid.

15. Grehan & Mace, op. cit., p.32

16. Clark, op. cit., p.279

17. Strawson, *The Battle for North Africa*, p.31

CHAPTER 6: FOX IS KILLED

1. Macksey, *Beda Fomm*, p.47

2. Gilbert, *The Desert War*, p.2

3. Perrett, *Wavell's Offensive*, p.39

4. Ibid.

5. Ibid., p.44

6. Ibid.

7. Ibid.

8. Gilbert, op. cit., p.4

9. Pitt, *The Crucible of War*, p.180

10. Macksey, op. cit., p.155

11. Ibid, p.151

12. Moorehead, *Mediterranean Front*, p.191

13. Ibid., p.192

14. Ibid.

15. Schofield, *Wavell: Soldier & Statesman*, p.171

16. Churchill, *The Second World War*, Vol III, *The Grand Alliance*, pp.56–8

17. Gilbert, op. cit., p.13

18. Strawson, *The Battle for North Africa*, p.40

19. Pitt, *Churchill and the Generals*, p.59

20. Shirer, *The Rise and Fall of the Third Reich*, p. 819

21. Bullock, *Hitler: A Study of Tyranny*, p.609

22. Ibid.

23. Shirer, op. cit., p.819

24. Ibid., p.821

CHAPTER 7: BACK AT SEA

1. Churchill, *The Second World War*, Vol III, *The Grand Alliance*, p.84

2. Ibid.

3. Pack, *The Battle of Matapan*, p.19

4. Ibid.

5. McKay, *The Secret Life of Bletchley Park*, p.132

6. Ibid., p.131

7. Ibid.

8. Grehan & Mace, *The War at Sea in the Mediterranean 1940-1944*, p.53

9. Pack, op. cit., p.21

10. Ibid., p.78

11. Ibid.

12. Ibid., p.81

13. Ibid., p.99

14. Ibid., p.101

15. Kerrigan, *How Bletchley Park Won World War II*, p.73

16. Pack, op. cit., p.133

17. Ibid., p.134

18. Ibid., p.166

19. Kerrigan, op. cit., p.78

20. Churchill, op. cit., p.194

21. Holland, *Fortress Malta: An Island Under Siege 1940-1943*, p.84

22. Neil, *Onward to Malta: Memoirs of a Hurricane pilot in Malta 1941*, p.93

23. Holland, op. cit., p.197

24. Bradford, *Siege: Malta 1940-1943*, p.113

25. Liddell Hart, *The Rommel Papers*, p.151

26. Turner, *Periscope Patrol: The Saga of the Malta Force Submarines*, p.204

27. Newby, *Something Wholesale*, p.202

28. Ibid., p.203

29. Laffin, *Raiders: Elite Forces Attacks*, p.168

30. Ibid., p.165

CHAPTER 8: UNWANTED DISTRACTIONS

1. Churchill, *The Second World War*, Vol III, *The Grand Alliance*, p.192

2. Schofield, *Wavell: Soldier & Statesman*, p.156

3. Pitt, *Churchill and the Generals*, p.62

4. Ibid.

5. Ibid.

6. De Guingand, *Operation Victory*, p.58

7. Clark, *The Fall of Crete*, p.17

8. Ibid.

9. Plowman, *Greece 1941: The Death Throes of Blitzkrieg*, p.17

10. Ibid., p.156

11. Beevor, *Crete: The Battle and the Resistance*, p.54

12. De Guingand, op. cit., p.80

13. Farrell, *Mussolini: A New Life*, p.349

14. Churchill, op. cit., p.220

15. Farrell, op. cit., p.350

CHAPTER 9: FALLING FROM THE SKIES

1. Liddell Hart, *The Other Side of the Hill*, pp.238–9

2. Churchill, *The Second World War*, Vol III, *The Grand Alliance*, p.241

3. Ibid.

4. Ibid., p.243

5. Bekker, *The Luftwaffe War Diaries*, p.249

6. Liddell Hart, op. cit., p.241

7. Moorehead, *Mediterranean Front*, pp.264–5

8. Ibid.

9. Liddell Hart, op. cit., p.240

10. Churchill, op. cit., Vol III, p.262

11. Beevor, *Crete: The Battle and the Resistance*, p.210

12. Schofield, *Wavell: Soldier & Statesman*, p.202

13. Ibid.

14. Beevor, op. cit., p.228

15. Schofield, op. cit., p.202

16. Liddell Hart, *History of the Second World War*, p.135

17. Churchill, op. cit., p.268

18. Cunningham, *A Sailor's Odyssey*, p.64

19. Ibid., p.292.

CHAPTER 10: ADVENTURES IN THE LEVANT

1. Shirer, *The Rise and Fall of the Third Reich*, p.829

2. Ibid.

3. Griffiths, *Marshal Pétain*, p.287

4. Churchill, *The Second World War*, Vol III, *The Grand Alliance*, p.82

5. Ibid., p.289

6. De Guingand, *Operation Victory*, p.87

7. Churchill, op. cit., p.291

8. Ibid., p.296

9. Barnett, *The Desert Generals*, p.74

10. Pitt, *The Crucible of War*, p.297

11. Liddell Hart, *The Rommel Papers*, p.144

12. Schmidt, *With Rommel in the Desert*, p.51

13. Liddell Hart, op. cit., p.145

14. Ibid., p.145

15. Ibid., p.147

16. Schmidt, op. cit., p.51

17. Churchill, op. cit., p.307

18. Pitt, op. cit., p.309

19. Churchill, op. cit., p.309

20. Liddell Hart, op. cit., p.146

21. Churchill, op. cit., p.775

22. Schmidt, op. cit., p.93

CHAPTER 11: MALTESE SICKNESS

1. Churchill, *The Second World War*, Vol III, *The Grand Alliance*, p.54

2. Moorehead, *A Year of Battle*, p.162

3. Tucker-Jones, *The Desert Air War 1940-1943*, p.74

4. Elliot, *The Cross and the Ensign: A Naval History of Malta 1798-1979*, p.126

5. Churchill, op. cit., p.54

6. Douglas-Hamilton, *The Air Battle for Malta: The Diaries of a Fighter Pilot*, p.10

7. Fabri, 'Our Daily Round in War-torn Malta,' *The War Illustrated*, 7 August 1942, p.120

8. Lucas, *Malta: The Thorn in Rommel's Side*, p.281

9. Neil, *Onward to Malta*, p.104

10. 'Malta: So Small in Size, So Great in Spirit,' *The War Illustrated*, 1 May 1942, p.659

11. Ibid.

12. Fabri, 'Our Daily Round in War-torn Malta,' *The War Illustrated*, 7 August 1942, p.120

13. Niven, *The Moon's a Balloon*, p.70

14. Moorehead, op. cit., p.161

15. 'Malta: So Small in Size, So Great in Spirit,' op. cit., p.659

16. Bradford, *Siege: Malta 1940-1943*, p.169

17. Ibid.

18. Lucas, *Malta: The Thorn in Rommel's Side*, pp.133–4

19. Moorehead, op. cit., p.163

20. Douglas-Hamilton, *The Air Battle for Malta*, p.56

21. Moorehead, *A Year of Battle*, p.164

22. Douglas-Hamilton, op. cit., p.58

23. Bekker, *The Luftwaffe War Diaries*, p.310

24. Ibid., pp.311–12

25. Ibid., p.312

26. Fabri, op. cit., p.120

27. Arthur, *Forgotten Voices of the Second World War*, p.171

28. Macmillan, 'The War in the Air,' *The War Illustrated*, 4 September 1942

29. Arthur, op. cit., p.173

30. Douglas-Hamilton, op. cit., p.94

31. Elliot, op. cit., pp.178–9

32. Tucker-Jones, *The Desert Air War*, p.76

33. Kesselring, *The Memoirs of Field Marshal Kesselring*, p.123

34. Macmillan, 'The War in the Air,' *The War Illustrated*, 22 January 1943, p.502

35. 'Malta: So Small in Size, So Great in Spirit,' op. cit., p.659

CHAPTER 12: BACK TO TRIPOLI

1. Warner, *Alamein*, p.192

2. Moorehead, *A Year of Battle*, p.217

3. Newby, *On the Shores of the Mediterranean*, p.131

4. Cooper, *Cairo in the War 1939-1945*, p.193

5. Ibid., p.190

6. Dimbleby, *Destiny in the Desert: The Road to El Alamein – The Battle that Turned the Tide*, p.289

7. Liddell Hart, *The Rommel Papers*, p.525

8. Cooper, op. cit., p.196

9. Farrell, *Mussolini: A New Life*, p.356

10. Liddell Hart, op. cit., pp.293–4

11. Eisenhower, *Crusade in Europe*, p.102

12. Ibid., p.90

13. Liddell Hart, op. cit., p.365

14. Atkinson, *An Army at Dawn, The War in North Africa, 1942-1943*, p.256

15. Eisenhower, op. cit., p.116

16. Churchill, *A Life*, p.737

17. Tompkins, *The Murder of Admiral Darlan*, p.186

18. Ibid., p.195

19. Ibid., p.202

20. Tute, *The Reluctant Enemies*, p.309

21. Ponting, *Churchill*, p.588

22. Jeffrey, *MI6*, pp.745–6

23. Tute, op. cit., p.313

24. Weitz, *Hitler's Diplomat: The Life and Times of Joachim von Ribbentrop*, p.291

25. De Guingand, *Operation Victory*, p.323

26. Barnett, *The Desert Generals*, p.298

27. Liddell Hart, op. cit., p.418

28. Alexander, *The Alexander Memoirs*, p.71

29. Whicker, *Whicker's War*, p.34

30. Moorehead, *The End in Africa*, p.209

31. Schmidt, *With Rommel in the Desert*, p.192

32. Pitt, *Churchill and the Generals*, p.144

33. Tute, *The North African War*, p.213

34. Ibid.

35. Kesselring, *The Memoirs of Field Marshal Kesselring*, p.157

CHAPTER 13: WHERE NEXT?

1. Kesselring, *The Memoirs of Field Marshal Kesselring*, p.161

2. Pack, *Operation 'Husky': The Allied Invasion of Sicily*, p.26

3. Alexander Clifford, 'Why the White Flag Went Up on Pantelleria,' *The War Illustrated*, 9 July 1943, p.70

4. Ibid.

5. Denis Martin, 'Now They Call Me "The King of Lampedusa,"' *The War Illustrated*, 9 July 1943, p.92

6. Sitwell & Jones, *Malta*, p.61

7. Alexander, *The Alexander Memoirs 1940-45*, p.106

8. Ibid., p.105

9. Kesselring, op. cit., p.162

10. Pack, op. cit., p.60

11. Whicker, *Whicker's War*, p.59

12. Farrell, *Mussolini: A New Life*, p.377

13. Shirer, *The Rise and Fall of the Third Reich*, p.997

14. Pitt, *Churchill and the Generals*, p.158

15. Skorzeny, *Skorzeny's Special Missions*, p.88

16. Shirer, op. cit., p.997

17. Kesselring, op. cit., p.165

18. Whicker, op. cit., p.67

CHAPTER 14: IL DUCE RESURRECTED

1. Shirer, *The Rise and Fall of the Third Reich*, p.999

2. Liddell Hart, *The Rommel Papers*, p.436

3. Ibid., p.439

4. Churchill, *The Second World War*, Vol V, *Closing the Ring*, p.102

5. Elliot, *The Cross and the Ensign: A Naval History of Malta 1798-1979*, p.202

6. Liddell Hart, op. cit., p.445

7. Djilas, *Wartime*, p.330

8. Newby, *A Small Place in Italy*, p.1

9. Churchill, op. cit., p.104

10. Gander, 'I Saw Nazi Paratroops attack in Leros Battle,' *The War Illustrated*, December 1943, p.442

11. Grehan & Mace, *The War at Sea in the Mediterranean 1940-1944*, p.244

12. Ibid., p.245

13. Pitt, *Churchill and the Generals*, p.179

14. Skorzeny, *Skorzeny's Special Missions*, p.83

15. Ibid., p.88

16. Farrell, *Mussolini: A New Life*, p.430

17. Churchill, op. cit., p.104

CHAPTER 15: AIR, SEA AND LAND

1. Alexander, *The Alexander Memoirs*, p.152
2. Ibid., p.127
3. Whicker, *Whicker's War*, p.183
4. Alexander, op. cit., p.127
5. Trevelyan, *Rome '44: The Battle for the Eternal City*, p.307
6. D'Este, *Eisenhower*, p.551
7. Ibid., p.566
8. Ibid.
9. Ibid., p.567
10. Eisenhower, *Crusade in Europe*, p.312
11. Djilas, *Wartime*, p.327
12. Kesselring, *The Memoirs of Field Marshal Kesselring*, pp.226–7

CHAPTER 16: DEADLY SIDESHOW

1. Skorzeny, *Skorzeny's Special Missions*, p.108
2. Ibid.
3. Kesselring, *The Memoirs of Field Marshal Kesselring*, p.237
4. Whicker, *Journey of a Lifetime*, p.267
5. Whicker, *Whicker's War*, p.221
6. Ibid.
7. Alexander, *The Alexander Memoirs*, p.152
8. Forty, *Fifth Army at War*, p.142
9. Whicker, *Whicker's War*, p.222
10. Clark, *Mussolini*, p.293
11. Thompson, *Forgotten Voices: Desert Victory*, p.356
12. Ibid., p.353
13. Liddell Hart, *The Rommel Papers*, p.232
14. Kesselring, op. cit., p.157
15. Strawson, *The Battle for North Africa*, p.210
16. Kesselring, op. cit., p.157
17. Liddell Hart, op. cit., p.422
18. Kesselring, op. cit., p.157
19. Liddell Hart, *The Other Side of the Hill*, p.81
20. Griffiths, *Marshal Pétain*, p.335.

Bibliography

AIRBORNE WARFARE

Beevor, Antony. *Crete: The Battle and the Resistance*. London: Penguin, 1992

Bekker, Cajus. *The Luftwaffe War Diaries*. London: Corgi, 1972

Bradford, Ernle. *Siege: Malta 1940-1943*. London: Hamish Hamilton, 1985

Burns, Michael G. *Bader*. London: Rigel, 2003

Clark, Alan. *The Fall of Crete*. London: Cassell, 2004

Douglas-Hamilton, James. *The Air Battle for Malta: The Diaries of a Fighter Pilot*. Shrewsbury: Airlife, 1990

Gregory, Barry & Batchelor, John. *Airborne Warfare 1918-1941*. London: Phoebus, 1978

Holland, James. *Fortress Malta: An Island Under Siege 1940-1943*. London: Weidenfeld & Nicolson, 2004

Lucas, Laddie. *Malta: The Thorn in Rommel's Side*. London: Penguin, 1993

MacDonald, Callum. *The Lost Battle: Crete 1941*. London: Macmillan, 1993

Quarrie, Bruce. *Fallshirmjäger: German Paratrooper 1935-39*. Oxford: Osprey, 2001

Quarrie, Bruce. *German Airborne Troops 1939-45*. Oxford: Osprey, 1983

Simpson, Tony. *Operation Mercury: The Battle for Crete, 1941*. London: Hodder and Stoughton, 1981

Tucker-Jones, Anthony. *The Desert Air War 1940-1943*. Barnsley: Pen & Sword, 2018

BIOGRAPHY

Blumenson, Martin. *Patton: The Man Behind the Legend 1885-1945*. London: Jonathan Cape, 1986

Bullock, Alan. *Hitler: A Study in Tyranny*. Harmondsworth: Penguin, 1978

Clark, Martin. *Mussolini*. Harlow: Pearson Longman, 2005

Clark, Brigadier Stanley. *The Man who is France: The Story of Charles de Gaulle*. London: George G. Harrap, 1960

D'Este, Carlo. *Eisenhower*. London: Weidenfeld & Nicolson, 2003

Farrell, Nicholas. *Mussolini: A New Life*. London: Weidenfeld & Nicolson, 2003

Griffiths, Richard. *Marshal Pétain*. London: Constable, 1994

Hamilton, Nigel. *Monty: Master of the Battlefield 1942-1944*. London: Hamish Hamilton, 1983

Hamilton, Nigel. *Monty: The Making of a General 1887-1942*. London: Hamish Hamilton, 1981

Hastings, Max. *Finest Years: Churchill as Warlord 1940-45*. London: Harper Press, 2009

Irving, David. *The Trail of the Fox: The Life of Field Marshal Erwin Rommel*. London: Weidenfeld & Nicolson, 1977

Packwood, Allen. *How Churchill Waged War: The Most Challenging Decisions of the Second World War*. Barnsley: Frontline, 2019

Pitt, Barrie. *Churchill and the Generals*. Barnsley: Pen & Sword, 2004

Ponting, Clive. *Churchill*. London: Sinclair-Stevenson, 1994

Schofield, Victoria. *Wavell: Soldier & Statesman*. London: John Murray, 2006

Sixsmith, E.K.G. *Eisenhower as Military Commander*. London: B.T. Batsford, 1973

Toland, John. *Adolf Hitler*. Ware: Wordsworth, 1997

Tompkins, Peter. *The Murder of Admiral Darlan*. New York: Simon and Schuster, 1965

Viotti, Andrea. *Garibaldi: The Revolutionary and his Men*. Poole: Blandford, 1979

Weitz, John. *Hitler's Diplomat: The Life and Times of Joachim von Ribbentrop*. New York: Ticknor & Fields, 1992

INTELLIGENCE WAR

Hastings, Max. *The Secret War: Spies, Codes and Guerrillas 1939-1945*. London. William Collins, 2017

Jeffrey, Keith. *MI6: The History of the Secret Intelligence Service 1909-1949*. London: Bloomsbury, 2011

Kerrigan, Michael. *How Bletchley Park Won World War II*. London: Amber, 2018

McKay, Sinclair. *The Secret Life of Bletchley Park*. London: Aurum Press, 2011

Paterson, Michael. *Voices of the Codebreakers*. Barnsley: Greenhill, 2018

Smith, Michael. *Station X: The Codebreakers of Bletchley Park*. London: Pan 2004

LAND CAMPAIGNS

Adleman, Robert H. & Walton, Colonel George. *The Champagne Campaign*. Boston: Little Brown 1969

Atkinson, Rick. *An Army at Dawn: The War in North Africa, 1942-1943*. London: Little Brown, 2003

Barnett, Correlli. *The Desert Generals*. London: Pan, 1983

Buckingham, William F. *Tobruk: The Great Siege 1941-2*. Stroud: Tempus, 2008

Carver, Michael. *Tobruk*. London: Pan, 1972

Clark, Lloyd. *Anzio: The Friction of War, Italy and the Battle for Rome 1944*. London: Headline Review, 2006

Clayton, Tim & Craig, Phil. *End of the Beginning*. London: Hodder & Stoughton, 2002

Cooper, Artemis. *Cairo in the War 1939-1945*. London: Hamish Hamilton, 1992

D'Este, Carlo. *Bitter Victory: The Battle for Sicily 1943*. London: Collins, 1988

D'Este, Carlo. *Fatal Decision: Anzio & The Battle for Rome*. London: Aurum Press, 2007

Dimbleby, Jonathan. *Destiny in the Desert: The Road to El Alamein – The Battle that Turned the Tide*. London: Profile, 2013

Ellis, John. *Cassino The Hollow Victory: The Battle for Rome January-June 1944*. London: Andre Deutsch, 1984

Ford, Ken. *El Alamein 1942: The Turning of the Tide*. Oxford: Osprey, 2001

Ford, Ken. *Operation Crusader 1941: Rommel in Retreat*. Oxford: Osprey, 2010

Forty, George. *Fifth Army at War*. Shepperton: Ian Allan, 1980

Gilbert, Adrian. *The Imperial War Museum Book of the Desert War*. London: Sidgwick & Jackson, 1995

Gooderson, Ian. *A hard way to make war: the Italian campaign in the second world war*. London: Conway, 2008

Harokopos, George. *The Fortress Crete: The Secret War 1941-1944*. Athens: Giannikos & Caldis, 2001

Harrison, Frank. *Tobruk: The Great Siege Reassessed*. London: Brockhampton Press, 1999

Holland, James. *Italy's Sorrow: A Year of War, 1944-1945*. London: Harper Press, 2008

Holland, James. *Together We Stand: Turning the Tide in the West – North Africa 1942-1943*. London: Harper Collins, 2005

Kershaw, Andrew & Close, Ian (ed). *The Desert War*. London: Phoebus, 1975

Linklater, Eric. *The Campaign in Italy*. London: HMSO, 1977

Lucas, James. *War in the Desert: The Eighth Army at El Alamein*. London: Arms and Armour Press, 1982

Macksey, Kenneth. *Afrika Korps*. London: Pan/Ballatine, 1972

Macksey, Kenneth. *Beda Fomm*. London: Pan/Ballatine, 1972

Macksey, Kenneth. *Rommel: Battles and Campaigns*. London: Arms and Armour Press, 1979

Miller, Robert A. *August 1944: The Campaign for France*. Novato, CA: Presidio Press, 1996

Ministry of Information. *The Campaign in Greece and Crete*. London: HMSO, 1942

Perrett, Bryan. *Armour in Battle: Wavell's Offensive*. Shepperton: Ian Allan, 1979

Pitt, Barrie. *The Crucible of War: Western Desert 1941*. London: Futura, 1981

Plowman, Jeffrey. *Greece 1941: The Death Throes of Blitzkrieg*. Barnsley: Pen & Sword, 2018

Quarrie, Bruce. *Afrika Korps*. Cambridge: Patrick Stephens, 1975

Rogers, Anthony. *Kos and Leros 1943: The German Conquest of the Dodecanese*. Oxford: Osprey, 2019

Sanders, John. *8th Army in the Desert*. Cambridge: Patrick Stephens, 1976

Strawson, John. *The Battle for North Africa*. London: B.T. Batsford, 1969

Trevelyan, Raleigh. *Rome '44: The Battle for the Eternal City*. London: Secker & Warburg, 1981

Tucker-Jones, Anthony. *Armoured Warfare in the North African Campaign*. Barnsley: Pen & Sword, 2011

Tute, Warren. *The North African War*. London: Sidgwick and Jackson, 1976

Tute, Warren. *The Reluctant Enemies: The story of the last war between Britain and France 1940-42*. London: Collins, 1990

Warner, Philip. *Alamein*. London: William Kimber, 1979

Whiting, Charles. *First Blood: The Battle of the Kasserine Pass*. London: Leo Cooper, 1984

MARITIME OPERATIONS

Bishop, Chris & Chant, Chris. *Aircraft Carriers: The world's greatest naval vessels and their aircraft*. St Paul, MN: Motorbooks International, 2004

Breuer, William B. *Operation Dragoon: The Allied Invasion of the South of France*. Shrewsbury: Airlife, 1988

Breuer, William B. *Operation Torch: The Allied Gamble to Invade North Africa*. New York: St Martin's Press, 1985

Breyer, Siegfried. *Battleships and Battle Cruisers 1905-1970*. London: Macdonald and Jane's, 1973

Chapman, A.J. *War of the Motor Gun Boats*. Barnsley: Pen & Sword, 2013

Elliot, Peter. *The Cross and the Ensign: A Naval History of Malta 1798-1979*. London Harper Collins, 1994

Grehan, John & Mace, Martin. *The War at Sea in the Mediterranean 1940-1944*. Barnsley: Pen & Sword, 2014

Herder, Brian Lane. *Operation Torch 1942: The invasion of French North Africa*. Oxford: Osprey, 2017

Konstam, Angus. *Taranto 1940: The Fleet Air Arm's precursor to Pearl Harbor*. Oxford: Osprey, 2015

Pack, S.W.C. *Operation Husky: The Allied Invasion of Sicily*. New York: Hippocrene, 1977

Pack, S.WC. *The Battle of Matapan*. London: B.T. Batsford, 1961

Parker, John. *Task Force: Untold Stories of the Heroes of the Royal Navy*. London: Headline, 2004

Pearson, Michael. *The Ohio and Malta: The Legendary Tanker that Refused to Die*. Barnsley: Pen & Sword, 2019

Preston, Anthony (foreword). *Jane's Fighting Ships of World War II*. London: Bracken, 1989

Roskill, Stephen. *Churchill and the Admirals*. Barnsley: Pen & Sword, 2013

Smith, Peter C. *The Great Ships: British Battleships in WWII*. Mechanicsburg, PA: Stackpole, 2008

Tucker-Jones, Anthony. *Operation Dragoon: The Liberation of Southern France 1944*. Barnsley: Pen & Sword, 2009

Turner, John Frayn. *Periscope Patrol: The Saga of the Malta Force Submarines.*
Barnsley: Pen & Sword, 2008

Tute, Warren. *The Deadly Stroke.* London: Collins, 1973

Vader, John. *The Fleet Without a Friend. London*: New English Library, 1971

Whitley, M.J. *Cruisers of World War Two.* London: Brockhampton, 1999

Wragg, David. *Second World War Carrier Campaigns.* Barnsley: Pen & Sword, 2004

Wragg, David. *Sink the French!* Barnsley: Pen & Sword, 2007

MEMOIRS & REPORTAGE

Alexander, Field Marshal. *The Alexander Memoirs 1940-1945.* London: Cassell, 1962

Arthur, Max. *Forgotten Voices of the Second World War.* London: Ebury Press, 2004

Bormann, Martin. *Hitler's Table Talk.* Oxford: Oxford University Press, 1988

Clifford, Alexander. *Crusader.* London: George G. Harrap, 1942

Cunningham, Admiral of the Fleet Viscount. *A Sailor's Odyssey: The Autobiography of Admiral of the Fleet Viscount Cunningham of Hyndhope.* London: Hutchinson, 1951

De Guingand, Major-General Sir Francis. *Operation Victory.* London: Hodder and Stoughton, 1947

Djilas, Milovan. *Wartime.* London: Secker & Warburg, 1977

Eisenhower, Dwight D. *Crusade in Europe.* London: William Heinemann, 1948

Halifax, Viscount. *Speeches on Foreign Policy.* London: Oxford University Press, 1940

Horrocks, Lieutenant-General Sir Brian. *A Full Life.* London: Collins, 1960

Kesselring, Field Marshal Albert. *The Memoirs of Field-Marshal Kesselring.* London: William Kimber, 1974

Liddell Hart, B.H. *The Other Side of the Hill.* London: Pan, 1983.

Liddell Hart, B.H. (ed). *The Rommel Papers.* London: Collins, 1953

Moorehead, Alan. *A Year of Battle.* London: Hamish Hamilton, 1943

Moorehead, Alan. *Mediterranean Front.* London: Hamish Hamilton, 1941

Moorehead, Alan. *The End in Africa.* London: Hamish Hamilton, 1943

Neil, Wing Commander T.F. *Onward to Malta: Memoirs of a Hurricane pilot in Malta – 1941.* Shrewsbury: Airlife, 1992

Newby, Eric. *A Small Place in Italy*. London: Picador, 1995

Newby, Eric. *On the Shores of the Mediterranean*. London: Harper Press, 2011

Newby, Eric. *Something Wholesale*. London: Picador, 1985

Niven, David. *The Moon's a Balloon*. London: Cornet, 1972

Schmidt, Heinz Werner. *With Rommel in the Desert*. London: Panther 1968

Skorzeny, Otto. *Skorzeny's Special Missions. The Memoirs of Hitler's Most Daring Commando*. Barnsley: Frontline, 2011

Thompson, Julian. *Forgotten Voices: Desert Victory*. London: Ebury Press, 2011

Whicker, Alan. *Journey of a Lifetime*. London: Harper Collins, 2009

Whicker, Alan. *Whicker's War*. London: Harper Collins, 2005

OTHER PUBLISHED SOURCES

Ball, Simon. *The Bitter Sea: The Struggle for Mastery in the Mediterranean, 1935-1949*. London: Harper Press, 2009

Beevor, Antony. *The Second World War*. London: Weidenfeld & Nicolson, 2012

Beevor, Antony. *The Spanish Civil War*. London: Orbis, 1982

Bradford, Ernle. *The Great Siege*. London: Hodder and Stoughton, 1961

Bradford, Ernle. *The Shield and the Sword: The Knights of Malta*. London: Fontana, 1974

Brendon, Piers. *The Dark Valley: A Panorama of the 1930s*. London: Jonathan Cape, 2000

Carr, Raymond. *Images of the Spanish Civil War*. London: Allen & Unwin, 1986

Churchill, W.S. *The Second World War*. Vols I-VI. London: Cassell, 1948-54

Crowley, Roger. *Empires of the Sea: The Final Battle for the Mediterranean 1521-1580*. London: Faber and Faber, 2008

Hills, George. *The Battle for Madrid*. London: Vantage, 1976

Laffin, John. *Raiders: Elite Forces Attacks*. London: Chancellor Press, 2000

Liddell Hart, B.H. *History of the First World War*. London: Cassell, 1970

Liddell Hart, B.H. *History of the Second World War*. London: Cassell, 1970

Mitchell, David. *The Spanish Civil War*. London: Granada, 1982

Overy, Richard & Wheatcroft, Andrew. *The Road to War*. London: Macmillan, 1989

Scurr, John. *The Spanish Foreign Legion*. London: Osprey, 1985

Shirer, William. *The Rise and Fall of the Third Reich*. London: Secker & Warburg, 1973

Sitwell, Sacheverell & Jones, Tony Armstrong. *Malta*. London: B.T. Batsford, 1958

Smyth, Brigadier Sir John. *The Valiant*. London: A.R. Mowbray, 1970

Sommerville, Christopher. *Our War: How the British Commonwealth fought the Second World War*. London: Weidenfeld & Nicolson, 1998

Taylor, A.J.P. *The Origins of the Second World War*. London: Hamish Hamilton, 1962

Thomas, Hugh. *The Spanish Civil War*. London: Eyre & Spottiswoode, 1961

Thompson, Robert Smith. *Pledge to Destiny*. New York: McGraw-Hill, 1974

Turnbull, Patrick. *The Spanish Civil War 1936-39*. London: Osprey, 1978

Windrow, Martin. *French Foreign Legion*. Reading: Osprey, 1971

DOCUMENTARIES & NEWSREELS

Barrett, Matthew. *WWII in Colour*. Episode 6 *The Mediterranean and North Africa*. Negus Martin Productions/IMG Entertainment, 2009

Bonello, Adam. *The Siege of Malta*. AAB Films, 2014

Carruthers, Bob. *Naval Warfare in World War II*. Episode 5 *War in the Mediterranean*, Episode 8 *Mediterranean Command 1940-42* & Episode 9 *Invasion of North Africa*. Visions of War, 2014

Grinberg, Sherman. *Battlezone WWII*. Episode I *Malta*, Episode 2 *Sicily*, Episode 4 *Anzio*, Episode 5 *Monte Cassino* & Episode 7 *The Gothic Line*. Timeless Television, 1963/2014

PERIODICALS

The War Illustrated

Index

Adriatic 25, 26, 75, 79–80, 84, 119, 218

Aegean 18, 25, 45, 78, 106, 122, 127, 183, 187, 197, 202, 203–5, 226, 228

Ajaccio 62

Albacores 107–9, 165

Albania 43–5, 73, 74–6, 79, 86, 119, 120–1, 185, 188, 202, 217–18, 228

Alexander, General Harold 9, 171, 182, 183, 189–90, 206, 209, 211–12, 221, 222

Alexandria 45, 55–6, 62, 74, 77, 80, 81–2, 103, 105, 106, 107, 111, 112, 113, 121, 124, 131, 134, 135, 152, 154, 155, 156, 167, 168–71, 222, 224

Algeria 10, 25, 26, 37, 62–3, 71, 172–3, 177–8, 180, 189, 226, 228

Algiers 16, 62, 64, 67, 68, 162, 173–4, 177–8, 179, 180, 225

Al-Husayni, Grand Mufti Mohammad Amin 39–40

Aliakmon Line 118, 120

Ambrosio, General Vittorio 123, 186, 192–3

Anfuso, Filippo 45

Athens 118, 121, 122, 127, 128, 171, 217

Auchinleck, General Claude 166, 167, 168, 169, 170–1

Auphan, Admiral Paul 63, 64–5

Baade, Colonel Ernst-Günther 194

Badoglio, Marshal Pietro 29, 30, 35, 73, 74, 75, 192–4, 197, 198, 200, 203, 205, 206

Balbo, Air Marshal Italo 16, 28, 29, 35, 38, 50–2, 54–5, 57, 223

Balearic Islands 35, 36, 40–1, 200, 224

Balkans 9, 10, 14, 16, 18, 25–6, 42, 46, 50, 72, 74, 87, 98, 118–23, 126, 128, 183, 185, 186, 197, 202, 207, 209, 210, 211, 217–18, 224, 227

Balkan League 25–6

Barcelona 62

Bardia 53, 54, 55, 56, 60, 93–4

Bardini, General 97

Bari 43

Barone, Rear Admiral Pietro 190–1, 194–5

Batey, Mavis 105

Beda Fomm 17, 95–7, 99, 104, 115, 227

Benghazi 25, 28, 54, 70, 95–7, 98, 112

Berbers 25, 27–8

Bergamini, Admiral Carlo 200

Beresford-Peirse, General Sir 142, 143

Berkane 37

Bethouart, General Antoine 172

Bignani, General 97

Bizerte 62, 177

Bletchley Park 105, 110, 212, 227

Bonnier de la Chapelle, Fernand 179

Borghese, Count Julio Valerio 113

Brindisi 43, 84, 106, 203

British & Commonwealth Forces

  Armies

    1st 177, 180, 182, 183

    8th 9, 147, 171, 180, 182, 190, 193, 227–8

  Brigades

    1st Armoured Brigade 120, 121

3rd Armoured Brigade 115, 116, 117–18
4th Armoured Brigade 53, 90, 93, 95, 96
7th Armoured Brigade 90, 142, 143, 144
5th Indian Infantry Brigade 91, 140
5th New Zealand Brigade 129, 130, 132
22nd Guards Brigade 125
Divisions
  1st Airborne 215
  1st Cavalry 160
  1st South African Division 138
  2nd Armoured Division 115, 116, 118, 125, 217
  2nd New Zealand Division 120
  4th Indian Division 52, 90, 91, 92, 93, 138, 142
  5th Indian Division 138
  6th Australian Division 52, 93, 95, 120
  7th Armoured Division 52, 57, 90, 92, 95, 96, 115, 124, 142, 145–6, 182
  7th Australian Division 120, 140
  11th African Division 138
  12th African Division 138
Losses
  in Crete 133–4
  in French North Africa 176
  in Greece 110
  in Italy 195, 221
  in North Africa 144–5, 171
  in Sicily 195
British Somaliland 32, 52
Brown, Trooper 'Topper' 96
Bulgaria 26, 76, 87, 104, 119, 120, 122, 217
Buq Buq 59, 92, 93
Burt-Smith, Captain 168

Cádiz 35
Cadogan, Sir Alexander 180
Caesar, Julius 13, 23
Cairo 16, 17, 97, 98–9, 118, 119, 134, 140, 167, 168, 169, 170, 224, 226
Calabria 69–70
Calato 78
Campioni, Admiral 69, 78, 80, 82, 85, 203–4
Canary Islands 70
Caneva, General Carlo 25

Cap Bon 17, 112, 162, 182, 183
Cape Spartivento 85
Capuzzo 52, 53, 55, 56, 57, 93, 125, 142–4
Carta, General Angelo 133
Cartagena 36
Carthage 24, 183
Caruana, Joseph 152
Casablanca 24, 62, 173, 174
Catania 158, 159, 188, 189–90, 193
Cattaneo, Admiral Carlo 106
Cavallero, Marshal Ugo 164, 178, 186, 225
Ceuta 23, 35, 36, 228
Chamberlain, Prime Minister Neville 15, 44
Chirieleison, General Domenico 188
Churchill, Winston 11, 15–16, 17, 29–30, 31–3, 50, 52, 61, 62, 63–4, 68, 69, 72, 74, 77, 80, 89, 97–8, 100, 104, 110, 117–18, 119, 122, 123–4, 129, 132, 135, 138, 139, 140, 141, 142, 144–7, 151, 152, 158, 159, 168, 170, 171, 172, 178–9, 180, 183, 187, 200, 202–3, 206, 207, 209–10, 211, 213–14, 215, 222, 225, 227
Ciano, Count Galeazzo 37–8, 41, 42, 44, 45, 50, 55, 73, 74, 84, 112, 160
Cohen, Sergeant Pilot Sydney 187–8
Constantinople 13, 25
Coonan, Jane & Margaret 168–9
Corbett, Lieutenant-General Thomas 169, 171
Corinth Canal 121
Corsica 42, 50, 185, 189, 207
Cos 204–5
Creagh, Major-General Michael O'Moore 124, 141–2
Crete 8, 17, 18, 74, 76, 78, 87, 104, 106, 108, 118, 121–2, 124, 127–36, 140, 160–1, 203, 204, 205, 211, 217, 226, 228
Croatia 62, 119, 218
Cunningham, Admiral Andrew 9–10, 18, 64, 69, 70, 74, 77–82, 83–4, 104, 105, 106, 107, 108, 109–10, 111–12, 113, 121, 131, 132, 134, 135–6, 138, 154, 157, 168, 179, 190, 191, 196, 200, 201, 206
Cyrenaica 23, 24, 29, 51, 97, 98–9, 104, 105, 120, 140, 178
Cyprus 42, 52, 135, 140

Da Zara, Admiral Alberto 201
Damascus 141
Darlan, Admiral Jean François 15, 18, 50, 63,

64, 68–9, 101, 137–8, 139, 172, 174, 176, 178–80

Dardanelles 25

Davies, Lieutenant-Commander 66

D'Avanzo, Colonel 53–4

de Gaulle, General Charles 68, 69, 70, 139, 141, 178–9, 180, 228

de Guingand, Colonel 'Freddie' 118, 122, 140

De Vecchi, Governor Cesare Maria 74, 78

Dentz, General Henri 137–8, 140, 141

Derna 25, 55, 94–5, 116, 171

Dobbie, General Sir William 152

Dodecanese 18, 25, 78, 85, 86, 110, 122, 133, 217

Douglas-Hamilton, Squadron Leader David 159, 163

Dufay, Lieutenant Bernard 64

Easter Agreement 60–2, 64

Eden, Foreign Secretary Anthony 118–19

Egypt 10, 15, 17, 23, 30, 38, 51–6, 57–60, 62–3, 73–4, 79, 84, 90–2, 97–9, 104, 115, 117, 123, 124, 126, 137, 140–1, 147–8, 153, 167–71, 223, 224, 225, 226

Eisenhower, General Dwight D. 9, 18, 172–3, 179, 180, 183, 189, 192, 196, 201, 206, 209, 211, 213–14, 215

El Alamein 10, 17, 116, 167, 169, 170, 171, 178, 181, 227

Esteva, Admiral Jean Pierre 176–7

Ethiopia (Abyssinia) 14, 29, 30–2, 40, 138, 223

Eritrea 29, 32, 138, 140

Fabri, George 153, 156, 161

Feller, Colonel Bonner 171

Ferrini, Lieutenant-Commander Renato 163

Fez 24

Fezzan 29

Florence 39, 73

Fougier, General Rino Corso 162

French Empire 18, 24, 62–3, 72, 101, 225, 228

French fleet
    French warships
        Bretagne 66, 68
        Dunkerque 64, 65, 67, 68
        Mogador 67
        Richelieu 68, 70
        Strasbourg 67

Franco, General Francisco 14, 18, 27, 35–8,

41–3, 46, 70–2, 84, 99–101, 115, 186, 224–5, 227, 228

French Morocco 37, 71, 172–6

French Somaliland 29, 50

Freyberg, Major-General Sir Bernard 127, 129, 130, 134

Gabès Gap 178

Gallina, General Sebastiano 90, 91–2

Gensoul, Admiral Marcel 64–5, 67, 68

Gibraltar 15, 17, 23, 24, 30, 36, 41, 42, 45, 63, 70–2, 79, 82, 84, 85, 99–100, 113, 123, 153, 154, 155, 157, 159, 161, 174, 186, 222, 224

Gibson, Lieutenant Donald 108

Giuliano, General 97

Gerbina 195

Genoa 27, 50, 86, 190, 221

Genovese, Vito 190

Germany 13, 16, 17, 29, 35, 37, 40, 42, 46, 62, 71, 87, 198, 202, 205–6, 207, 210, 220, 226

German Army
    Armies
        1st 210
        19th 210
    Divisions
        1st Parachute 192
        1st SS Panzer 199
        3rd Panzergrenadier 198
        5th Light 124, 143, 144
        5th Mountain 128, 131
        7th Parachute 128, 129
        11th Panzer 211, 214, 215, 216
        15th Panzer 124, 125, 143, 144, 147
        15th Panzergrenadier 188, 189
        17th SS Panzergrenadier 211, 212
        21st Panzer 126, 147
        29th Panzergrenadier 192
        44th Infantry 198
        65th Infantry 199
        148th Infantry 215, 216
        189th Infantry 216
        198th Infantry 216
        242nd Infantry 215, 216
        Hermann Göring 189, 191
    Losses
        in Crete 135, 160, 226
        in Italy 195, 218, 221

in North Africa 10, 116, 143, 171, 182
in Sicily 195
Godfrey, Admiral John 110
Gort, General Lord 44, 160, 206
Grand Harbour (Malta) 154, 155, 159, 163, 201
Graziani, Marshal Maresciallo Rodolpho 28, 29, 32, 51, 55–7, 59–60, 73, 89, 92, 94, 99, 223
Greece 10, 14, 17, 26, 44, 72, 73–6, 78, 79, 87, 98–9, 104–5, 115, 118–23, 127, 128–9, 138, 140, 185, 187, 203–5, 211, 217, 223, 225, 228
Greek Army 74, 75, 105, 120, 121, 228
Greek Navy 74, 121, 122
Guzzoni, General Alfredo 188–9, 191, 194, 195

Hafid Ridge 142–3, 144
Hale, Lieutenant-Commander 'Ginger' 83
Halfaya Pass 56, 57–8, 117, 125, 142, 143, 144–5, 147–8
Halifax, Lord 15, 32, 37, 40, 44
Halim, Prince Abbas 169
Hargest, Brigadier James 129
Harmon, General Ernest N. 174
Harwood, Admiral Sir Henry 168
Hassell, Ambassador Ulirch von 37
Haworth, Lieutenant Mike 107, 109
Heraklion 127, 128, 130, 133, 134
Hendaye 71, 72, 224
His Majesty's Ships *see also* Royal Navy
    HMS *Ajax* 107, 121, 131, 133
    HMS *Argus* 62, 153, 157
    HMS *Ark Royal* 61, 62, 64, 65, 67, 68, 70, 82, 85, 86, 153, 157
    HMS *Barham* 82, 103, 106, 109, 135, 157
    HMS *Cairo* 163
    HMS *Carlisle* 131
    HMS *Courageous* 61
    HMS *Decoy* 132, 133
    HMS *Dido* 131, 133
    HMS *Eagle* 61, 77, 80–1, 103, 157, 158, 159, 160, 162
    HMS *Fiji* 131, 132
    HMS *Formidable* 61–2, 103, 106–7, 108, 110, 132, 135
    HMS *Gloucester* 94, 131, 132
    HMS *Greyhound* 131, 132
    HMS *Griffin* 131
    HMS *Hereward* 133
    HMS *Hood* 30, 64, 66, 67
    HMS *Indomitable* 62, 162
    HMS *Illustrious* 61–2, 77, 78, 79, 80–1, 82, 94, 103, 108, 151–2, 157, 201
    HMS *Kandahar* 132
    HMS *Kashmir* 132
    HMS *Kelly* 132
    HMS *Kent* 56
    HMS *Kingston* 132
    HMS *Ladybird* 56, 155
    HMS *Malaya* 56, 86
    HMS *Naiad* 131
    HMS *Nigeria* 163
    HMS *Orion* 78, 131, 133–4
    HMS *Queen Elizabeth* 113
    HMS *Renown* 30, 85, 86
    HMS *Sheffield* 86
    HMS *Southampton* 94
    HMS *Valiant* 64, 77, 103, 105, 106, 109, 113, 131, 201
    HMS *Victorious* 61–2, 162
    HMS *Warspite* 56, 77, 79, 103, 106, 109, 110, 131, 132, 135, 162, 201
    HMS *Welshman* 159
Hitler, Adolf 10, 11, 14, 15–16, 17–18, 31, 32, 35, 36–7, 40–3, 44, 46, 50–1, 62, 63, 64, 70–3, 74, 76, 84, 87, 99–101, 115, 116, 118, 119, 120, 125–6, 127, 128, 135, 137, 151, 154, 157, 160, 167, 169–71, 178, 180, 183, 185, 186–7, 192, 193–4, 197–8, 200, 202–3, 205–7, 210, 211, 212, 217, 221, 223–7
Holland, Captain Cedric 'Hooky' 64, 65, 66
Hopkins, Lieutenant F.H.E. 107, 108
Hoxha, Enver 217

Iachino, Admiral Angelo 85
Iraq 26, 52, 137–8, 140–1, 170
Italy 9, 10–11, 13, 14–18, 23–7, 29–31, 32–3, 37–9, 43–4, 49, 78, 86, 87, 99, 100, 119, 125, 154, 156, 164, 183, 185–207, 209–18, 219–21, 224, 226
Italian Air Force 37, 45, 51, 52, 55, 56, 57, 61, 67, 72, 78–9, 80, 82, 94, 108, 133, 140, 157, 162–4, 171, 183, 190
Italian Army
    Armies
        1st 185
        2nd 119, 123

5th 51, 185
6th 185, 188
8th 126
9th 120, 185
10th 51, 56, 97, 185
11th 185, 119, 120
Divisions
  1st Blackshirt 57, 59, 92
  2nd Blackshirt 93
  4th Blackshirt 57, 59, 93
  1st Colonial 51–2
  1st Libyan 53, 58, 90, 92, 93
  2nd Libyan 91, 93
  4th Colonial 138
  4th Livorno 188, 191
  51st Sienna 133
  60th Sabratha 95
  61st Sirte 94
  62nd Marmarica 93
  63rd Cirene 93
  64th Catanzaro 57, 93
  Ariete Armoured 116–17, 124
  Centauro Armoured 116
  Littorio Armoured 116
  Babini Armoured Brigade 95–6
  Group Maletti 90–1, 93
Losses
  in Greece 122, 123
  in North Africa 10, 25, 50, 55, 54, 59,
  91, 97, 182, 185, 223
  in Sicily 195
Italian Naval Enigma 105
Italian Navy 25–6, 29–30, 54, 61, 74, 80, 84,
  85, 86, 94, 103–4, 105–10, 112, 119, 122,
  123, 133, 135, 154, 190–1, 195, 201, 222,
  226
Italian warships
  Audace 200–1
  Banda Nere 112
  Bolzano 105–7, 163, 201
  Caio Duilio 83–4
  Conte di Cavour 83–4
  Diaz 112
  Fiume 105–6, 109
  Giosuè Carducci 109
  Gorizia 201
  Giulio Cesare 85, 201
  Littorio 83–4
  Pola 105, 109

  Raimondo Montecuccoli 112, 201
  Trento 84, 105–6, 107
  Trieste 106, 107, 112
  Vittorio Alfieri 109
  Vittorio Veneto 83, 84, 85, 105, 108–9
  Zara 105, 109
  Submarines
    Axum 163
Italian Somaliland 29, 78, 138, 168

Jordan 26, 52
Kalamata 121
Kerisc, Iusuf 38–9
Kesselring, Field Marshal Albert 148, 151,
  154, 158, 159, 162, 164, 178, 183, 185–6,
  188–9, 190, 192, 193, 194, 195, 197, 198,
  199, 200, 201–2, 206–7, 211–12, 218,
  219–20, 226–7
Kleemann, General Ulrich 203–4
Knox, Dillwyn 'Dilly' 105, 110
Kuneitra 141

La Spezia 87, 190, 199, 200, 201
Lampedusa 151, 187–8
Lampson, Ambassador Sir Miles 16, 167, 170
Laval, Foreign Minister Pierre 29, 71, 101, 172
Lebanon 26, 139, 141
Le Luc, Admiral 64–5
Leros 122, 204–5
Levant 16, 29, 62, 137–48, 225
Libya 10, 13, 14, 15, 16, 17, 24–6, 27, 28–9, 32,
  38–9, 40, 50–1, 56–7, 72, 75–6, 89–101,
  115–18, 122, 123, 124–5, 126, 141–8,
  155, 164, 167, 177, 178, 180–1, 223, 225,
  226, 228
Lloyd, Air Vice-Marshal Hugh 154, 158, 159,
  161, 165
Longmore, Air Chief Marshal Sir Arthur 153
Lucas, Squadron Leader Laddie 154
Luftwaffe 72, 80, 87, 94, 100, 103, 108, 110,
  119–20, 121–2, 129–32, 133, 137, 140,
  151–3, 154–5, 158–9, 161, 164, 168,
  178, 187, 188, 189–90, 200, 202, 204–5,
  214–15
Luciano, Charles 'Lucky' 190

Macedonia 26, 120
Macmillan, Captain Norman 162, 164
Maddalena 52–3, 147

Madrid 42–3, 99, 199

Maffei, General Achille 187

Majorca 40, 42

Maleme 127, 128, 129, 130, 132

Malta 15, 42, 45, 60, 70, 79, 80, 81, 85, 86, 94, 105, 123–4, 135, 151–65, 170, 200–1, 222, 223, 224, 225–6, 227

Mannella, General Patessi 94

Mareth Line 16, 29, 32, 182

Marseilles 50, 214–16, 217

Mason, Captain Dudley 163

Mast, General Emmanuel Charles 172, 173

Mechili 95, 116

Meindl, Brigadier Eugen 128

Melilla 27, 36, 228

Menzies, Sir Stewart 180

Mers-el-Kébir 62, 64, 65, 69, 71, 139, 179, 225

Mersa Matruh 57, 59, 73, 140

Messe, General Giovanni 126

Messina 105–6, 188, 189–90, 192, 193, 194–5, 196

Metaxas, Prime Minister General Ioannis 74, 118

Metaxas Line 120

Milan 11, 50, 198, 219, 220, 221

Molinaro, General Giuseppe 193

Montgomery, General Bernard 9, 17, 18, 38, 171, 181–2, 183, 195, 196, 227

Montoire-sur-le-Loire 71–2, 101, 224

Moorehead, Alan 77, 78, 79, 80, 97, 131, 151, 158, 159, 168, 182–3

Morocco 10, 23, 24, 27–8, 36–7, 62–3, 71, 172–5, 189, 228 *see also* Spanish Morocco

Mount Olympus 121

Al-Mukhtar, Omar 28, 60

Mussolini, Benito 9, 10–11, 14–17, 18, 23, 25, 26–7, 28–33, 35, 36, 37–46, 49, 50, 52, 54, 55–6, 57, 69, 70, 71–6, 77, 79, 80, 84, 86, 89, 92, 93, 99–101, 104, 110–11, 115, 118–19, 120, 122, 123, 125, 128–9, 138, 151, 154, 155, 156, 162–3, 170, 171, 177, 178, 180, 182, 183, 185–7, 190, 191–4, 197, 205–7, 212, 219, 220, 222–7

Nazi-Soviet Pact 46

Negroni, General 97

Neil, Fighter Pilot Tom 111

Neumann, Dr Heinrich 130

Newby, Lieutenant Eric 112, 167–8, 201, 202

Nezuet Ghirba 53–4

Nibeiwa 90–1

Nile, River 13, 29, 73, 97–8, 169, 170

Noguès, General Auguste 172

O'Connor, General Richard 18, 52, 53, 55, 57, 59–60, 89, 90, 92–4, 95, 97, 98, 117

Operations
 Anvil 209–10, 213–14
 Battleaxe 141–7
 Catapult 64–7
 Crusader 147–8
 Dragoon 209, 212–17
 Hercules 160–1, 225–6
 Hurry 157
 Husky 189–92
 Isabella 70
 Lustre 104–10
 Mincemeat 187
 Orient 169–70
 Pedestal 161–5
 Torch 172–8, 203
 White 157–60

Oran 62, 64, 65, 67, 173–4, 176, 225

Ottoman Empire 15, 23, 26, 155–6, 169

Pact of Steel 45

Palazzo Venezia 31, 49, 220

Palestine 26, 38, 40, 52, 139, 140, 168–9, 170, 228

Palermo 25, 112, 158, 188, 190, 193, 194

Palma 40–1

Pantelleria 45, 151, 187, 188, 191

Park, Air Vice-Marshal Keith 161

Patton, General George 9, 18, 176, 193, 194, 195, 217

Pavesi, Admiral Gino 187

Pétain, Marshal 18, 62, 63, 69, 71, 72, 101, 137, 173, 176, 178, 224, 225, 228

Piraeus 106, 119

Poland 9, 16, 46, 51, 52, 120

Polic, Vice-Admiral Marjan 119

Portugal 70, 71

Prague 45

Prasca, General Sebastiano Visconti 74, 75

Price, Ward 31

Pridham-Wippell, Admiral 106, 107, 109, 121

Puntoni, General Paolo 192

Raeder, Admiral Erich 84, 137

Rahn, Ambassador Rudolf von 206

Raw, Captain 'Sammy' 111–12

Rew, Major Henry 91

Rhodes 15, 25, 77–9, 104, 106, 108, 110,
203–4, 228

Ribbentrop, Ambassador Joachim von 70

Riccardi, Admiral Arturo 162

Richthofen, Field Marshal von 202

Rif War 27–8

Ringel, Major-General Julius 130

Roatta, General Mario 38, 186, 188, 199, 201

Roman Empire 10, 15, 23, 222, 227

Romania 44, 76, 126, 127, 211, 217

Rome 15, 23, 27, 28, 31, 40, 51, 55, 104, 138,
148, 159, 171, 178, 182, 185, 192–3, 196,
197, 198, 199–200, 201, 203, 205, 206,
211–12

Rommel, General Erwin 9, 10, 17–18, 98–9,
112, 115–18, 124–5, 126, 137, 142,
143–5, 146, 147–8, 154, 160–1, 164,
167–72, 178, 180, 182, 183, 185, 192,
194, 198–9, 202, 210, 223, 226, 227

Rommel, Manfred 169

Roosevelt, President Franklin 72, 158, 159,
209, 212, 213

Royal Air Force 38, 45, 50, 52, 58, 71, 74, 97,
99, 104, 108, 139, 151, 152, 153, 154–5,
156, 157, 158, 159–60, 161, 165

Royal Navy see also His Majesty's Ships
Fleet Air Arm 45, 65, 80, 82, 83, 107–8,
155–6, 161
Home Fleet 30
Mediterranean Fleet 10, 29–30, 31–2, 38,
42, 45, 61–2, 64, 70, 77, 80–5, 100, 103,
105, 106–10, 131–2, 135–6, 157, 168, 190,
222, 224, 277–8
1st Submarine Flotilla 112
10th Submarine Flotilla 111

Salerno 200, 206, 221

Salonika 120, 122

Sansonetti, Admiral Luigi 105

Sarajevo 120

Sardinia 15, 37, 45, 61, 82, 85, 162, 185,
189–90, 199, 200, 207

Schmidt, Lieutenant Heinz 144, 145, 147–8,
183

Serbia 26

Seville 35

Shepherd's Hotel 16

Sicilian Channel 17, 111, 225

Sicily 9, 10, 15, 17, 45, 61, 72, 77, 85, 111, 151,
152, 158, 161, 162, 165, 176, 188–94,
195–6, 200, 225, 226

Sidi Azeiz 53, 55, 125, 147

Sidi Barrani 54, 59–60, 89–90, 91–2

Simpson, Commander George 111, 112

Sinclair, Secretary of State for Air Sir Archibald
154–5

Skorzeny, SS-Sturmbannführer Otto 205, 219

Skua 65

Smith, Eve 168

Sollum 54, 55–6, 57–9, 142, 144

Somerville, Admiral 18, 64, 65–6, 70, 77, 85,
86–7

Spain
Spanish Civil War 14, 35–8, 42–3
Spanish Foreign Legion 27, 36–7
Spanish Nationalist Air Force 36
Spanish Nationalist Navy 35–6, 41
Spanish Republic 27, 35–8, 40–2, 46, 224
Spanish Republican Navy 14, 41
Spanish Morocco 23, 24, 27–8, 36, 174,
183, 225 see also Morocco

Special Boat Section 112

Stalin, Joseph 11, 46, 52, 100, 209, 211, 213,
215

Student, General Kurt 72, 128–9, 130, 131,
135, 160–1, 226

Suda Bay 104, 130

Sudan 52, 92, 138

Suez Canal 10, 17, 29, 38, 42, 54, 103, 104,
123, 126, 135, 137, 140, 147, 160, 170,
224, 228

Suner, Minister of the Interior Ramon Serrano
70

Süssman, Major-General Wilhelm 128, 129–30

Swordfish 65, 67, 78, 82–3, 85, 106, 107,
108–9, 155, 161

Syracuse 25, 188, 190

Syria 26, 63, 139–41, 228

Syrian Legion 160

Taranto 9, 80–4, 85, 86, 97, 99, 103, 106, 135,
190, 200, 201, 222

Theobold, Petty Officer 108

Thermopylae 121

Thoma, General von 73

Thrace 26, 122

Tiger Convoy 123–4, 146–7

Tiger Cubs 124–5, 142, 143, 144, 145–7

Tirana 43, 45, 119, 218

Tito, Josip Broz 218

Tobruk 25, 52, 54, 55, 56–7, 81, 89, 91, 93–5, 112, 117, 160, 167, 225

Toulon 50, 62, 63, 64, 67, 101, 214–15, 216–17, 225

Tripoli 13, 16, 17, 23, 25, 29, 38–9, 54, 69, 73, 92, 98–9, 111, 114, 120, 151, 180–1, 220–1, 226

Tripoli Grand Prix 13, 16, 38

Tripolitania 24, 29, 51, 165, 178, 226

Tunis 16, 157, 164–5, 176–7, 182, 185–6, 187–8

Tunisia 17, 18, 23, 29, 38, 42, 45, 51, 52, 63, 69, 71, 72, 111, 114, 126, 165, 173, 176–8, 179, 180, 182–3, 185–6, 189, 191, 192, 194, 223, 225–7

Turf Club 16

Turkey 13, 14, 24–6, 45–6, 72, 87, 98, 118, 120, 203

Turin 50, 219

US Army

    Armies

        3rd 217

        5th 200, 211–12

        7th 193, 214, 215, 216, 217, 221

    Divisions

        1st Armored 176

        2nd Armored 175

        3rd Infantry 215, 217

        36th Infantry 215, 216–17

        45th Infantry 215

        82nd Airborne 191

    Losses

        in French North Africa 176

        in Italy 195, 221

        in Sicily 195

US Navy 174, 195

USS *Wasp* 158, 159

Valencia 41

Valletta 111, 153, 154, 155

Via Balbia 38

Vichy 18, 62–3, 69, 71, 72, 101, 137–41, 172–8, 179–80, 210

Victor Emmanuel III, King 44, 191–4, 198, 203

Vienna 45, 213

Vietinghoff, General von 220

Villanis, General 97

Vizzini, Don Calogero 190

Wanklyn, Lieutenant-Commander Malcolm 111–12

Wavell, General Sir Archibald 18, 38, 52, 53, 55, 57, 60, 76, 87, 89–90, 92, 96, 97–8, 115, 116, 117–18, 120, 122, 123–4, 129, 132, 134–5, 138, 139–40, 145–6

Weichold, Admiral Eberhard 162

Wells, Admiral (rtd) Sir Gerard 168

Weygand, General Maxime 101, 140, 172

Whicker, Lieutenant Alan 182, 183, 191, 196, 211, 220

Williamson, Lieutenant-Commander Kenneth 83

Willis, Vice-Admiral Sir Algernon 204–5

Wilson, General Sir Henry Maitland 120, 160, 203, 210, 213

Wolff, SS-General Karl 206

Yugoslav Army 119, 120, 122

Yugoslav Navy 119

Yugoslavia 10, 17, 26, 63, 64, 87, 104, 116, 118–20, 122–3, 185, 202, 209, 218, 220, 228

Zog, King Ahmed 43–4, 168